Crochet One-Skein Wonders

101 Projects From Crocheters Around the World

Judith Durant & Edie Eckman

Photography by Keller + Keller Photography Inc.

Storey Publishing

The mission of Storey Publishing is to serve our customers by
publishing practical information that encourages
personal independence in harmony with the environment.

Edited by Melinda A. Sheehan, Pam Thompson, and Gwen Steege
Art direction and book design by Jessica Armstrong
Text production by Liseann Karandisecky

Photography by © Keller + Keller Photography Inc., except for pages 7, 27, 36, 83, 84,
    89, 90, 107, 113, 121, 143, 242, and 243 and all margins through page 262 by Mars Vilaubi
Charts and diagrams by Karen Manthey
Illustrations by Brigita Fuhrmann, except for adjustable ring sequence, page 273,
    by Alison Kolesar

Indexed by Catherine Goddard
Tech edit by Karen Manthey

Storey Publishing
210 MASS MoCA Way
North Adams, MA 01247
www.storey.com

Printed in China by R.R. Donnelley
10 9 8 7 6 5 4

Library of Congress Cataloging-in-Publication Data

Crochet one-skein wonders / edited by Judith Durant and Edie Eckman.
    pages cm
  Includes index.
  ISBN 978-1-61212-042-3 (pbk. : alk. paper)
  ISBN 978-1-60342-866-8 (ebook)
  1. Crocheting—Patterns. I. Durant, Judith, 1955- II. Eckman, Edie.
TT820.C892 2013
746.43'2041—dc23

2012044467

CONTENTS

Fine Weight

Light Weight

Medium Weight

Bulky Weight

Appendix

Welcome to *Crochet One-Skein Wonders*!

While each of the previous books in the One-Skein Wonders series has included crocheted projects, this is the first one devoted solely to crochet.

According to *Merriam-Webster's* dictionary, crochet is "needlework consisting of the interlocking of looped stitches formed with a single thread and a hooked needle." No one seems to know the origin of crochet (though the word comes from Middle French for "hook"), but it has been practiced for at least four centuries throughout the Western world to make lace fabrics. Modern stitchers ply their crochet hooks and yarn to create everything from lace to dolls to sweaters and more.

Carrying on the tradition of the One-Skein Wonders series, this volume offers a wide variety of projects including scarves and shawls, hats, gloves, socks, bags and purses, jewelry, items for baby and child, home decor, and several *amigurumi* projects. You'll find the projects organized according to yarn weight, with like projects together within the weight category. So if you have an abundance of DK- or light worsted-weight yarn, check out the Light Weight section where you'll find patterns such as the Ice-Cold Summer Scarf on page 117, the Bellisfaire Beanie on page 123, the Sunflower Pillow on page 135, and the Green Water-Bottle Holder on page 141. If worsted yarn is your thing, page through the Medium Weight section of 38 projects, from the Three-Round Scarf on page 146 to the Peacock Hat on page 174 to a Spiral Mesh Bag on page 184 and Louis the Lobster on page 234. For those of you who prefer threadwork, we've included a section with eight projects including jewelry, accessories, and home decor.

If it's hats you're after, you'll find 18 patterns, such as Blue Bow Hat on page 160 in Medium Weight, Pixie Hats on page 128 in Light Weight, Around-the-Post Hat on page 166 in Medium Weight, and Men's Snow Sports Headband on page 252 in the Bulky Weight section. If you're into home decor, check out Blooming Blossom Coaster Set on page 8 in Thread, Lovely Linen Place Mat on page 107 in Fine Weight, Napkin Rings on page 139 in Light Weight, Entwine Trivets on page 239 in Medium Weight, and Fuzzy Tea Cozy on page 259 in Bulky Weight. You'll also find projects for babies and children — hats, booties, dolls' clothes, stuffed toys, and a bib — scattered throughout the sections.

We've used the Craft Yarn Council's standards to classify the yarn weights, and you'll find a chart of these weights on page 277 of the appendix. Also in this section is a glossary of all the techniques you'll need to complete the projects, as well as a list of abbreviations we've used. Wherever we thought it helpful, we've included a diagram of the stitch pattern, and you'll also find a key to the symbols used in the appendix.

We hope you find plenty of projects within these pages to keep those hooks moving and those loops interlocking!

Judith Durant

Edie Eckman

Thread

Blooming Blossom Coaster Set

Designed by Melinda Miller

A pretty blossom is the centerpiece of this duo, one round and one square. The coasters would make a charming hostess gift, and one ball makes four coasters.

Crocheting the Square Coaster

» Chain 6, join with slip st to form a ring.

» **RND 1 (RS):** Ch 1, 12 sc in ring, join with slip st to first sc.

» **RND 2:** Ch 3 (counts as dc), dc in same st, 2 dc in each sc around, join with slip st to top of ch-3. *You now have* 24 dc.

» **RND 3:** Ch 1, sc between next 2 dc posts, ch 3, skip next 3 dc, *sc in space between last dc skipped and next dc, ch 3, skip next 3 dc; repeat from * six more times, join with slip st to first sc. *You now have* 8 sc and 8 ch-3 spaces.

» **RND 4:** Ch 1, sc in same sc, *(hdc, dc, 3 tr, dc, hdc) in next space**, sc in next sc; repeat from * around, ending last repeat at **, join with slip st to first sc. *You now have* eight petals.

» **RND 5:** Ch 6 (counts as dc, ch 3), *sc in center tr of next petal, ch 3,** dc in next sc, ch 3, repeat from * around, ending last repeat at **, join with slip st to 3rd ch of ch-6.

» **RND 6:** Slip st in next ch-3 space, ch 1, 4 sc in same space, *5 sc in next ch-3 space**, 4 sc in next ch-3 space, repeat from * around, ending last repeat at **, join with slip st to first sc. *You now have* 72 sc.

» **RND 7:** Ch 1, sc in same st, *sc in next 3 sts, hdc in next 3 sts, dc in next 2 sts, 3 tr in next st, dc in next 2 sts, hdc in next 3 sts, sc in next 4 sts; repeat from * around, omitting last sc, join with slip st to first sc. Fasten off. *You now have* 20 sts on each side. Weave in ends.

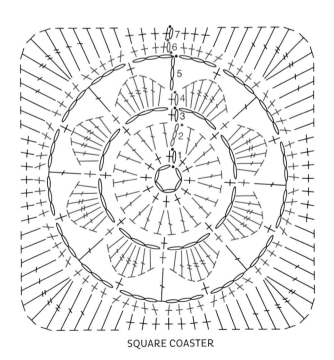

SQUARE COASTER

Crocheting the Round Coaster

» Work as for Square Coaster through Rnd 6.

» **RND 7:** Ch 1, sc in same st and in each remaining st around, join with slip st to beg sc. Fasten off. Weave in ends.

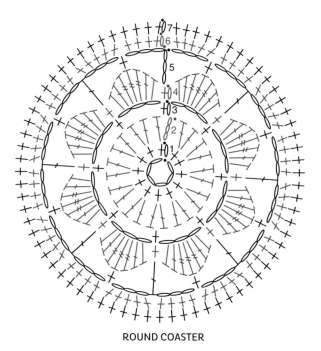

ROUND COASTER

Golden Ray of Sunshine Trivet

Designed by Susan McCabe

This little trivet is constructed of two simple hexagon motifs that are crocheted together. It is shown here in one color, but color changes on various rounds would add a little pizzazz.

Crocheting the Motifs
(make 2)

See chart on page 13.

» Loosely ch 6, join with slip st to form ring.

» **RND 1 (RS):** Ch 3 (counts as a dc throughout), 3 dc in ring, ch 2, *4 dc in ring, ch 2; repeat from * four more times, join with slip st to top of ch-3, ch 1, turn. *You now have 24 dc and 6 ch-spaces.*

» **RND 2 (WS):** Slip st in ch-2 space, beg shell in same space, ch 2, *shell in next space, ch 2; repeat from * four more times, join with slip st to top of ch-3, ch 1, turn. *You now have 6 shells.*

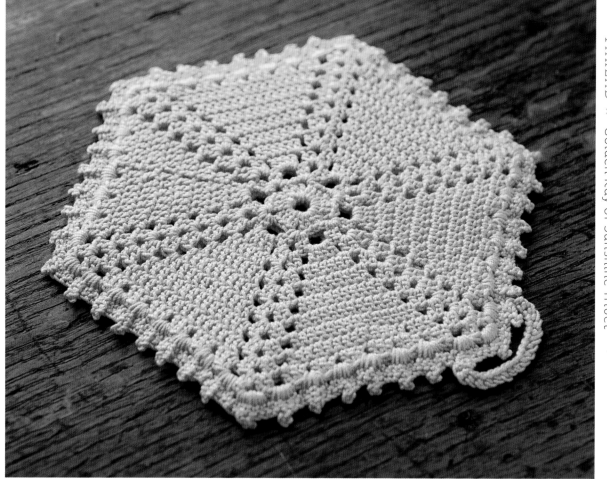

FINISHED MEASUREMENTS
6"/15 cm in diameter at widest point

YARN
Red Heart Classic Crochet Thread size 10, 100% mercerized
   cotton, 300 yds (274 m) per ball, Color 0421 Goldenrod

CROCHET HOOK
Steel US 8 (1.5 mm) *or size you need to obtain correct gauge*

GAUGE
Rounds 1–3 = 2"/5 cm in diameter

OTHER SUPPLIES
Tapestry needle

PATTERN ESSENTIALS

Beg shell (Ch 3, dc, ch 2, 2 dc)
in same space.

Shell (2 dc, ch 2, 2 dc) in same
space.

Tight picot-3 Ch 3, slip st to
top of dc at base of ch.

Picot shell (3 dc, tight picot-
3, 2 dc) in same space.

» **RND 3 (RS):** For the remaining rounds, do not turn the motif while working. Slip st in ch-2 space, ch 3 (counts as dc), 3 dc in same space, ch 1, shell in next shell space, ch 1, *4 dc in next space, ch 1, shell in next shell space, ch 1; repeat from * four more times, join with slip st to top of ch-3.

» **RND 4:** Ch 3 (counts as dc), dc in next 3 dc, *dc in next space, ch 1, shell in next shell space, ch 1, dc in next space**, dc in next 4 dc; repeat from * around, ending last repeat at **, join with slip st to top of ch-3.

» **RND 5:** Ch 3 (counts as dc), dc in next 4 dc, *dc in next space, ch 1, shell in next shell space, ch 1, dc in next space**, dc in next 6 dc; repeat from * around, ending last repeat at **, dc in next dc, join with slip st to top of ch-3.

» **RND 6:** Ch 3 (counts as dc), dc in next 5 dc, *dc in next space, ch 1, shell in next shell space, ch 1, dc in next space**, dc in next 8 dc; repeat from * around, ending last repeat at **, dc in last 2 dc, join with slip st to top of ch-3.

» **RND 7:** Ch 3 (counts as dc), dc in next 6 dc, *dc in next space, ch 1, shell in next shell space, ch 1, dc in next space**, dc in next 10 dc; repeat from * around, ending last repeat at **, dc in last 3 dc, join with slip st to top of ch-3.

» **RND 8:** Ch 3 (counts as dc), dc in next 7 dc, *dc in next space, ch 1, shell in next shell space, ch 1, dc in next space**, dc in next 12 dc; repeat from * around, ending last repeat at **, dc in last 4 dc, join with slip st to top of ch-3.

» **RND 9:** Ch 3 (counts as dc), dc in next 8 dc, *dc in next space, ch 1, shell in next shell space, ch 1, dc in next space**, dc in next 14 dc; repeat from * around, ending last repeat at **, dc in last 5 dc, join with slip st to top of ch-3.

» **RND 10:** Ch 3 (counts as dc), dc in next 9 dc, *dc in next space, ch 1, shell in next shell space, ch 1, dc in next space**, dc in next 16 dc; repeat from * around, ending last repeat at **, dc in last 6 dc, join with slip st to top of ch-3.

» Fasten off. Weave in ends.

Joining the Motifs

» With WS facing, line up and match edges. Join thread with slip st in ch-1 space before any shell, making sure to crochet through both motifs here and throughout. Ch 3 (counts as dc), (2 dc, tight picot-3, 2 dc) in same space — *beg picot shell made,* *picot shell in next shell space, picot shell in next ch-1 space, (skip next 3 dc, picot shell between the 3rd and 4th dc) five times, picot shell in next ch-1 space; repeat from * around, omitting the last picot shell, join with slip st to top of ch-3.

» Do not fasten off. *You now have* 48 picot shells.

Making the Hanging Loop *(optional)*

» Fsc 18 (see page 273). Skip next 2 picot shells. Slip st in last dc of the next picot shell. Fasten off and weave in ends.

Finishing

» Block.

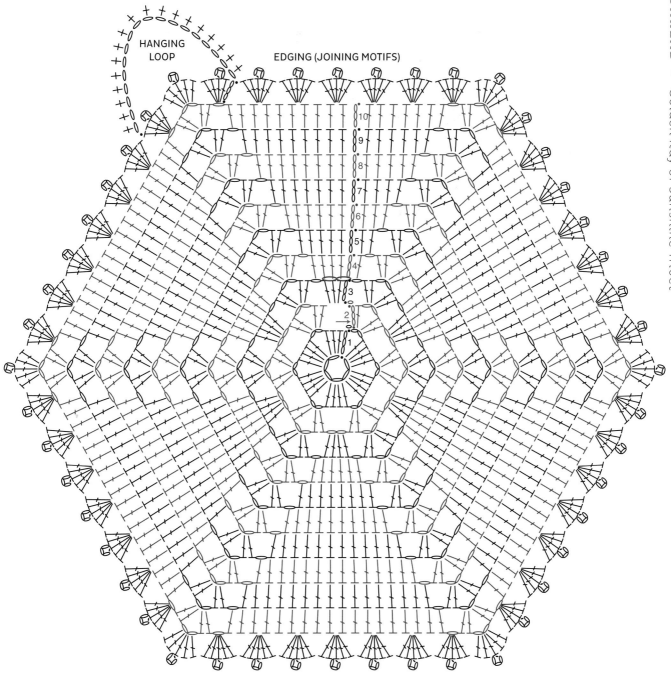

HANGING LOOP

EDGING (JOINING MOTIFS)

TRIVET

FINISHED MEASUREMENTS
As desired; sample fits 22½"/57 cm waist

YARN
DMC Cebelia Crochet Cotton size 20, 100% mercerized
cotton, 416 yds (380 m)/1.75 oz (50 g), Color 0001 White

CROCHET HOOK
Steel US 10 (1.15 mm) *or size you need to obtain correct
gauge*

GAUGE
Rows 1–14 = 3"/7.5 cm long (*Note:* Widest part of motif
should be 1½"/3.8 cm wide to fit belt properly.)

OTHER SUPPLIES
Suede strip measuring 1½"/3.8 cm wide and 3½"/9 cm
longer than desired finished waist size, sewing thread to
match belt and crochet thread (sample used black and
white), sewing needle, two 1"/2.5 cm D rings, thimble

Lacy Pineapple Belt

Designed by Bendy Carter

*This lovely belt will dress up any
simple black dress — all you need
are the pearls. Alternatively, it
would look great with jeans and
a T-shirt. (You could still wear the
pearls, too.)*

Preparing the Belt

» Cut the ends of the suede strip according to illustration.

Crocheting the Lace

See chart on page 16.

» **ROW 1:** Ch 4, (dc, ch 2, 2 dc) in 4th ch from hook, turn.

» **ROW 2–10:** Slip st in first 2 dc, slip st in ch-2 space, ch 3 (counts as dc), (dc, ch 2, 2 dc) in ch-2 space, turn.

» **ROW 11:** Slip st in first 2 dc, slip st in ch-2 space, ch 3 (counts as dc), [dc, (ch 2, 2 dc) three times] in ch-2 space, turn.

» **ROW 12:** Slip st in first 2 dc, slip st in ch-2 space, ch 3 (counts as dc), dc in same space, ch 3, 7 dc in next ch-2 space, ch 3, 2 dc in last ch-2 space, turn.

» **ROW 13:** Slip st in first 2 dc, slip st in ch-3 space, ch 3 (counts as dc), dc in same space, ch 3, dc in first dc of 7-dc group, (ch 1, dc in next dc) six times, ch 3, 2 dc in last ch-3 space, turn.

» **ROW 14:** Slip st in first 2 dc, slip st in ch-3 space, ch 3 (counts as dc), dc in same space, (ch 3, sc in next ch-3 space) six times, ch 3, 2 dc in last ch-3 space, turn.

» **ROW 15:** Slip st in first 2 dc, slip st in ch-3 space, ch 3 (counts as dc), dc in same space, (ch 3, sc in next ch-3 space) five times, ch 3, 2 dc in last ch-3 space, turn.

» **ROW 16:** Slip st in first 2 dc, slip st in ch-3 space, ch 3 (counts as dc), dc in same space, (ch 3, sc in next ch-3 space) four times, ch 3, 2 dc in last ch-3 space, turn.

» **ROW 17:** Slip st in first 2 dc, slip st in ch-3 space, ch 3 (counts as dc), dc in same space, (ch 3, sc in next ch-3 space) three times, ch 3, 2 dc in last ch-3 space, turn.

» **ROW 18:** Slip st in first 2 dc, slip st in ch-3 space, ch 3 (counts as dc), dc in same space, (ch 3, sc in next ch-3 space) two times, ch 3, 2 dc in last ch-3 space, turn.

» **ROW 19:** Slip st in first 2 dc, slip st in ch-3 space, ch 3 (counts as dc), dc in same space, ch 3, sc in next ch-3 space, ch 3, 2 dc in last ch-3 space, turn.

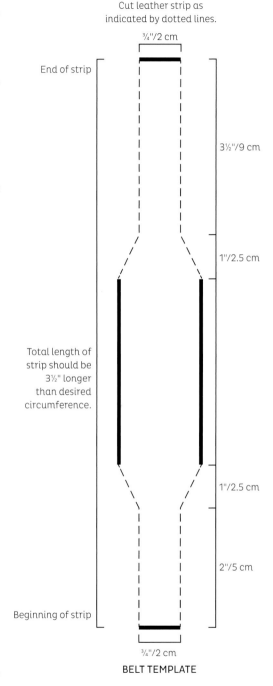

Cut leather strip as indicated by dotted lines.

¾"/2 cm

End of strip

3½"/9 cm

1"/2.5 cm

Total length of strip should be 3½" longer than desired circumference.

1"/2.5 cm

2"/5 cm

Beginning of strip

¾"/2 cm

BELT TEMPLATE

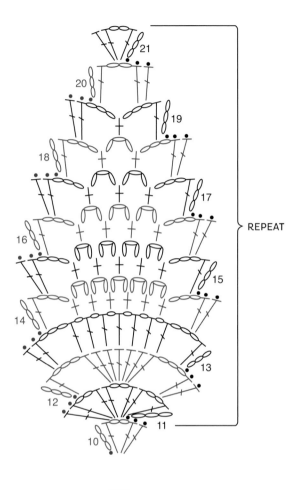

REPEAT

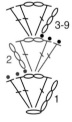

PINEAPPLE LACE

» **ROW 20:** Slip st in first 2 dc, slip st in ch-3 space, ch 3 (counts as dc), dc in same space, ch 2, 2 dc in last ch-3 space, turn.

» **ROW 21:** Repeat Row 2.

» Repeat Rows 11–21 until lace is 3¼"–5¼"/8.5–13.5 cm less than length of suede strip, ending with Row 21.

» Repeat Row 2 until lace is 3½"/9 cm longer than suede strip. Fasten off.

Attaching the Lace

» Place lace on suede strip so that Row 1 is centered at beginning of strip. Using thread to match crochet thread, sewing needle, and thimble, sew straight down middle of lace to end of strip. Fold the extra 3½"/9 cm of lace to the WS of the end of strip and sew in place.

Finishing

» Fold top 1"/2.5 cm of beginning of strip down with two D rings inside fold. Using thread to match belt, sew in place.

Burgundy Lace Hoops

Designed by Brenda K. B. Anderson

Here's a quick project that yields amazing results — thread crochet over purchased two-inch hoops. You can make a pair for every color in your wardrobe. (Or with one ball, you can make a pair for absolutely everyone you know.)

FINISHED MEASUREMENTS
2"/5 cm in diameter

YARN
Coats & Clark Aunt Lydia's Classic Crochet Thread size 10, 100% mercerized cotton, 350 yds (320 m)/ 3.5 oz (100 g), Color 0492 Burgundy

CROCHET HOOK
Steel US 6 (1.6 mm) *or size you need to obtain correct gauge*

GAUGE
Motif = 1¾"/4.5 cm in diameter before joining to hoop

OTHER SUPPLIES
2"/5 cm hoop earrings (see note on next page), embroidery needle

PATTERN ESSENTIALS

Puff st (Yo, insert hook into indicated ch-1 space, yo, pull loop through to front of work) five times, yo and pull through all but 1 loop on hook, yo and pull through remaining 2 loops on hook. *Note:* If you have trouble pulling through the puff stitches, make your yarn overs looser by holding your hook a little farther away from the work.

Working into the back of the chain With the WS of the chain facing, insert hook into the bumps on the back of the chain. *Note:* The RS of the chain is a series of horizontal Vs.

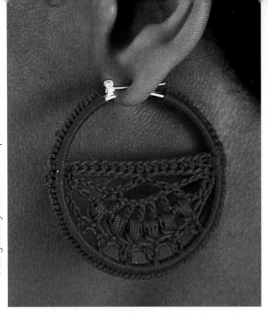

Crocheting the Motif

» **ROW 1 (WS):** Ch 16; working into the back of the ch, hdc in the 3rd ch from hook (first 2 ch sts count as first hdc), hdc in each ch across, turn. *You now have 15 sts.*

» **ROW 2 (RS):** Ch 5, skip first 7 hdc, (tr, ch 5, tr) in next hdc, ch 5, skip next 6 hdc, slip st into top of ch-2 at end of row, turn.

» **ROW 3 (WS):** Ch 4, skip ch-5 space, dc in next tr, ch 1, (dc into next ch, ch 1) five times, dc in next tr, ch 4, slip st in ch st at end of row, turn.

» **ROW 4 (RS):** Ch 4, skip (ch-space, dc), (puff st in next space, picot-4) six times, ch 4, slip st ch st at end of row. *Do not fasten off.*

Attaching Motif to Hoop

» Place motif inside hoop with working yarn coming out from the back of the hoop. Sc around hoop and motif to join them together as follows: With RS of motif facing, work 3 sc sts into the side of the motif working toward the top of the hoop, work 15 sc sts around hoop, ending at the top of the earring, fasten off.

» Starting at top (on other side of hinged post), work 15 sc sts around hoop. Now make 3 sc sts into the other side of motif, work 10 sc around hoop, sc in next picot, (work 5 sc around hoop, sc into next picot) five times, work 10 sc around hoop, slip st to first sc around hoop to join. Fasten off. Weave in ends.

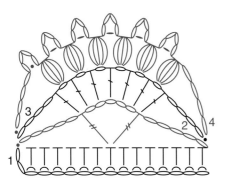

✳ **NOTE:** Hoop earrings with a front hinge work best. The kind with a hinged backing doesn't allow for the motif to be centered, and a hoop without hinges makes it difficult to keep the single crochet stitches from sliding around, although you could improvise with a small dab of Super Glue on each end.

Butterfly Necklace

Designed by Myra Wood

This butterfly will go anywhere and will be right at home with an elegant evening dress or with your turtleneck and jeans. Try crocheting with various sizes of thread — you can find just the right size for many applications.

FINISHED MEASUREMENTS
5"/12.5 cm at widest point and
4"/10 cm long, excluding ties

YARN
Coats & Clark Aunt Lydia's Fashion
Crochet Thread size 3, 100%
mercerized cotton, 150 yds (137 m)
per ball, Color 175 Warm Blue

CROCHET HOOK
US C/2 (2.75 mm) *or size you need
to obtain correct gauge*

GAUGE
Gauge is not crucial in this project

OTHER SUPPLIES
Yarn needle; T-pins; two 1"/2.5 cm plastic
rings; coordinating upholstery thread;
sewing needle; two 10 mm crystal beads;
five 6 mm crystal beads; seven beads of
varying shapes, approximately 3 mm and
4 mm; several seed beads, sizes 11º and 8º

PATTERN ESSENTIALS

Picot-3 Ch 3, slip st in 3rd ch from hook.

Tight picot-3 Ch 3, slip st in st at base of ch.

Crocheting the Left Wing

Note: Row 1 is RS on left wing and WS on right wing.

» Chain 11, join with slip st to first ch to form a ring.

» **ROW 1 (RS):** Working in ring, ch 3, tr, ch 1, 2 tr, (ch 1, 2 dc) four times, turn.

» **ROW 2:** Ch 3 (counts as dc), dc in next dc, ch 1, 2 dc in next dc, dc in next dc, ch 1, dc in next 2 dc, ch 1, dc in next dc, ch 1, 2 dc in next dc, ch 1, tr in next 2 tr, ch 1, tr in next tr, tr in top of ch-3, turn.

» **ROW 3:** Ch 4 (counts as tr), 2 tr in next tr, ch 2, 2 tr in next 2 tr, ch 1, dc in next 2 dc, ch 1, dc in next dc, ch 1, dc in next 2 dc, ch 2, dc in next 2 dc, ch 1, 2 dc in next dc, ch 2, dc in next dc, dc in top of ch-3, turn.

» **ROW 4:** Ch 1, sc in first dc, tight picot-3, sc in next dc, 2 sc in next ch-2 space, sc in next dc, tight picot-3, sc in next dc, sc in next ch-1 space, sc in next 2 dc, tight picot-3, 2 sc in next ch-2 space, sc in next dc, tight picot-3, sc in next dc, slip st in next ch-1 space, sc in next dc, ch 5, 2 dc in next dc, dc in next dc, (ch 1, tr in next 2 tr) two times, ch 2, tr in next 2 tr, tr in top of ch-4, turn.

» **ROW 5:** Ch 1, sc in next 3 tr, 2 sc in next ch-2 space, (sc in next 2 tr, sc in next ch-1 space) two times, sc in next 3 dc, 3 sc in next ch-5 space, turn.

» **ROW 6:** Ch 3, picot-3, ch 2, skip first 4 sc, sc in next sc, (ch 2, picot-3, ch 2, skip 3 sc, sc in next sc) two times, ch 2, picot-3, ch 2, skip 3 sc, slip st in last sc. Fasten off. Weave in ends.

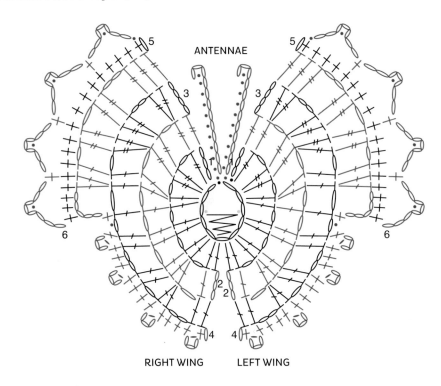

RIGHT WING   LEFT WING

Crocheting the Right Wing

» With WS of left wing facing, leaving an 8"/20.5 cm tail, join yarn in ring adjacent to first st of left wing.

» Work Rows 1–6 as for left wing.

Joining the Wings

» Using starting tail from right wing, thread yarn needle and weave back through bottom of 5 sts around to yellow dots on chart, sew opening between wings together from yellow dots to bottom of body. Weave in end.

Antennae

» Join thread at top of body between wings, (ch 9, picot-3, slip st in next 9 chs, slip st to ring to join) two times. Fasten off. Weave in ends. Block, stretching open the picot points with T-pins.

Covering the Rings
(make 2)

» Tie thread to ring, insert hook into ring, yo and pull loop through, place hook above ring, yo, pull through loop on hook.

» Insert hook into ring, yo, pull through — *2 loops on hook*, yo above ring, pull through both loops — *1 sc made*. Crochet over tail as you work. Repeat this step as many times as needed to cover entire ring, join with slip st to first sc. Fasten off, leaving a 6"/15 cm tail.

Making the I-Cord

MAKING THE RIGHT CORD

» Leaving a 6"/15 cm tail, ch 3.

» **ROW 1:** Insert hook in 2nd ch from hook, pull loop through, insert hook in 3rd ch from hook, pull loop through. *You now have 3 loops on hook.*

» **ROW 2:** Drop loops 2 and 3 (those just made) from hook and secure them between thumb and index finger, ch 1, replace loop 2 on hook, ch 1, replace loop 3 on hook, ch 1. *You now have 3 loops on hook.*

» Repeat Row 2 until cord measures 8"/20.5 cm, yo, pull through all 3 loops, ch 12 or length needed for bead closure; join with slip st to first ch, cut yarn, pull through loop, weave in end.

MAKING THE LEFT CORD

» Work as for right cord until cord measures 8"/20.5 cm, yarn over, pull through 3 loops, cut thread leaving a 6"/15 cm tail, pull through loop.

Assembling the Butterfly

» Using tail, sew each covered ring to top picot on butterfly wings; sew tail of each cord to tops of ring; weave in tails.

» Thread 10 mm crystal bead onto tail of left cord and sew to cord. Using upholstery thread, sew beads to center of butterfly from head to tail, in the following order: 6 mm, 10 mm, 6 mm, 4 mm, 3 mm. *Thread 10–12 beads on upholstery thread from small to large, placing a seed bead at the end, insert needle into next-to-last bead and up through remaining beads to top of strand, secure to butterfly body; repeat from * forming a second strand of beads, cut thread, and weave in end.

FINISHED MEASUREMENTS
Approximately 6.5"/16.5 cm inside circumference, unstretched

YARN
Coats & Clark Aunt Lydia's Fashion Crochet Thread size 3, 100% mercerized cotton, 150 yds (137 m) per ball, Color 65 Warm Teal

CROCHET HOOK
Steel US 1 (2.75 mm) *or size you need to obtain correct gauge*

GAUGE
7 rounds = 1"/2.5 cm in tubular slip-stitch bead crochet

OTHER SUPPLIES
Big eye beading needle; size 6° seed beads, for unembellished bangle: 290 turquoise/emerald mix, about 1 oz (30 g); for embellished bangle: 290 transparent emerald, about 1 oz/30 g, and 140 turquoise/emerald mix, about ½ oz/15 g); yarn needle

Beady Bangles

Designed by Judith Durant

Here's a great introduction to tubular slip-stitch bead crochet, using larger-than-traditional materials. Using size 6° seed beads and size 3 cotton crochet thread, you can whip up a bracelet in very little time. An optional tubular embellishment sits atop the bangle join.

PATTERN ESSENTIALS

Bch (beaded chain stitch) Slide a bead up against the hook and then make a chain stitch, keeping the bead behind the stitch.

Slip-stitch bead crochet *Holding a bead, insert hook into loop and position the bead to the right of the hook; push a bead up to the hook, making sure the yarn and bead are above the old bead; yo hook, pull through both loops on hook. Repeat from * to desired length. *Note:* You'll be working from inside the tube.

Crocheting the Bangle

» Thread the yarn onto the big eye beading needle and string all 290 emerald or turquoise/emerald mix beads. Chain 5 with beads. Work slip-stitch bead crochet into the first beaded chain to form a ring. Continue in the round with slip-stitch bead crochet until all strung beads have been worked or until bangle is desired length; sample is 8"/20.5 cm. Fasten off, leaving a 6"/15 cm tail.

Crocheting the Embellishment *(optional)*

» Thread yarn onto the big eye needle and string the 140 mixed beads. Chain 14 with beads. Work slip-stitch bead crochet into the first beaded chain to form a ring. Continue in the round with slip-stitch bead crochet until all strung beads have been worked; the sample has 10 rounds. Fasten off and weave in the tails.

Finishing

» Slide embellishment over bangle. Join ends of bangle to form a ring and weave in tails. Slide embellishment over join.

Beaded Lariat

Designed by Judith Durant

Tubular slip-stitch crochet with beads is a great technique for creating straps of all kinds. This lariat has a tassel at each end and looks great worn around the neck and looped in front. This rope has a very subtle spiral pattern; this could be more pronounced by using more contrasting beads or eliminated by using all one color.

23

PATTERN ESSENTIALS

Bch (beaded chain stitch) Slide
a bead up against the hook and
then make a chain stitch, keeping
the bead behind the stitch.

Slip-stitch bead crochet *Holding
a bead, insert hook into loop and
position the bead to the right of
the hook; push a bead up to the
hook, making sure the yarn and
bead are above the old bead; yo
hook, pull through both loops on
hook. Repeat from * to desired
length. Note: You'll be working
from inside the tube.*

Stringing the Beads

» Set aside 288 beads for the tassels,
144 of each color. Thread the yarn onto
the big eye beading needle and *string
three A beads, and three B beads;
repeat from * until all remaining beads
are strung.

Note: You may have more of one color
than the other; just string as many six-
bead sequences as possible. If you want
to adjust the length of the rope, plan
on stringing 6"/15 cm of beads for each
1"/2.5 cm of beaded rope.

Crocheting the Rope

» Leaving a 12"/30.5 cm tail for a tassel,
chain 6 with beads. Work slip-stitch
crochet into first beaded chain to form
a ring. Continue in the round with
slip-stitch bead crochet until all strung
beads have been worked. Fasten off,
leaving a 12"/30.5 cm tail.

Making the Tassels

» Thread a tail onto the beading needle.
*Pick up 24 beads and pass from out-
side to inside through the loop of the
next beaded stitch; repeat from * to add
six 24-bead loops. Weave in tail. Repeat
on the other end of the rope.

Nana's Hanky

Designed by Gwen Steege

Gwen's grandmother was never without a hanky with a crocheted edge — either up her sleeve or in progress on her hook! This simple edging was designed in her honor. Handkerchief blanks are widely available online as well as in some fabric and craft stores. Take care not to let the first round of single crochet stitches pull in too tightly, or the edges will "cup."

PATTERN ESSENTIALS

Blanket st Thread embroidery needle with perle cotton. Working from left to right along edge, insert needle from WS to RS at very edge of fabric. *Holding thread to the left, insert needle from RS to WS at a point ⅛"/3 mm in from edge of fabric and ⅛"/3 mm to left of first st, then tilt top of needle away so that needle tip peeks out at edge of fabric and is *in front of thread*; pull needle through and adjust stitch to fit snugly but not tightly against edge of fabric. Repeat from * around edge. (See illustration on next page.)

FINISHED MEASUREMENTS

The edging is approximately ½"/13 mm wide; total measurement depends on handkerchief measurement

YARN

DMC cotton perle size 8, 100% cotton, 95 yds (87 m)/0.35 oz (10 g,) Color 818

CROCHET HOOK

Steel US 5 (1.9 mm) *or size you need to obtain correct gauge*

GAUGE

7 repeats = 3"/7.5 cm in pattern

OTHER SUPPLIES

Water-erasable marking pen (optional), ruler (optional), hemmed fabric handkerchief (sample is 11"/28 cm square), embroidery needle for blanket stitching, yarn needle

Setting Up for the Edging

» To create a guide for blanket stitching, use a water-erasable marking pen to make small ⅛"/3 mm marks around the entire edge of the handkerchief. If the existing hemstitches are about ⅛"/3 mm apart, use them as a guide.

» Using the perle cotton and embroidery needle, work blanket sts all the way around the handkerchief, spaced ⅛"/3 mm apart. At each corner, stitch into the same spot three times. Work a multiple of 3 blanket sts plus 2 across each side, counting 1 corner st.

Crocheting the Edging

» **RND 1:** With hook, join yarn 1 st to the left of any corner blanket st, ch 1, sc in each blanket st around, placing 3 sc in each corner st, join with slip st to first st. *You now have* a multiple of 3 plus 1 sc across each side, plus 3 sc in each corner.

» **RND 2:** *Ch 3, skip 2 sc, slip st in next sc; repeat from * across to 1 sc before corner st; at the corner, ch 5, skip 3 sc, slip st in next sc; repeat from * around, join with slip st in first slip st.

» **RND 3:** (3 sc, hdc, 3 sc) in each ch-3 space and (3 sc, 2 hdc, dc, 2 hdc, 3 sc) in each ch-5 corner space around, join with slip st to first sc. Fasten off.

» Weave in ends.

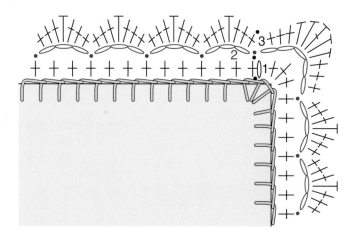

NANA'S HANKY

Lace
Weight

Bristleberry Scarf ∗ The Gratitude Scarf ∗
Bead Crochet Mesh Möbius ∗ Shell Net Cowl

Bristleberry Scarf

Designed by Mike Horwath

Crocheted in a hand-dyed lace-weight wool, this scarf is a gift to both sight and touch. Seemingly complex, the pattern is easily remembered and combines single crochet, double crochet, and chains.

FINISHED MEASUREMENTS
76"/193 cm long and 6"/15 cm wide

YARN
Madelinetosh Prairie, 100% superwash merino wool, 840 yds (768 m)/4 oz (115 g), Color Sequoia

CROCHET HOOK
US G/6 (4 mm) *or size you need to obtain correct gauge*

GAUGE
2 pattern repeats and 12 rows = 2½"/6.5 cm

OTHER SUPPLIES
Yarn needle

Crocheting the Scarf

» Chain 42.

» **ROW 1:** Sc in 2nd ch from the hook and in each ch across, turn.

» **ROW 2:** Ch 1, sc in first 3 sc, *ch 5, skip 3 sc**, sc in next 5 sc; repeat from * across, ending last repeat at **, sc in last 3 sc, turn.

» **ROW 3:** Ch 1, sc in first 2 sc, *ch 3, sc in next ch-5 space, ch 3, skip 1 sc**, sc in next 3 sc; repeat from * across, ending last repeat at **, sc in last 2 sc, turn.

» **ROW 4:** Ch 1, sc in first sc, *ch 3, skip 1 sc, sc in next space, sc in next sc, sc in next space, ch 3, skip 1 sc, sc in next sc; repeat from * across, turn.

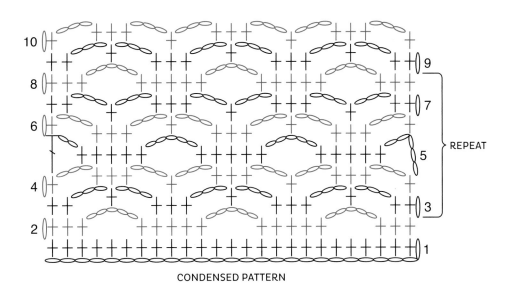

CONDENSED PATTERN

» **ROW 5:** Ch 5, *sc in next space, sc in next 3 sc, sc in next space**, ch 5; repeat from * across, ending last repeat at **, ch 2, dc in last sc, turn.

» **ROW 6:** Ch 1, sc in dc, ch 3, *skip 1 sc, sc in next 3 sc, ch 3, skip 1 sc**, sc in next space, ch 3; repeat from * across, ending last repeat at **, sc in 3rd ch of ch-5, turn.

» **ROW 7:** Ch 1, sc in first sc, *sc in next space, ch 3, skip 1 sc, sc in next sc, skip 1 sc, ch 3, sc in next space, sc in next sc; repeat from * across, turn.

» **ROW 8:** Ch 1, sc in first 2 sc, sc in next space, *ch 5, skip 1 sc, sc in next space**, sc in next 3 sc, sc in next space; repeat from * across, ending last repeat at **, sc in last 2 sc, turn.

» Repeat Rows 3–8 until piece measures 80"/203 cm or desired length, ending with Row 8 of pattern.

» **LAST ROW:** Ch 1, sc in first 2 sc, skip next sc, 5 sc in next space, *skip next sc, sc in next 3 sc, skip next sc, 5 sc in next space; repeat from * across, ending skip next sc, sc in last 2 sc.

Finishing

» Fasten off. Weave in ends and lightly block to even out edge stitches.

The Gratitude Scarf

Designed by René E. Wells

Gratitude can be defined as "with a readiness to return kindness." This reversible pattern, lovely from either side, is worked from the center back to the ends, making the most of a small skein.

FINISHED MEASUREMENTS
28"/71 cm long and 3½"/9 cm wide

YARN
Windy Valley Muskox Majestic Blend, 80% extra-fine merino wool/15% qiviut/5% mulberry silk, 144 yds (132 m)/1 oz (28 g), Color 5037

CROCHET HOOK
US G/6 (4 mm) *or size you need to obtain correct gauge*

GAUGE
1 front post double crochet plus shell of (2 dc, 1 ch, 2 dc) plus 1 front post double crochet = 1"/2.5 cm; 11 rows = 4"/10 cm

OTHER SUPPLIES
Yarn needle

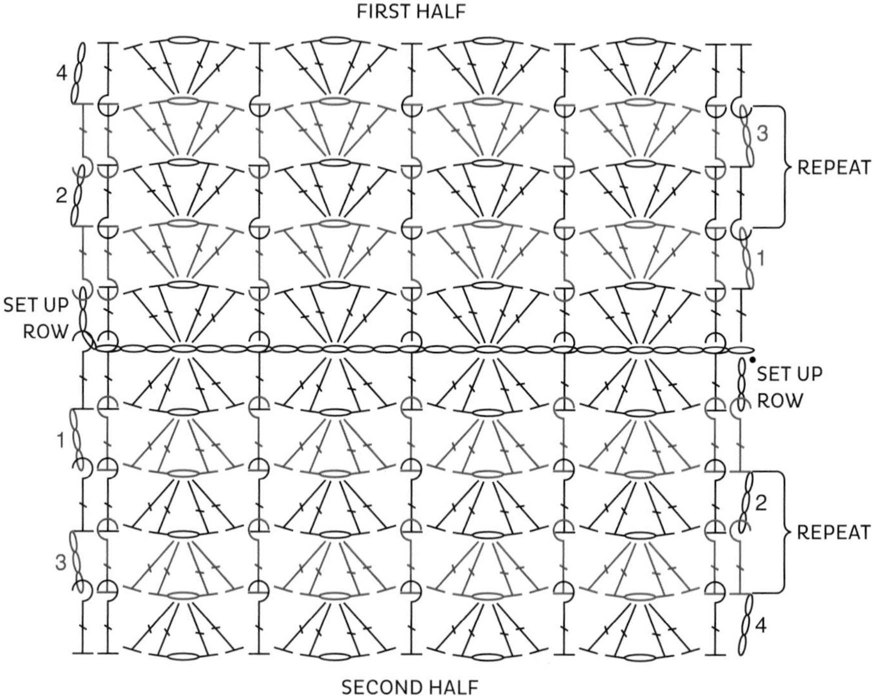

PATTERN ESSENTIALS

Shell (2 dc, ch 1, 2 dc) in same st or space.

FIRST HALF

SET UP ROW

REPEAT

SET UP ROW

REPEAT

SECOND HALF

✳ **NOTE:** The scarf is worked from the back neck down so the ends will match. Wind a second ball from the first, stopping when both balls are the same size. Do not cut the yarn. When you make the starting chain from the midpoint, you can work each half of the scarf from its own ball, and there will be no ends in the middle to darn in.

Crocheting the First Half

» Chain 26, plus 3 for first dc.

» Work Setup Row from chart or written instructions.

» **SETUP ROW:** Dc in 4th ch from hook, *skip 2 ch, shell in next ch, skip 2 ch, dc in next ch; repeat from * three more times, dc in last ch, turn.

» **ROW 1 (RS):** Ch 3 (counts as dc), *FPdc in next dc, shell in center space of next shell; repeat from * across, ending FPdc in last 2 dc, turn.

» **ROW 2:** Ch 3 (counts as dc), *BPdc in next st, shell in center space of next shell; repeat from * across, ending BPdc in last 2 sts, turn.

» **ROW 3:** Ch 3 (counts as dc), *FPdc in next st, shell in center space of next shell; repeat from * across, ending FPdc in last 2 sts, turn.

» Repeat Rows 2 and 3 until half of yarn has been used (sample is worked for 38 rows). Fasten off. Weave in end.

Crocheting the Second Half

» **SETUP ROW:** With WS facing, join yarn in first ch, ch 3 (counts as dc), *BPdc in dc of row below, skip 2 ch, shell in next ch, skip 2 ch; repeat from * across, ending BPdc in dc of row below, BPdc in last st.

» **ROW 1:** Ch 3 (counts as dc), *FPdc in next st, shell in center space of next shell; repeat from * across, ending FPdc in last 2 sts.

» **ROW 2:** Ch 3 (counts as dc), *BPdc in next st, shell in center space of next shell; repeat from * across, ending BPdc in last 2 sts.

» Repeat Rows 1 and 2 until second half measures same as first half. Fasten off. Weave in end.

Bead Crochet Mesh Möbius

Designed by Nancy Brown

A simple mesh-stitch scarf becomes a work of art with the addition of a beaded picot edging. Wrap the scarf once or twice to suit your desired look.

FINISHED MEASUREMENTS

Approximately 56"/142 cm in circumference and 4"/10 cm wide

YARN

Fly Designs Cashmara, 80% merino wool, 10% cashmere, 10% nylon, 590 yds (540 m)/4 oz (113 g), Color Teal

CROCHET HOOK

US F/5 (3.75 mm) *or size you need to obtain correct gauge*

GAUGE

Approximately 7 mesh blocks and 5 rows = 2"/5 cm

OTHER SUPPLIES

Yarn needle, approximately 500 size 6 mm glass seed beads (about 50 g), big eye beading needle or dental floss threader

Crocheting the Strip

» Chain 26.

» **ROW 1:** Dc in 6th chain from hook, (ch 1, skip 1 ch, dc in next ch) 10 times, turn. *You now have 11 ch-1 spaces.*

» **ROW 2:** Ch 4 (counts as dc and ch 1), dc in next dc, (ch 1, dc in next dc) 10 times, ending with dc under turning ch, turn.

» Repeat Row 2 until piece measures approximately 56"/142 cm or desired length, ending with an even number of rows. Fasten off.

continued on page 34

PATTERN ESSENTIALS

Join yarn with sc Make a slip knot on hook, insert hook in st, yo, pull up a loop, yo, draw through both loops.

Bead picot (Slide a bead up close to work, ch 1) three times, slip st in the 2 front loops at top of next dc.

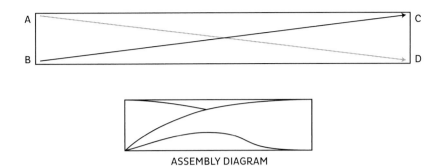

ASSEMBLY DIAGRAM

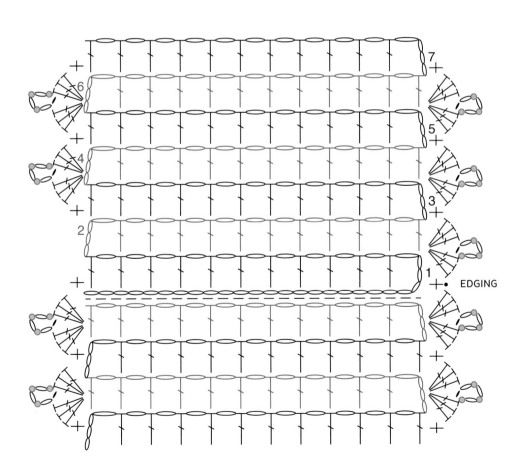

Joining the Möbius

» Sew last row to first row to seam the strip into a Möbius with a half twist by joining corners A to D and corners B to C (see illustration on page 33).

Crocheting the Edging

» Thread the yarn onto the big eye beading needle or floss threader and string all beads.

» The edging is worked on ends of rows either over the beg ch-3 or over the ending dc.

» Join yarn with sc over the end of any row; *(3 dc, bead picot, 3 dc) over end of next row, sc over end of next row; repeat from * around, ending with slip st in beg sc. Fasten off. Weave in ends.

Finishing

» Place Möbius on a padded surface, cover with damp cloths, and allow to dry thoroughly.

Shell Net Cowl

Designed by Ryan Hollist

This wide Möbius cowl is worked continuously in the round from the inside of the circle to the outside. The pattern comprises double crochet shells separated by chain stitches.

Crocheting the Cowl

» Chain 362. Be careful not to twist chain.

» **RND 1:** 4 dc in back loop of beg ch — *shell made*, *ch 4, skip 6 ch, 4 dc in back of next ch; repeat from * around to last 4 ch. *You now have* 52 shells.

» **RND 2:** Working on the opposite side of the base chain, ch 4, 4 dc in the base of first shell made, *ch 4, skip 6 ch, 4 dc in base of next shell; repeat from * around. (A shell is made into the base of each shell made in Rnd 1.)

» **REMAINING RNDS:** Ch 4, 4 dc in third dc of first shell made (from Rnd 1), *ch 4, skip next ch-4 space, 4 dc in third dc of next shell; repeat from * until cowl is desired size (sample has 13 rounds). Ch 4, skip next ch-4 space, slip st in third dc of next shell. Fasten off. Weave in ends.

> ✳ **NOTE:** For alternate lengths, chain a multiple of 7 plus 5.

FINISHED MEASUREMENTS
Approximately 60"/152.5 cm circumference and 9"/23 cm wide

YARN
Knit Picks Shimmer, 70% baby alpaca/30% silk, 440 yds (402 m)/1.75 oz (50 g), Color E766 Eucalyptus

CROCHET HOOK
US B/1 (2.25 mm) *or size you need to obtain correct gauge*

GAUGE
4 pattern repeats (shell, ch-4 space) and 11 rounds = 4"/10 cm; exact gauge is not essential

OTHER SUPPLIES
Yarn needle

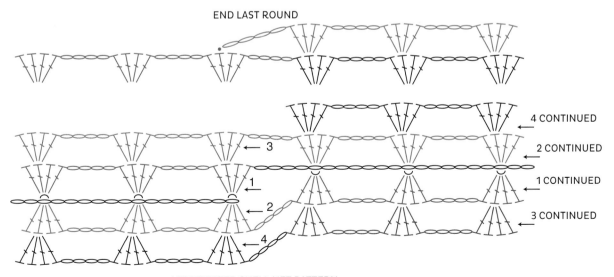

END LAST ROUND

4 CONTINUED

2 CONTINUED

1 CONTINUED

3 CONTINUED

ABBREVIATED SHELL NET PATTERN

Super-Fine Weight

JoAnn's Scarf * Switchback Scarf * "Practice Makes Perfect" Scarf *
Simply Elegant Scarf * Autumn Camouflage Scarf * Easy-to-Wear Cowl *
Sea Breeze Shawlette * Secret Garden Shrug * Autumn Leaves Shawlette *
Flower Power Purse * WIP Project Bag * Tunisian Pouch * Shell Stitch
Fingerless Gloves * Astra Gloves * Elegant Fingerless Gloves * Bangle
Bracelets * One-Skein Doll Wardrobe * Rainbow Doll Ensemble *
V-Stitch Sundress * French Toast with Maple Sugar Jacket

JoAnn's Scarf

Designed by Marcia Sommerkamp

This scarf was stitched for a friend who is an avid sock knitter, so the material was obvious! Easy enough for a beginner and soft enough to double and loop through, this makes a great gift idea for men or women.

FINISHED MEASUREMENTS
84"/213.5 cm long and 4½"/11.5 cm wide

YARN
Berroco Comfort Sock, 50% super fine nylon/50% super fine acrylic, 447 yds (412 m)/3.5 oz (100 g), Color 1816

CROCHET HOOK
US E/4 (3.5 mm) *or size you need to obtain correct gauge*

GAUGE
11 stitches and 6 rows = 2"/5 cm in pattern

OTHER SUPPLIES
Yarn needle

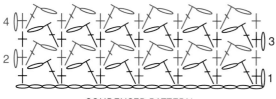

CONDENSED PATTERN

Crocheting the Scarf

» Chain 26.

» **ROW 1:** Sc in 2nd chain from hook, dc in same st; *ch 1, skip next 2 ch, (sc, dc) in next ch; repeat from * across to last 3 sts, ch 1, skip 2 ch, sc in last ch, turn.

» **ROW 2:** Ch 1, (sc, dc) in first st, ch 1, *(sc, dc) in next sc, ch 1; repeat from * across, ending with sc in last sc, turn.

» Repeat Row 2 for pattern to desired length.

Finishing

» Fasten off. Weave in ends. Block lightly.

Switchback Scarf

Designed by Ryan Hollist

The innovative color effect in this scarf is created by crocheting with alternating ends of the skein, and the switchback design emphasizes the varying colors. The extra-long length is great for wrapping!

FINISHED MEASUREMENTS
Approximately 130"/330 cm long and 3"/7.5 cm wide

YARN
Noro Taiyo Sock, 50% cotton/ 17% wool/17% nylon/16% silk, 459 yds (420 m)/3.5 oz (100 g), Color 06

CROCHET HOOK
US D/3 (3.25 mm) *or size you need to obtain correct gauge*

GAUGE
20 stitches and 9 rows = 4"/10 cm in double crochet; exact gauge is not essential

OTHER SUPPLIES
Yarn needle

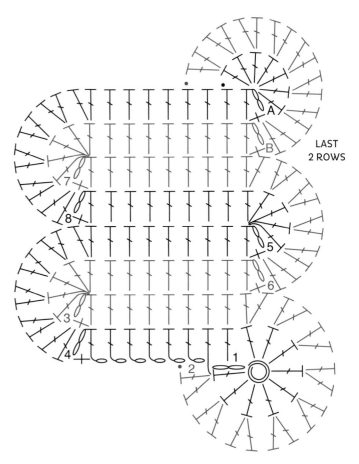

LAST 2 ROWS

CONDENSED PATTERN

Crocheting the Scarf

Note: When switching strands, rotate the work so that the strand is being picked up with the same side facing that was last worked.

» With Strand 1, make an adjustable ring (see page 271).

» **ROW 1 (RS):** Ch 2 (does not count as st), 9 dc in ring, close ring, dc in beg ch-2 space, dc in first dc, work 6 fdc, ch 2, sc in bottom of fdc just made, drop Strand 1 to be picked up later.

» **ROW 2:** With RS facing, join Strand 2 with a slip st in ch at base of second fdc, 2 dc in the first 9 dc of Row 1, dc in next 7 dc, (dc, ch 2, sc) in next dc.

» **ROW 3:** With Strand 2, turn, skip sc and ch-2 space at end of last row, 5 dc in next dc, dc in next 7 dc, (dc, ch 2, sc) in next dc, drop Strand 2 to be picked up later.

» **ROW 4:** Pick up Strand 1, turn, 2 dc in side of sc 2 rows below (insert hook under outside "leg" loops of sc), working across sts of previous row, 2 dc in next 5 dc, dc in next 7 dc, (dc, ch 2, sc) in next dc.

» **ROW 5:** With Strand 1, turn, skip sc and ch-2 space at end of last row, 5 dc in next dc, dc in next 7 dc, (dc, ch 2, sc) in next dc, drop Strand 1 to be picked up later.

» **ROW 6:** Rotate work, pick up Strand 2, 2 dc in side of sc 2 rows below (insert hook under outside "leg" loops of sc), working across sts of previous row, 2 dc in next 5 dc, dc in next 7 dc, (dc, ch 2, sc) in next dc.

» Repeat Rows 3–6 until scarf is desired length, ending with Row 4 of pattern.

» **ROW A:** With Strand 1, turn, skip sc and ch-2 space at end of last row, 7 dc in next dc, skip next dc, slip st in next dc. Fasten off Strand 1. Weave in end.

» **ROW B:** Rotate work, pick up Strand 2, turn, 2 dc in side of sc 2 rows below, working across sts of previous row, 2 dc in next 7 dc; working across 2 rows below, slip st in second dc from last slip st made. Fasten off Strand 2. Weave in end.

"Practice Makes Perfect" Scarf

Designed by Beth Graham

Tunisian simple stitch worked in subtly variegated shades of blue and purple combines with a picot edge to make this light and romantic scarf, which can also be worn as a shawlette.

FINISHED MEASUREMENTS
Approximately 60"/152.5 cm long and
7½"/19 cm wide

YARN
Dream in Color Smooshy Sock Yarn, 100% superfine
Australian merino wool, 450 yds (411 m)/4 oz (113 g),
Color 230 Deep Seaflower

CROCHET HOOKS
US H/8 (5 mm) afghan hook *or size you need to obtain
correct gauge* and crochet hook one size smaller

GAUGE
20 stitches and 17 rows = 4"/10 cm in pattern on
afghan hook

OTHER SUPPLIES
Yarn needle

Crocheting the First End of the Scarf

» With afghan hook, ch 3. Pick up loops in 2nd and 3rd chain from hook (3 loops total on hook). Work return row as for Tunisian simple stitch (TSS) (see page 274).

» **ROW 1 (INCREASE ROW):** Pick up loop in second vertical bar as usual for TSS (2 loops on hook); pick up loop in the space before next vertical bar (3 loops on hook); pick up loop in each st to end of forward row; work return row. ***Note:*** The extra stitch created in the space between vertical bars makes a small eyelet along the edge of the fabric.

» **ROW 2:** Work even in TSS.

» Repeat Rows 1 and 2 until you've completed 70 rows, or until scarf is approximately 7½"/19 cm wide, unblocked.

Crocheting the Back of the Scarf

» **ROW 1:** Pick up loop in second vertical bar (2 loops on hook); pick up loop in space before next vertical bar (3 loops on hook); skip next bar and pick up loop in following vertical bar (4 loops on hook); continue picking up loops normally to end of forward row; work return row. ***Note:*** Row 1 maintains the eyelet edging established in the first part of the scarf without increasing stitches.

» **ROW 2:** Work even in TSS.

» Repeat Rows 1 and 2 for 110 rows, or until total length of scarf is approximatley 43"/109 cm, unblocked.

Crocheting the Second End of the Scarf

» **ROW 1 (DECREASE ROW):** Pick up loop in second vertical bar (2 loops on hook); pick up loop in the space before the next vertical bar (3 loops on hook); skip next bar and pick up loop in following vertical bar (4 loops on hook); continue picking up loops normally to end of forward row; work return row until 3 loops remain on hook, yo and draw through all 3 loops. *Note:* The extra loop made between vertical bars on the forward row continues the established eyelet effect, while the last step of the return row decreases the row by 1 st.

» **ROW 2:** Work even in TSS.

» Repeat Rows 1 and 2 until 3 sts remain, ending with Row 1.

» **LAST ROW:** Bind off TSS (see page 274). Do not fasten off.

Crocheting the Border

Note: As you look along the edge of the scarf, notice that the edge stitches have created a V effect that mimics a single crochet stitch. You will treat these Vs like single crochet stitches for the purposes of the border. For example, when border instructions say "sc in back loop of each edge st," you will create a single crochet in the back loop of the V.

» With RS facing and smaller crochet hook, ch 1, 3 sc in same space as last bound-off st, sc in back loop of each edge st across, 3 sc in corner edge st, sc across to next corner, 3 sc in corner st, sc in next eyelet, tight picot-3, *sc in

next edge st, sc in next eyelet, tight picot-3 (see page 274); repeat from * to end of scarf, 3 sc in corner st, sc across to first sc, join with slip st to first sc. Fasten off.

Finishing

» Weave in ends. Wet block to shape.

Simply Elegant Scarf

Designed by Annalee Rose

This lovely double-layered scarf, suitable for a winter bride, features an open crochet pattern worked in the round. Beads are incorporated in a random pattern using the hook method.

FINISHED MEASUREMENTS
Approximately 48"/122 cm long and 5"/12.5 cm wide

YARN
Swans Island Organic Fingering Yarn, 100% merino wool, 580 yds (530 m)/3.5 oz (100 g), Color 111 Natural

CROCHET HOOKS
US K/10½ (6.5 mm) *or size you need to obtain correct gauge* and steel US 10 (1.15 mm) for beading

GAUGE
4 shells and 6 rounds = 4"/10 cm in shell pattern

OTHER SUPPLIES
Approximately 300 (about 15 g) size 6° opaque ivory luster seed beads, yarn needle

Crocheting the Scarf

» Loosely ch 40; being careful not to twist the chain, join in a ring with a slip st to first ch.

» **FOUNDATION RND:** Ch 1, sc in each ch around, join with a slip st to first sc. *You now have 40 sc.*

» **RND 1:** Ch 3 (counts as dc), (dc, ch 1, 2 dc) in same st, *skip next 3 sc**, shell in next st; repeat from * around, ending last repeat at **, join with slip st to top of ch-3.

» **RND 2:** Placing beads randomly using the hook method, slip st in next st, slip st in ch-1 space, ch 3, (dc, ch 1, 2 dc) in same space, *skip 4 dc, shell in next ch-1 space; repeat from * around, join with slip st to top of ch-3. Repeat Rnd 2 until piece measures 48"/122 cm or desired length from beginning.

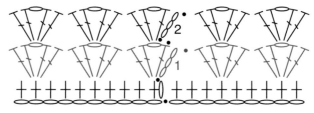

LAST ROUND

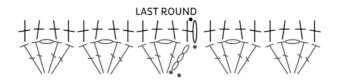

ABBREVIATED FOUNDATION ROUND

PATTERN ESSENTIALS

Shell (2 dc, ch 1, 2 dc) in same st.

Hooking beads To place a bead with the hook method, pick up a bead with the small steel hook. Slip the loop from working larger hook, pick up the loop with the small hook, slide one bead onto the loop, reinsert larger hook and continue with the stitch.

» **FINISHING RND:** Ch 1, sc in same st, sc in each dc around, skipping over each ch-1 space, join with slip st to top of first sc. *You now have* 40 sc. Do not fasten off.

Finishing

» **EDGING:** To close up the end, line up rows of the stitch pattern and slip st through both top loops of matching sc pairs, placing a bead in every other stitch. Join with a slip st to first st. Fasten off.

» Matching the pattern rows along the length to avoid twisting the scarf, join yarn and work edging across other end, working through the bottom loops of foundation chain. Fasten off. Weave in ends. Lightly block.

43

Autumn Camouflage Scarf

Designed by Janet Brani

The simple change from single crochet to treble and back creates a camouflage pattern with this autumn-hued sock yarn. The five button-on flowers can be scattered across the treble rows, or grouped tightly together to form one large flower embellishment.

FINISHED MEASUREMENTS
68"/172.5 cm long and 5½"/14 cm wide

YARN
Zitron Trekking XXL, 75% superwash wool/25% nylon, 459 yds (420 m)/ 3.5 oz (100 g), Color 470

CROCHET HOOK
US E/4 (3.5 mm) *or size you need to obtain correct gauge*

GAUGE
20 stitches and 20 rows = 4"/10 cm in single crochet

OTHER SUPPLIES
Five ¾"/19 mm buttons or size needed to snugly button through treble crochet rows

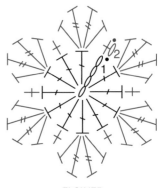

FLOWER

Crocheting the Scarf

» Chain 26.

» **ROW 1:** Sc in 2nd chain from hook and in each chain across, turn. *You now have* 25 sc.

» **ROWS 2–12:** Ch 1, sc in each sc across, turn.

» **ROWS 13–15:** Ch 4 (counts as tr), skip first st, tr in each st across, turn.

» **ROW 16:** Ch 1, sc in each st across, turn.

» Repeat Rows 2–16 thirteen more times, then work Rows 2–12 once more. Fasten off and weave in ends.

Crocheting the Flower Embellishments *(make 5)*

» Chain 4.

» **RND 1:** 11 dc into 4th ch from hook (beginning ch counts as first dc), join with slip st to top of beginning ch-4.

» **RND 2:** Ch 1, sc in same st, *(hdc, 2 tr, hdc) in next dc**, sc in next dc; repeat from * around, ending last repeat at **, join with slip st to first sc. *You now have* six petals. Fasten off. Weave in ends.

Finishing

» Sew each flower loosely to a button. Arrange four flowers in a circle around the fifth flower on the end treble section. Push buttons between stitches to secure.

Easy-to-Wear Cowl

Designed by Edie Eckman

It's amazing what one can do with a few simple stitches and a skein of lovely variegated yarn. This colorful striped cowl is worked mostly with chain stitches and single crochet, with the occasional double crochet.

FINISHED MEASUREMENTS

Approximately 28"/71 cm circumference
　and 12"/30.5 cm deep

YARN

Noro Silk Garden Sock, 40% lamb's
　wool/25% silk/25% nylon/10% kid mohair,
　328 yds (300 m)/35 oz (100 g), Color S302

CROCHET HOOK

US G/6 (4 mm) *or size you need to obtain correct gauge*

GAUGE

16 stitches or 8 repeats and 12 rows =
　4"/10 cm in Chain-Stitch pattern

OTHER SUPPLIES

Yarn needle

PATTERN ESSENTIALS

CHAIN-STITCH PATTERN

Chain a multiple of 4 plus 2.

Row 1: Sc in 2nd ch from hook, *ch 1, skip 1 ch, sc in next ch; repeat from * across, turn.

Row 2: Ch 5 (counts as dc and ch 2), sc in next space, *ch 5, sc in next space; repeat from * across, ch 2, dc in last sc, turn. *You now have 24 ch-spaces.*

Row 3: Ch 1, sc in first dc, ch 1, skip 1 space, sc in next space, *ch 1, sc in next space; repeat from * across, turn.

Row 4: Ch 1, sc in first sc, sc in next space, *ch 1, sc in next space; repeat from * to last sc, sc in last sc, turn.

Row 5: Ch 1, sc in first sc, ch 5, sc in next space; repeat from * across, ending ch 5, sc in last sc, turn.

Row 6: Ch 3 (counts as dc), sc in next space, *ch 1, sc in next space; repeat from * across, end dc in last sc, turn.

Row 7: Ch 1, sc in first dc, *ch 1, sc in next space; repeat from * across, end ch 1, sc in top of turning ch, turn.

Repeat Rows 2–7 for pattern.

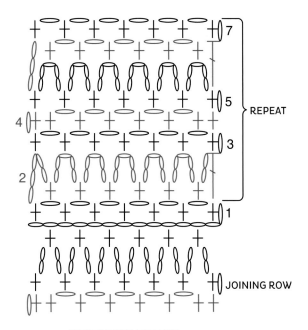

ABBREVIATED PATTERN

Crocheting the Cowl

» Chain 48.

» **ROW 1:** Work Row 1 of Chain-Stitch pattern. *You now have* 24 sc and 23 ch-1 spaces.

» Continue in Chain-Stitch pattern until piece measures approximately 27"/69 cm, ending with Row 4 of pattern. Fold cowl in half so that foundation chain is above last row worked. The Joining Row will be worked into next row and into ch-spaces formed by foundation chain and Row 1 of cowl.

» **JOINING ROW:** Ch 1, sc in first sc, ch 2, sc in first space of foundation chain, ch 2, sc in next space of current row, *ch 2, sc in next space of foundation chain, ch 2, sc in next space of current row; repeat from * across, ending with last sc in last sc. Do not fasten off.

Crocheting the Edging

» **ROW 1:** Working along edge of cowl, ch 1, sc in same st, ch 1, sc in edge of next ch-space; continue to (ch 1, sc) evenly along edge, spacing sts to allow edging to lie flat without bunching or rippling; end by joining with sc to first sc.

» **ROW 2:** Ch 1, sc in space formed by joining sc, ch 1, *sc in next space, ch 1; repeat from * around, join with slip st to first sc. Fasten off.

» Join yarn to opposite edge of cowl and work the edging. Weave in ends.

Sea Breeze Shawlette

Designed by Kristen Stoltzfus

This lacy half-moon-shaped cover-up is quick to make and easy to wear. It features an optional, amigurumi-like flower pin that can be used as a corsage or shawl closure. The yarn is easy to care for, too.

Crocheting the Shawlette

See charts on pages 50 and 51.

» **ROW 1:** Ch 4 (first 3 ch count as dc), work 10 dc in 4th ch from hook, turn. *You now have* 11 dc.

» **ROW 2 (RS):** Ch 5 (counts as tr and ch 1), tr in same st, ch 1, (tr, ch 1) two times in next 4 dc, (tr, ch 1) three times in next dc, (tr, ch 1) two times in next 4 dc, (tr, ch 1, tr) in last dc, turn. *You now have* 23 tr and 22 ch-1 spaces.

» **ROW 3:** Ch 5 (counts as dc and ch 2), *sc in next tr, ch 2, dc in next tr**, ch 2; repeat from * across, ending last repeat at **, turn. *You now have* 12 dc and 11 sc.

» **ROW 4:** Beg shell in first dc, (ch 2, shell in next dc) across, turn. *You now have* 12 shells.

» **ROW 5:** Slip st in next dc and in ch-2 space, beg shell in same space, (ch 3, shell in next shell) across, turn.

» **ROW 6:** Slip st in next dc and ch-2 space, beg V-st in same space, (ch 3, sc in next space, ch 3, V-st in next shell space) across, turn. *You now have* 12 V-sts.

» **ROW 7:** Slip st in V-st, ch 1, sc in same space, (ch 9, sc in next V-st) across, turn. *You now have* 11 ch-spaces.

» **ROW 8:** Slip st in first space, ch 3, dc in same space, (ch 2, 2 dc) three times in same space, [(ch 2, 2 dc) four times in next space] across, turn. *You now have* 88 dc.

FINISHED MEASUREMENTS
31"/79 cm from tip to tip, 13"/ 33 cm wide at center back

YARN
Kraemer Yarns Saucon Sock, 44% cotton/43% acrylic/13% nylon, 430 yds (393 m)/3.5 oz (100 g), Color Y5030 Turquoise

CROCHET HOOK
US E/4 (3.5 mm) *or size you need to obtain correct gauge*

GAUGE
First 10 rows = 4"/10 cm in diameter

OTHER SUPPLIES
Yarn needle, pins for blocking, pin back for flower

PATTERN ESSENTIALS

Beg shell (Ch 3, dc, ch 2, 2 dc) in same st.

Shell (2 dc, ch 2, 2 dc) in same st.

Beg V-st (Ch 6, dc) in same st.

V-st (Dc, ch 3, dc) in same st.

» **ROW 9:** Slip st in next dc and ch-2 space, ch 6 (counts as tr and ch 3), tr in next ch-2 space, (ch 3, tr in next ch-2 space) across, turn. *You now have* 43 tr.

» **ROW 10:** Beg V-st in first tr, (ch 2, sc in next tr, ch 2, V-st in next tr) across, ending with last V-st in 4th ch of beginning ch-7, turn. *You now have* 22 V-sts and 21 sc.

» **ROW 11:** Slip st in V-st, ch 1, sc in same space, (ch 7, sc in next V-st) across, turn. *You now have* 21 ch-spaces.

» **ROW 12:** Slip st to center of first ch-7 space, beg shell in same space, (ch 3, shell in next space) across, turn. *You now have* 21 shells.

» **ROW 13:** Slip st in next dc and ch-2 space, beg shell in same space, (ch 4, shell in next shell) across. *You now have* 21 shells.

» **ROWS 14–30:** Repeat Rows 6–13 twice. Repeat Row 6 once more. Do not turn or fasten off.

Crocheting the Edging

» Working across the neck edge, sc in side of last V-st, work (ch 2, sc) evenly across neck edge, join with slip st in 3rd ch of first V-st. Fasten off.

Finishing

» Weave in ends. Mist with water and pin, stretching fabric slightly to open up lace pattern. Let dry completely.

Crocheting the Flower
(optional)

CROCHETING THE FLOWER BASE

» **RND 1:** Leaving a long end for sewing, ch 2, work 8 sc in 2nd ch from hook; do not join. Work in a spiral.

» **RND 2:** Working in back loops only, sc in each sc around, increasing by working 2 sc in 1 sc as often as needed to keep the work flat; do not join.

» Repeat Rnd 2 until circle measures 2"/5 cm in diameter; slip st in next sc, do not fasten off.

CROCHETING THE PETALS

» Ch 1, turn, working first in both loops around edge and then in free front loops of circle, (sc, ch 3, sc) in first sc, skip next sc, *(sc, ch 3, sc) in next sc, skip next sc; repeat from * around, join with slip st down through center. Fasten off.

» Weave in the nonsewing end. With yarn needle threaded on sewing end, sew to pin back. Use as a corsage or as closure to shawlette.

continued on next page

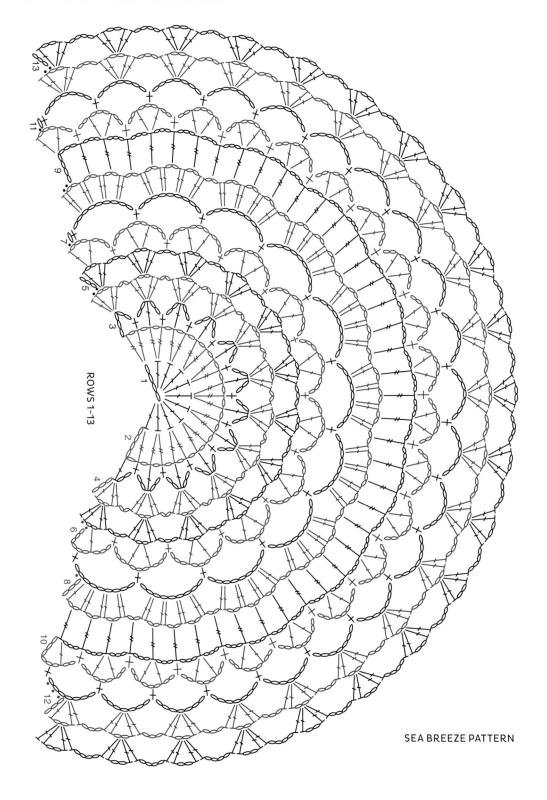

ROWS 1-13

SEA BREEZE PATTERN

50

CONTINUE INCREASING
UNTIL FLOWER BASE
MEASURES
2" (5.5 cm) IN DIAMETER

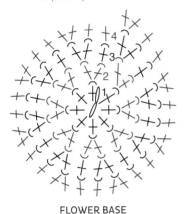

FLOWER BASE

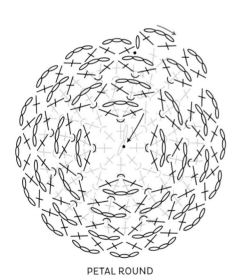

PETAL ROUND

Secret Garden Shrug

Designed by Erica Jackofsky

The Secret Garden Shrug is worked side to side in rows, and the sleeve sections are seamed together. A change in stitch pattern and hook size allows the back portion of the shrug to expand, and the openness and elasticity of the stitch allows for aggressive blocking to accommodate wider shoulders. The sample shown was not blocked to its full potential.

51

FINISHED MEASUREMENTS

Finished circumference of cuffs: 9¼" (11½", 12½")/23.5 (29, 32) cm

Finished width: 25½" (29½", 29½")/65 (75, 75) cm

Finished back depth: 14" (17¼", 19")/35.5 (44, 48.5) cm

YARN

Noro Kureyon Sock, 70% wool/30% nylon, 459 yds (420 m)/3.5 oz (100 g), Color S188

CROCHET HOOKS

US G/6 (4 mm) and US E/4 (3.5 mm) *or sizes you need to obtain correct gauge*

GAUGE

With smaller hook, 22 stitches and 20 rows = 4"/10 cm in Woven Stitch pattern; with larger hook, 21 stitches and 7 rows = 4"/10 cm in Rope Stitch pattern

OTHER SUPPLIES

Yarn needle

PATTERN ESSENTIALS

WOVEN STITCH PATTERN

Chain an even number of sts.

Row 1: Sc in 2nd ch from hook, *ch 1, skip 1 ch, sc in next ch; repeat from * across, turn.

Row 2: *Ch 1, sc in next ch-1 space; repeat from * across, turn.

Repeat Row 2 for pattern.

ROPE STITCH PATTERN

Chain a multiple of 2 plus 1 sts.

Row 1: Dc in 4th ch from hook, ch 1, dc in same ch, *skip next ch, (dc, ch 1, dc) in next ch; repeat from * across to last ch, dc in last ch, turn.

Row 2: Ch 3 (counts as dc), *(dc, ch 1, dc) in next ch-1 space, repeat from * across to last st, dc in top of turning ch, turn.

Repeat Row 2 for pattern.

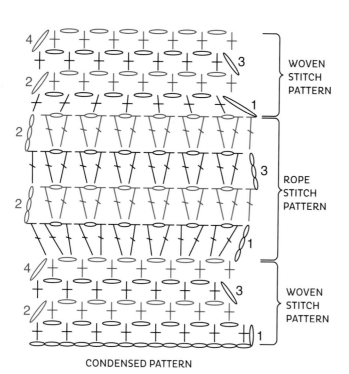

CONDENSED PATTERN

(Diagram labels: WOVEN STITCH PATTERN, ROPE STITCH PATTERN, WOVEN STITCH PATTERN)

Crocheting the First Cuff

» Using smaller hook, ch 52 (64, 70).

» Work in Woven Stitch pattern until cuff measures 2½" (3", 3")/ 6.5 (7.5, 7.5) cm) from beginning.

Crocheting the Back

» Change to larger hook.

» **ROW 1:** Ch 3 (counts as dc), *(dc, ch 1, dc) in next ch-1 space; repeat from * across, dc in last ch-1 space, turn.

» Beginning with Row 2, work in Rope Stitch pattern for 35 (40, 40) rows.

Crocheting the Second Cuff

» Change to smaller hook.

» **ROW 1:** Ch 1, *sc in next ch-1 space, ch 1; repeat from * across to last st, sc in top of turning ch, turn.

» **ROW 2:** *Ch 1, sc in next ch-1 space; repeat from * across, turn.

» Beginning with Row 2, work in Woven Stitch pattern until cuff measures 2½" (3", 3")/6.5 (7.5, 7.5) cm from beginning. Fasten off. Weave in ends.

Finishing

» Block shrug to match your desired proportions.

» Thread a needle with yarn. Lay the piece on a flat surface with the WS facing up. Seam together the side sections of cuffs.

Autumn Leaves Shawlette

Designed by Lindsey Stephens

This romantic triangular shawlette can double as a scarf. The stitch pattern is open and airy, and the motifs resemble hearts or butterflies. The fabric of the shawl may look crinkled as you crochet, but it will smooth out with blocking.

FINISHED MEASUREMENTS
51"/129.5 cm wide and 23"/58.5 cm deep, blocked

YARN
Juniper Moon Farm Findley, 50% merino
  wool/50% silk, 798 yds (730 m)/3.5
  oz (100 g), Color 09 Bittersweet

CROCHET HOOK
US D/3 (3.25 mm) *or size you need
  to obtain correct gauge*

GAUGE
Swatch = 5"/12.5 cm wide and 2½"/6.5
  cm tall after blocking

OTHER SUPPLIES
Four locking stitch markers,
  yarn needle

PATTERN ESSENTIALS

Dc pm Make 1 dc, then place marker in dc just
  made.

Large Shell (3 dc, ch 1, dc, ch 1, 3 dc) in same st.

Shell (3 dc, ch 3, 3 dc) in same st.

Sc pm Make 1 sc, then place marker in sc just made.

Crocheting the Swatch

» Chain 34.

» **ROW 1 (WS):** Sc in 2nd ch from hook and in
  each ch across. *You now have 33 sc.*

» **ROW 2:** Ch 4 (counts as dc and ch 1), 3 dc in
  same st, skip 3 sc, sc in next sc, *skip 3 sc,
  large shell in next sc, skip 3 sc, sc in next sc;
  repeat from * to last 4 sts, skip 3 sc, (3 dc, ch
  1, dc) in last sc, turn. *You now have* 3 large
  shells and 2 partial large shells.

» **ROW 3:** Ch 1, sc in first dc, ch 3, dc in next sc,
  *ch 3, sc in center dc of next shell, ch 3, dc in
  next sc; repeat from * two more times, ch
  3, sc in 3rd ch of ch-4, turn. *You now have* 8
  ch-3 spaces.

» **ROW 4:** Ch 1, sc in first sc, *large shell in
  next dc, sc in next sc; repeat from * across,
  turn. *You now have* 4 shells.

» **ROW 5:** Ch 6 (counts as dc and ch 3), *sc
  in center dc of next shell, ch 3, dc in next
  sc**, ch 3; repeat from * across, ending last
  repeat at **, turn.

» **ROW 6:** Ch 4 (counts as dc and ch 1), 3 dc in
  first dc, sc in next sc, *large shell in next dc,
  sc in next sc; repeat from * two more times,
  (3 dc, ch 1, dc) in 3rd ch of ch-6, turn.

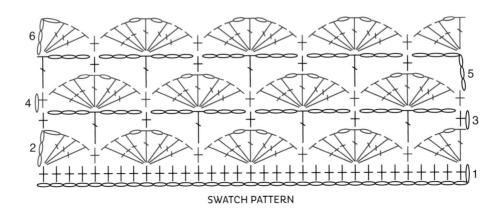

SWATCH PATTERN

Crocheting the Shawl Pattern

See chart on page 56.

» Chain 34.

» **ROW 1 (WS):** Sc in 2nd ch from hook and in each ch across, turn. *You now have 33 sc.*

» **ROW 2 (RS):** Ch 1, sc in first sc, *skip 3 sc, (3 dc, ch 1, dc, ch 1, dc pm, ch 1, 3 dc) in next sc, skip 3 sc, sc in next sc; repeat from * three more times, turn. *You now have 12 ch-1 spaces.*

» **ROW 3:** Ch 7 (counts as tr and ch 3), dc in first sc, *ch 3, sc in marked dc, remove marker, 3 sc in next ch-1 space, sc in next dc, ch 3**, dc in next sc; repeat from * across, ending last repeat at **, (dc, ch 3, tr) in last sc, turn. *You now have 10 ch-3 spaces.*

» **ROW 4:** Ch 1, sc in first st, shell in next dc, sc pm, ch 5, skip 3 sc, sc in next sc, shell in next dc, sc in next sc, ch 5, skip 3 sc, sc pm, shell in next dc, sc pm, ch 5, skip 3 sc, sc in next sc, shell in next dc, sc in next sc, ch 5, skip next 3 sc, sc pm, shell in next dc, sc in 4th ch of beg ch-7, turn.

» **ROW 5:** Moving each marker up to the dc made in that marked sc across, ch 6 (counts as dc and ch 3 here and throughout), sc in first ch-3 space, ch 3, dc in next sc, *ch 3, sc in next ch-3 space, ch 3, dc in next sc; repeat from * across, turn.

» **ROW 6:** *Note:* As you come to each marker on this row, remove it from the previous row and replace it in the designated st. Ch 4 (counts as dc and ch 1 here and throughout), 3 dc in first dc, sc in next sc, (3 dc, ch 1, dc, ch 1, dc pm, ch 1, 3 dc) in next marked dc, sc in next sc, *large shell in next dc, sc in next sc; repeat from * to marker, (3 dc, ch 1, dc, ch 1, dc pm, ch 1, 3 dc) in next marked dc, sc in next sc, (3 dc, ch 1, dc, ch 1, dc pm, ch 1, 3 dc) in next marked dc, sc in next sc, **large shell in next dc, sc in next sc; repeat from ** to marker, (3 dc, ch 1, dc, ch 1, dc pm, ch 1, 3 dc) in marked dc, sc in next sc, (3 dc, ch 1, dc) in last dc, turn.

» **ROW 7:** Ch 1, sc in first dc, ch 3, dc in next sc, ch 3, sc in marked dc, remove marker, 3 sc in next ch-1 space, sc pm in next dc, ch 3, dc in next sc, ch 3, *sc in center dc of next large shell, ch 3, dc in next sc, ch 3; repeat from * to marker, sc in marked dc, remove marker, 3 sc in next ch-1 space, sc pm in next dc, ch 3, dc in next sc, ch 3, sc in marked sc, remove marker, 3 sc in next ch-1 space, sc pm in next dc, ch 3, dc in next sc, ch 3, **sc in center dc of next large shell, ch 3, dc in next sc, ch 3; repeat from ** to marker, sc in marked dc, remove marker, 3 sc in next ch-1 space, sc pm in next dc, ch 3, dc in next sc, ch 3, sc in last dc, turn.

» **ROW 8:** Ch 1, sc in first sc, shell in next dc, sc pm in marked sc (moving up marker from last row), ch 5, skip 3 sc, sc in next sc, shell in next dc, * sc in next sc, shell in next dc; repeat from * to marker, sc in marked sc, remove marker, ch 5, skip 3 sc, sc pm in next sc, shell in next dc, sc pm in next marked sc (moving up marker from last row), ch 5, skip 3 sc, sc in next sc, shell in next dc, **sc in next sc, shell in next dc; repeat from ** to next marker, sc in marked sc, remove marker, ch 5, skip 3 sc, sc pm in next sc, shell in next dc; sc in last sc, turn.

» Repeat Rows 5–8 eleven more times; do not cut yarn.

continued on next page

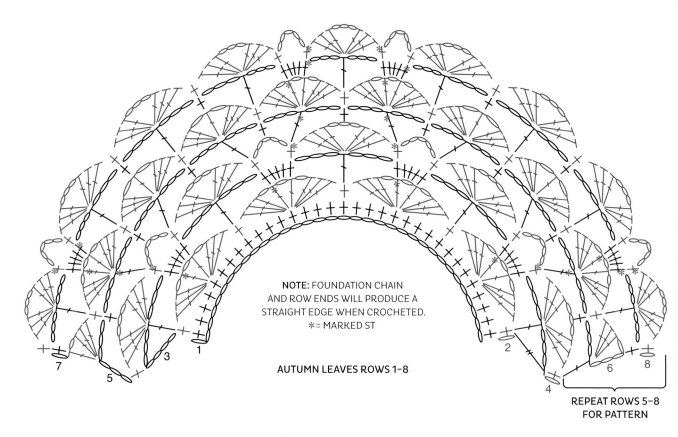

NOTE: FOUNDATION CHAIN
AND ROW ENDS WILL PRODUCE A
STRAIGHT EDGE WHEN CROCHETED.
✳ = MARKED ST

AUTUMN LEAVES ROWS 1-8

REPEAT ROWS 5-8
FOR PATTERN

Crocheting the Edging

» **ROW 1:** Work shawl body Row 5, removing markers.

» **ROW 2:** Ch 1, sc in first dc, *shell in next sc, sc in next dc; repeat from * across.

» **ROW 3:** Repeat edging Row 1.

» **ROW 4:** Repeat edging Row 2. Fasten off.

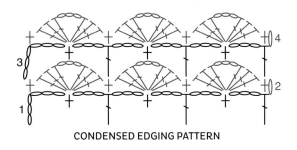

CONDENSED EDGING PATTERN

Finishing

» Block to finished measurements and weave in ends.

Flower Power Purse

Designed by Judith Durant

There's no end to the fun you can have choosing yarn and buttons for this purse. And while it's not the quickest project to stitch, it's very easy and very portable.

FINISHED MEASUREMENTS
Approximately 17"/43 cm in circumference and 5"/12.5 cm tall

YARN
Cascade Yarn Heritage, 75% superwash merino wool/25% nylon, 437 yds (400 m)/3.5 oz (100 g), Color 5627

CROCHET HOOK
US E/4 (3.5 mm) *or size you need to obtain correct gauge*

GAUGE
22 stitches and 18 rounds = 4"/10 cm in double crochet

OTHER SUPPLIES
Thirty locking stitch markers, yarn needle, thirty ½"/13 mm shank buttons, sewing needle, coordinating sewing thread

Crocheting the Flowers *(make 30)*

See chart on page 58.

» Chain 6; join with slip st to first ch to form a ring.

» **RND 1:** Ch 3 (counts as dc), 23 dc in ring, join with slip st to top of ch-3. *You now have 24 dc.*

» **RND 2:** Ch 1, sc in same st, FLsc in next 23 dc, join with slip st to first sc.

» **RND 3:** Ch 1, sc in first st, *(hdc, dc, tr) in next st, (tr, dc, hdc) in next st, sc in next st; repeat from * around, omitting last sc, join with slip st to first sc. Fasten off. Weave in ends.

Crocheting the Bag

- » Begin with an adjustable ring (see page 271).

- » **RND 1:** Work 12 dc into ring.

- » **RND 2:** Ch 3 (counts as dc), dc in same st, 2 dc in each dc around, join with slip st to top of ch-3. *You now have* 24 dc.

- » **RND 3:** Ch 3 (counts as dc), dc in same st, *dc in next st**, 2 dc in next dc; repeat from * around, ending last repeat at **, join with slip st to top of ch-3. *You now have* 36 dc.

- » **RND 4:** Ch 3 (counts as dc), dc in same st, *dc in next 2 dc**, 2 dc in next dc; repeat from * around, ending last repeat at **, join with slip st to top of ch-3. *You now have* 48 dc.

- » **RND 5:** Ch 3 (counts as dc), dc in same st, *dc in next 3 dc**, 2 dc in next dc; repeat from * around, ending last repeat at **, join with slip st to top of ch-3. *You now have* 60 dc.

- » **RNDS 6–9:** Continue in this manner, working 1 more dc between the increases on each rnd, until you have 7 dc between the increases. *You now have* 108 dc.

- » **RND 10:** Ch 3 (counts as dc), dc in same st, dc in next 53 dc, 2 dc in next dc, dc in next 53 dc, join with slip st to top of ch-3. *You now have* 110 dc. Mark this rnd.

- » **RNDS 11–27:** Ch 3 (counts as dc), dc in each dc around, join with slip st to top of ch-3.

- » **RND 28:** Ch 1, starting in first st, *sc in next 9 dc, sc2tog; repeat from * around; join with slip st to first sc. *You now have* 100 sts.

- » **RND 29:** Ch 1, starting in first st, *sc in next 8 dc, sc2tog; repeat from * around; join with slip st to first sc. *You now have* 90 sts. Do not fasten off.

Crocheting the Strap

- » **ROW 1:** Ch 1, sc in first 10 sts, turn. *You now have* 10 sts.

- » **ROW 2:** Ch 1, sc in each sc across, turn.

- » Repeat Row 2 until strap measures 16"/40.5 cm or desired length. Join with slip st to 10 sts directly opposite beg 10 sts. Weave in ends.

Attaching the Flowers

- » Mark the first st of Rnd 13 (3 rnds above marked rnd); mark every 9th st in this rnd. *You now have* 10 marked sts.

- » Mark the 5th st of Rnd 19; mark every 9th st after this marked st around. *You now have* 20 marked sts.

- » Mark the first st of Rnd 17; mark every 9th st after this marked st. *You now have* 30 marked sts.

- » Use sewing needle and thread to sew one button to each marked st and "button" one flower to each. ***Note:*** Because the flowers tend to curl in on themselves, the sample shows flowers attached with WS facing out.

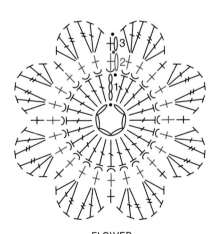

FLOWER

WIP Project Bag

Designed by Janet Brani

Take your latest WIP (work in progress) on the road! Perfectly sized for one-skein projects, this drawstring bag carries like a backpack. Though the stitch looks like Tunisian crochet or knitting, it's simply done with half double crochet in the round, splitting the stitches. The bag intentionally begins and ends with the dark brown portion of the color repeat. There's enough yarn in the skein to make I-cord straps if you prefer.

FINISHED MEASUREMENTS

Approximately 6½"/16.5 cm wide and 11"/28 cm tall

YARN

Zitron Unisono, 100% superwash wool, 330 yds (302 m)/3.5 oz (100 g), Color 1210

CROCHET HOOK

US D/3 (3.25 mm) *or size you need to obtain correct gauge*

GAUGE

16 stitches and 22 rows = 4"/10 cm) in half double crochet split stitch

OTHER SUPPLIES

Locking stitch marker, yarn needle, one set of 60"/152.5 cm shoelaces, two 10 mm wooden pony beads, three alphabet letters or other embellishment such as buttons or beads, blocking board and pins, fabric for lining (optional)

PATTERN ESSENTIALS

Split st Split stitches are worked into the middle of the stitch (between vertical bars) rather than the top loops of the stitch. This creates a denser fabric and a knitted look. Because you're working in the round with RS always facing, you'll always insert the hook between the two vertical bars on the face of the hdc stitch below.

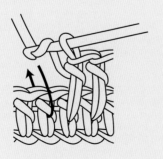

Crocheting the Bag

» Chain 24.

» **RND 1:** 2 hdc in 2nd ch from hook (place marker in first hdc), 2 hdc in next ch, hdc in next 19 ch, 2 hdc in next ch, 4 hdc in last ch (rounding the corner); working on opposite side of foundation ch, 2 hdc in next ch, hdc in next 19 ch, 2 hdc in next ch, work 2 hdc in last ch, do not join. *You now have* 54 hdc.

» **RND 2:** Work an hdc split st in marked hdc (first hdc of Rnd 1), then work a hdc split st in each hdc around.

» Repeat Rnd 2 until 10"/25.5 cm from beginning — it is not necessary to mark or count rows. To end, make a sc split st in next 3 hdc and then slip st in top of next 3 sts. Do not fasten off or turn.

Crocheting the Drawstring Mesh

» Chain 4 (counts as tr), work a tr split st in each st around, join with slip st to top of ch-4.

Crocheting the Picot Edge

» Chain 1, *sc in next 3 tr, tight picot-3 (see page 274); repeat from * around, join with slip st to first sc. Fasten off. Weave in ends.

Finishing

» The slight skew created when working in the round can be easily corrected when blocking. Completely wet the bag and squeeze out excess water. Tug the bag into shape against the skew and pin it to a blocking board.

Crocheting the Flowers *(make 3)*

» Begin with an adjustable ring (see page 271).

» **RND 1:** Ch 1, 7 sc in ring, join with slip st to first sc.

» **RND 2:** Ch 1, (sc, tight picot-3, sc) in each st around. *You now have* seven petals.

» Tighten the adjustable ring, fasten off, and weave in the ends.

Finishing

» Sew the flowers to the bag in a row with the letters *WIP* as shown (or use button centers if you prefer). Thread the shoelaces through the top mesh, working one lace from the left side fully around and back out the same slot, and one lace from the RS around and out the same slot. Sew a wooden pony bead to each bottom corner of the bag, thread the lace ends through the beads, and tie a knot close to the beads. Sew beaded ends to lower corners of bag.

» Line the bag if desired.

FLOWER

RESOURCES

Laces used in the sample are Kiwi Outdoor 60"/152.5 cm Round Brown, product #2121. Shorter laces can be used if you don't want to use the bag as a backpack.

The metal *WIP* letters are Alphabet Ribbon Charm alphabets by Making Memories, product #25778.

Tunisian Pouch

Designed by Laura Hontz

Unique construction makes this little purse stand out from the rest. Four pieces of Tunisian crochet are joined together and topped off with a lovely scalloped edge above the drawstring. Crocheted flowers finish the ends of the drawstrings.

FINISHED MEASUREMENTS
Approximately 10½"/26.5 cm circumference and 6"/15 cm deep

YARN
Patons Stretch Socks, 41% cotton/39% wool/13% nylon/7% elastic, 239 yds (218 m)/1.75 oz (50 g), Color 31222 Spearmint

CROCHET HOOK
US F/5 (3.75 m) afghan hook *or size you need to obtain correct gauge*

GAUGE
15 stitches = 2½"/6.5 cm in Tunisian simple stitch

OTHER SUPPLIES
Yarn needle

Crocheting the Strips *(make 4)*

» Chain 15. Work in Tunisian simple stitch (TSS) (see page 274) until piece measures 6"/15 cm.

» Bind off as follows: Skip first vertical bar, sc under each vertical bar across. Fasten off.

Assembling the Pieces

» Arrange strips as shown in diagram below.

» Thread the yarn needle with a long piece of yarn. Beginning at center where all pieces meet and with WS together, use

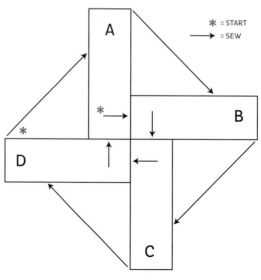

✳ = START
→ = SEW

ASSEMBLY DIAGRAM

whipstitch and sew A to B, then B to C, then C to D, and D to A. This forms the bottom of the bag.

» Next, with WS together, line D up along the side of A and slip st the edges together. Next, line A up along the side of B and slip st the edges together. Line B up along side of C and slip st the edges together, and finally line C up with D and slip st the edges together. The top edge of the bag will have four triangles.

Trimming the Top Edge

» With WS facing, join yarn at top edge of bag.

» **RND 1 (WS):** Ch 1, sc in same st and in each st around, working a multiple of 4 sts, join with slip st to first sc.

» **RND 2:** Ch 2 (does not count as st), hdc in same st and in each st around, join with slip st to first hdc, turn. **Note:** Turning at the end of this and the next round forms holes for the drawstring.

» **RND 3 (RS):** Ch 2 (does not count as hdc), hdc in same st and in next 2 hdc, ch 1, skip 1 st, *hdc in next 3 sts, ch 1, skip 1 st; repeat from * around, join with slip st in first hdc, turn.

» **RND 4:** Ch 2 (does not count as st), hdc in each st and space around, join with slip st to first hdc.

» **RND 5:** Ch 1, sc in same st, skip 2 sts, *5 dc in next st, skip 2 sts; repeat from * as evenly as possible around, join with slip st in first sc. Fasten off.

continued on next page

Crocheting the Flowers and Drawstrings *(make 2)*

» **RND 1:** Make adjustable ring (see page 271), ch 2 (does not count as st), 12 dc in ring, join with slip st in top of first dc, pull loop tight.

» **RND 2:** Ch 1, BLsc in first st, ch 3, skip 1 dc, *BLsc in next dc, ch 3, skip 1 dc; repeat from * around, join with slip st to first sc. *You now have* 6 spaces.

» **RND 3:** (Sc, hdc, dc, 2 tr, dc, hdc, sc) in each space around, join with slip st to first sc.

» Ch 120. Fasten off.

Finishing

» Weave ends without flower through Round 3 of top edge trim, each drawstring threaded through the opposite way from the other. Tie chain end to opposite flower ends and secure. Weave in all ends on bag and drawstrings.

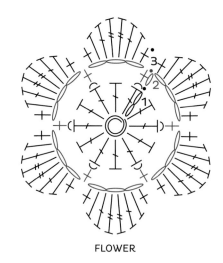

FLOWER

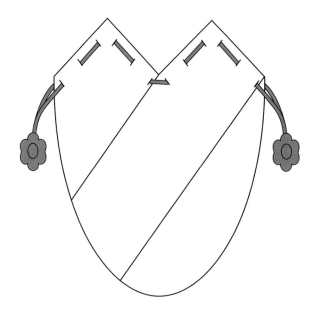

THREADING THE DRAWSTRINGS

Shell Stitch Fingerless Gloves

Designed by Gail Tanquary

These gloves are crocheted with a post stitch and shell stitch design on the back of the hand and plain double crochet on the palm. After finishing the cuff, join to work in the round and shape a thumb gusset — no sewing required!

FINISHED MEASUREMENTS
7"/18 cm circumference
  and 9½"/24 cm long

YARN
Crystal Palace Sausalito, 80% merino
  wool/20% nylon, 198 yds (181 m)/1.75
  oz (50 g), Color 8108 Mediterranean

CROCHET HOOK
US D/3 (3.25 mm) *or size you need
  to obtain correct gauge*

GAUGE
18 stitches and 10 rounds = 4"/10
  cm in double crochet

OTHER SUPPLIES
Yarn needle, two ¾"/19 mm buttons

PATTERN ESSENTIALS

Shell (2 dc, ch 2, 2 dc) in same st.

65

Crocheting the Right Glove

» Chain 34.

» **ROW 1:** Hdc in 3rd ch from hook and each ch across, turn. *You now have* 32 hdc.

» **ROW 2:** Ch 2 (counts as hdc), hdc in each hdc across, turn.

» **ROWS 3 AND 4:** Repeat Row 2.

» Work now progresses in rounds.

» **RND 5:** Ch 3 (counts as dc here and throughout), dc in next 3 hdc, 2 dc in next hdc, dc in next 7 hdc, 2 dc in next hdc, dc in next 6 hdc, 2 dc in next hdc, dc in next 7 hdc, 2 dc in next hdc, dc in last 4 hdc, join with slip st to top of beg ch-3. *You now have* 36 sts.

» **RND 6:** Ch 3, dc in next 2 dc, (FPdc in next st, skip 2 dc, shell in next dc, skip 2 dc) twice, FPdc in next dc, dc in next 20 dc; join with slip st to top of beg ch-3.

» **RND 7:** Ch 3, dc in next 2 dc, (FPdc in next FPdc, shell in center of next shell) twice, FPdc in next FPdc, dc in next 20 dc; join with slip st to top of beg ch-3.

» **RNDS 8–14:** Repeat Rnd 6.

SHAPING THE THUMB GUSSET

» **RND 1:** Ch 3, dc in next 2 dc, (FPdc in next st, shell in center of next shell) twice, FPdc in next FPdc, dc in next 5 dc, (2 dc in next dc) twice, dc in each dc to end of rnd, join with slip st to top of beg ch-3.

» **RND 2:** Ch 3, dc in next 2 dc, (FPdc in next st, shell in center of next shell) twice, FPdc in next FPdc, dc in next 5 dc, 2 dc in next dc, dc in next 2 dc, 2 dc in next dc, dc in each dc to end of rnd, join with slip st to top of beg ch-3.

» **RND 3:** Ch 3, dc in next 2 dc, (FPdc in next st, shell in center of next shell) twice, FPdc in next FPdc, dc in next 5 dc, 2 dc in next dc, dc in next 4 dc, 2 dc in next dc, dc in each dc to end of rnd, join with slip st to top of beg ch-3.

» **RND 4:** Work as established through third FPdc, dc in next 5 dc, 2 dc in next dc, dc in next 6 dc, 2 dc in next dc, dc in each dc to end of rnd, join with slip st to top of beg ch-3.

» **RND 5:** Work as established through third FPdc, dc in next 5 dc, 2 dc in next dc, dc in next 8 dc, 2 dc in next dc, dc in each dc to end of rnd, join with slip st to top of beg ch-3.

» **RND 6:** Work as established through third FPdc, dc in next 5 dc, 2 dc in next dc, dc in next 10 dc, 2 dc in next dc, dc in each dc to end of rnd, join with slip st to top of beg ch-3.

» **RND 7:** Work as established through third FPdc, dc in next 6 dc, skip 12 sts of thumb gusset, dc in each dc to end of rnd, join with slip st to top of beg ch-3.

» **RNDS 8–11:** Work as established through third FPdc, dc in each dc and ch around, join with slip st to top of beg ch-3. Fasten off.

Crocheting the Left Glove

» **RNDS 1–5:** Work as for right glove.

» **RND 6:** Ch 3, dc in next 19 dc, (FPdc in next dc, skip 2 dc, shell in next dc, skip 2 dc) twice, FPdc in next dc, dc in next 3 dc, join with slip st to top of beg ch-3.

» **RND 7:** Ch 3, dc in next 19 dc, (FPdc in next FPdc, shell in center of next shell) twice, FPdc in next FPdc, dc in next 3 dc, join with slip st to top of beg ch-3.

» **RNDS 8–14:** Repeat Rnd 7.

SHAPING THE THUMB GUSSET

» **RND 1:** Ch 3, dc in next 12 dc, (2 dc in next dc) twice, dc in next 5 dc, (FPdc in next st, shell in center of next shell) twice, FPdc in next FPdc, dc in next 3 dc, join with slip st to top of beg ch-3.

» **RND 2:** Ch 3, dc in next 12 dc, 2 dc in next dc, dc in next 2 dc, 2 dc in next dc, dc in next 5 dc, (FPdc in next st, shell in center of next shell) twice, FPdc in next FPdc, dc in next 3 dc, join with slip st to top of beg ch-3.

» **RND 3:** Ch 3, dc in next 12 dc, 2 dc in next dc, dc in next 4 dc, 2 dc in next dc, dc in next 5 dc, work in established pattern to end of rnd, join with slip st to top of beg ch-3.

» **RND 4:** Ch 3, dc in next 12 dc, 2 dc in next dc, dc in next 6 dc, 2 dc in next dc, dc in next 5 dc, work in established pattern to end of rnd, join with slip st to top of beg ch-3.

» **RND 5:** Ch 3, dc in next 12 dc, 2 dc in next dc, dc in next 8 dc, 2 dc in next dc, dc in next 5 dc, work in established pattern to end of rnd, join with slip st to top of beg ch-3.

» **RND 6:** Ch 3, dc in next 12 dc, 2 dc in next dc, dc in next 10 dc, 2 dc in next dc, dc in next 5 dc, work in established pattern to end of rnd, join with slip st to top of beg ch-3.

» **RND 7:** Ch 3, dc in next 13 dc, skip next 12 dc of thumb gusset, dc in next 6 dc, work in established pattern to end of rnd, join with slip st to top of beg ch-3.

» **RNDS 8–11:** Ch 3, dc in each dc and ch to next FPdc, work in established pattern to end of rnd, join with slip st to top of beg ch-3. Fasten off.

Crocheting the Button Loops

» Join yarn at inside corner of cuff opening (Rnd 5 of glove). Ch 5, slip st at outside corner of cuff opening, turn. Ch 1, 7 sc in ch-space, slip st in same st as beginning of chain. Fasten off. Repeat for other glove.

Finishing

» Weave in ends. Sew buttons opposite button loops.

Astra Gloves

Designed by Jana Whittle

These fingerless gloves are worked in a shell pattern; they have a cuff and are accented with a scalloped edge along the fingers. Originally designed to fit the average woman's hands, directions are also included for smaller or larger versions. One skein of yarn can make two pairs of gloves.

SIZES AND FINISHED MEASUREMENTS

Small (child or small woman):
6"/15 cm wrist circumference and 6"/15 cm long

Medium (average woman):
7"/18 cm wrist circumference and 7"/18 cm long

Large (average man):
8"/20.5 cm wrist circumference and 8"/20.5 cm long

YARN

Knit One Crochet Too Crock-O-Dye, 65% superwash wool/20% nylon/15% silk, 416 yds (380 m)/3.5 oz (100 g), Color 798 Currant

CROCHET HOOK

US D/3 (3.25 mm) *or size you need to obtain correct gauge*

GAUGE

6 shells and 12 rounds = 4"/10 cm

OTHER SUPPLIES

Two stitch markers, yarn needle

PATTERN ESSENTIALS

Shell (Sc, ch 3, 3 dc) in same st.

Crocheting the Cuff (make 2)

» **ROW 1:** Ch 13, sc in 2nd chain from hook, sc in each chain across, turn. *You now have* 12 sc.

» **ROW 2:** Ch 1 (does not count as first st, here or throughout), BLsc in each sc across.

» **ROWS 3–36 (44, 52):** Repeat Row 2 until piece measures approximately 5½" (6½", 7½")/14 (16.5, 19) cm.

» Fold so that top edge of Row 36 (44, 52) meets bottom of the foundation row. Slip st in both Row 36 (44, 52) and foundation row through back loops to form the cuff.

Crocheting the Hand

» **RND 1:** Ch 1, sc in each row-end st along top edge of cuff, join with slip st to top of first sc, turn. *You now have* 36 (44, 52) sc.

» **RND 2:** Ch 1, shell in first sc, skip next 3 sc, *shell in next sc, skip 3 sc; repeat from * around, join with slip st in first sc, turn. *You now have* 9 (11, 13) shells.

» **RND 3:** Ch 3 (does not count as st, here or throughout), shell in ch-3 space of first shell, *shell in ch-3 space of next shell; repeat from * around, join with slip st to first sc of first shell, turn.

» **RNDS 4 AND 5:** Repeat Rnd 3.

» **RND 6 (GUSSET):** Repeat Rnd 3, do not slip st to join, shell in the ch-3 space of turning chain; join with slip st in first sc of first shell, turn. *You now have* 10 (12, 14) shells.

» **RNDS 7–9 (7–10, 7–11):** Repeat Rnd 3.

CROCHETING THE THUMB

» **RND 10 (11, 12):** Ch 3, shell in first ch-3 space of first shell, shell in next ch-3 space of next shell, pm, skip next 6 (8, 9) shells, pm, (shell in ch-3 space of next shell) 2 (2, 3) times, join with slip st to first sc of first shell, turn. *You now have 4 (4, 5) shells.*

» **RND 11 (12, 13):** Ch 3, shell in ch-3 space of first shell, *shell in ch-3 space of next shell; repeat from * around, join with slip st to first sc of first shell. Fasten off.

FINISHING THE HAND

» **RND 10 (11, 12):** Join yarn with slip st in first marked st, shell into marked st, remove marker, shell into ch-3 space of next shell (the first of the 6, [8, 9] skipped shells), *shell into ch-3 space of next shell; repeat from * around to next marker, shell into 2nd marked st, remove marker, join with slip st to first sc of first shell. *You now have 8 (10, 11) shells.*

» **RNDS 11–15 (12–17, 13–19):** Repeat Rnd 3. Fasten off.

Finishing

» Weave in ends.

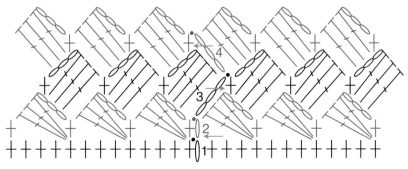

ABBREVIATED HAND PATTERN

Elegant Fingerless Gloves

Designed by Melody Fulone

Fingerless gloves, worked with black in a lacy pattern, make an elegant accessory for special occasions. The gloves are worked in the round from the wrist up, increased for a thumb gusset, and then each finger is worked individually. A wrist edging makes a beautiful finish.

FINISHED MEASUREMENTS

Approximately 7"/18 cm circumference and 6½"/16.5 cm from wrist to top of middle finger, unstretched

YARN

Patons Stretch Socks, 41% cotton/39% wool/13% nylon/7% elastic, 239 yds (218 m)/1.75 oz (50 g), Color 31041 Black Taffy

CROCHET HOOK

US F/5 (3.75 mm) *or size you need to obtain correct gauge*

GAUGE

6 V-stitches and 12 rows = 4"/10 cm in V-stitch pattern

OTHER SUPPLIES

Yarn needle

PATTERN ESSENTIALS

V-st (Dc, ch 3, dc) in same st or space.

❊ **NOTES:**
• Stretchy yarn makes gloves that will fit a variety of sizes.
• A larger or smaller hook may be used to customize sizing.

Crocheting the Gloves
(make 2)

» Chain 36. Chain should measure approximately 7"/18 cm, slightly stretched. Without twisting the chain, join with slip st to form a ring.

» **RND 1:** Ch 1, sc in each ch around, join with slip st in first sc. *You now have 36 sc.*

» **RND 2:** Ch 6 (counts as dc and ch 3), dc in same st, *ch 1, skip 3 sc, V-st in next st; repeat from * around to last 3 sts, skip last 3 sts, join with sc to 3rd ch of beg ch-6. *You now have 9 V-sts.*

» **RND 3:** Ch 6, dc in space made by joining sc, *ch 1, V-st in next ch-1 space; repeat from * around, ending join with sc to 3rd ch of beg ch-6.

» **RND 4 (INCREASE RND):** Ch 6, dc in space made by joining sc, ch 1, (V-st, ch 1, V-st) in next ch-1 space (increase made), *ch 1, V-st in next ch-1 space; repeat from * around; sc in 3rd ch of beg ch-6. *You now have 10 V-sts.*

» **RND 5:** Repeat Rnd 3.

» **RND 6 (INCREASE RND):** Ch 6, dc in space made by joining sc, ch 1, V-st in next ch-1 space, ch 1, increase in next ch-1 space, ch 1, increase in next ch-1 space, *ch 1, V-st in next ch-1 space; repeat from * around, join with sc to 3rd ch of beg ch-6. *You now have* 12 V-sts.

» **RND 7:** Repeat Rnd 3.

» **RND 8:** Ch 6, dc in space made by joining sc, (ch 1, V-st in next ch-1 space) three times, ch 1, skip 3 V-sts for thumb, V-st in next ch-1 space, *ch 1, V-st in next ch-1 space; repeat from * around, join with sc to 3rd ch of beg ch-6. *You now have* 10 V-sts.

» **RNDS 9–15:** Repeat Rnd 3. Fasten off.

» Flatten out glove, centering thumb opening on one side and aligning V-stitches and chain spaces on top edge.

Crocheting the Little Finger

» **RND 1:** With RS facing, skip 1 dc to the left of joining of last rnd, join yarn with slip st in next dc, ch 2, turn; skip next 4 dc, slip st in next dc (corresponding dc on opposite side of glove).

» **RND 2:** Slip st in next ch-3 space, ch 6, dc in same space, (ch 1, V-st in next V-st) two times, ch 1, V-st in next ch-2 space; join with slip st to 3rd ch of beg ch-6. Fasten off.

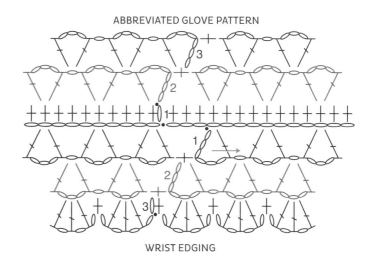

ABBREVIATED GLOVE PATTERN

WRIST EDGING

Crocheting the Ring Finger

» **RND 1:** With RS facing, join yarn with slip st in next dc to the right of where you joined yarn for little finger, ch 2, skip little finger, slip st in next corresponding dc on opposite side of glove, slip st in next 3 ch sts, slip st in next dc, ch 2, skip next 6 V-sts, slip st in next corresponding dc on opposite side of glove.

» **RND 2:** Slip st in next ch-3 space, ch 6, dc in same space, ch 1, V-st in next ch-2 space, ch 1, V-st in next V-st, ch 1, V-st in next ch-2 space, join with slip st to 3rd ch of beg ch-6.

» **RND 3:** Slip st in next ch-3 space, ch 6, dc in same space, *ch 1, V-st in next V-st; repeat from * around, join with slip st to 3rd ch of beg ch-6. Fasten off.

Crocheting the Middle Finger

» **RND 1:** With RS facing, join yarn with slip st in next ch-1 space to the right of where you joined yarn for ring finger, ch 2, skip ring finger, slip st in next corresponding ch-1 space on opposite side of glove, slip st in next dc, slip st in next 3 ch sts, slip st in next dc, ch 2, skip next 4 V-sts, slip st in next corresponding dc on opposite side of glove.

» **RNDS 2 AND 3:** Repeat Rnds 2 and 3 of ring finger.

Crocheting the Index Finger

» **RND 1:** With RS facing, join yarn with slip st in next dc to the right of where you joined yarn for middle finger, ch 2, skip middle finger, slip st in next dc on opposite side of glove, slip st in next ch-3 space.

» **RND 2:** Ch 6, dc in same space, (ch 1, V-st in next V-st) twice, ch 1, V-st in ch-2 space, ch 1, join with slip st to 3rd ch of beg ch-6.

» **RND 3:** Slip st in next ch-3 space, ch 6, dc in same space, *ch 1, V-st in next V-st; repeat from * around, ch 1, join with slip st to 3rd ch of beg ch-6. Fasten off.

Crocheting the Thumb

» With RS facing, join yarn in first V-st of thumb gusset (first V-st of 3 V-sts skipped for thumb gusset).

» **RND 1:** Ch 6, dc in same space, (ch 1, V-st in next V-st) twice, (ch 1, V-st in side of next dc) twice, join with slip st to 3rd ch of beg ch-6.

» **RNDS 2 AND 3:** Slip st in next ch-3 space, ch 6, dc in same space, *ch 1, V-st in next V-st, repeat from * around; join with slip st to 3rd ch of beg ch-6. At the end of Rnd 3, fasten off.

Adding the Wrist Edging

» **RND 1:** Working across opposite side of foundation ch, join yarn in ch at base of any V-st, ch 6, dc in same space, *ch 1, skip next 3 ch sts, V-st in next ch; repeat from * around, join with sc to 3rd ch of beginning ch-6.

» **RND 2:** Ch 6, dc in space formed by joining sc, *ch 1, V-st in next ch-1 space; repeat from * around, join with sc to 3rd ch of beg ch-6.

» **RND 3:** Ch 1, sc in space formed by joining sc, *(ch 1, dc) three times in next ch-3 space, ch 1**, sc in next ch-1 space, ch 1; repeat from * around, ending last repeat at **, join with slip st to first sc. Fasten off. Weave in ends.

Bangle Bracelets

Designed by Susan Levin

Cover your old bracelets, mailing tubes, or foam can cozies to make these fun-to-wear bangles. Linked double crochet makes a sturdy fabric, and the variegated sock yarn guarantees that every bracelet will be one-of-a-kind. They're perfect for quick gifts or to personalize every outfit.

FINISHED MEASUREMENTS
3¼"/8.5 cm in diameter and 1¼"/3 cm wide

YARN
Patons Kroy Socks Jacquards, 75% washable wool/25% nylon, 166 yds (152 m)/1.75 oz (50 g), Color 243455 Fern Rose; 1 skein makes 3 bracelets

CROCHET HOOK
US D/3 (3.25 mm) *or size you need to obtain correct gauge*

GAUGE
24 stitches and 20 rows = 4"/10 cm in alternating rows of single crochet and linked double crochet

OTHER SUPPLIES
Yarn needle, new or vintage bangle bracelet or plastic or cardboard tube with approximately 3"/7.5 cm diameter and 1"/2.5 cm (or desired) width. (The bracelets shown were made from 3"/7.5 cm flexible plastic tubing cut 1"/2.5 cm wide.)

❊ **NOTE:** To maximize stripes, cut yarn and change colors as desired.

Horizontal Stripe Bracelet

» Chain 16 (or number of stitches needed to snugly cover the girth of your bracelet plus 1).

» **ROW 1:** Sc in 2nd ch from hook and in each ch across, turn. *You now have 15 sc.*

» **ROW 2 (RS):** Ch 3, Ldc (see page 74) in each sc across, turn.

» **ROW 3:** Ch 1, sc in each Ldc across.

continued on next page

73

PATTERN ESSENTIALS

Ldc (linked double crochet) Ch 3, insert hook in second chain from hook, yo and draw loop through, insert hook into first st in row below, yo and draw loop through, yo and draw loop through first 2 loops on hook, yo and draw loop through remaining 2 loops on hook — *first Ldc complete.* *Insert hook into horizontal cross bar of Ldc just worked, yo and draw loop through, insert hook into next st in row below, yo and draw loop through, yo and draw loop through first 2 loops on hook, yo and draw loop through remaining 2 loops on hook — *next Ldc complete.* Repeat from * across row.

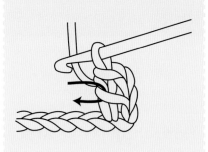

» Repeat Rows 2 and 3 for pattern until strip measures about ¼"/6 mm less than the circumference of your bracelet. Fasten off leaving a 12"/30.5 cm tail.

Finishing

» Sew ends together to form a circle. Gently stretch the circle over the bracelet and bring the edges together. Sew the long edges together to completely cover the bracelet. Twist the seam to the center on the inside of the bracelet.

Vertical Stripe Bracelet

» Chain 61 (or number of stitches needed to snugly cover the outer circumference of your bracelet plus 1).

» **ROW 1:** Sc in second ch from hook and in each ch across, turn. *You now have 60 sc.*

» **ROW 2 (RS):** Ch 3, Ldc in each sc across, turn.

» **ROW 3:** Ch 1, sc in each Ldc across.

» Repeat Rows 2 and 3 for pattern until strip measures about ¼"/6 mm less than the girth of your bracelet. Fasten off leaving a 12"/30.5 cm tail.

Finishing

» Finish as for Horizontal Stripe Bracelet above.

One-Skein Doll Wardrobe

Designed by Marcia Sommerkamp

Make any little girl happy with an entire wardrobe for her doll, and it's all made from a single skein of sock yarn! The sample was done in circus-like colors, but the patterns work equally well with a single color or a handpainted colorway with long repeats.

SIZE AND FINISHED MEASUREMENTS
To fit an 18"/45.5 cm doll; see individual piece measurements on the following pages

YARN
Opal Socken Zirkus, 75% wool/25% nylon, 465 yds (425 m)/3.5 oz (100 g), Color 2005

CROCHET HOOKS
US G/6 (4 mm) *or size you need to obtain correct gauge* and 2 sizes smaller for socks (optional)

GAUGE
10 stitches and 5 rows = 2"/5 cm in skirt pattern with larger hook. *Note:* Gauge may vary with stitch pattern.

OTHER SUPPLIES
¼"/6 mm elastic cut to fit around doll's waist, sewing needle and thread for joining elastic

✳ **NOTE:** Two options are given for the vest and hat. By omitting the top of the hat, you can make a ski band for the doll that allows a ponytail to be pulled through. For small tots who may have trouble dressing their dolls, make an open-front vest, or make two sides alike for a pullover vest. There's enough yarn to make both versions.

Crocheting the Skirt

Finished measurements are approximately 5"/12.5 cm long and 14½"/37 cm around before seaming.

» With larger hook, ch 66.

» **ROW 1 (RS):** Sc in 2nd ch from hook, *dc in next ch, sc in next ch; repeat from * across, turn.

» **ROW 2 (WS):** Ch 3 (counts as dc), *sc in next dc, dc in next sc; repeat from * across, turn.

» **ROW 3:** Ch 1, sc in first dc, *dc in next sc, sc in next dc; repeat from * across, ending with last sc in top of ch-3, turn.

» Repeat Rows 2 and 3 six more times, or until piece measures approximately 3½"/9 cm from beginning.

» **NEXT ROW:** *(Sc, hdc, dc, hdc, sc) in first st — *shell made*, skip 1 st, *shell in next st, skip 1 st; repeat from * across. Fasten off, leaving a sewing length.

CROCHETING THE WAISTBAND

» **ROW 1:** With RS facing, using larger hook, join yarn with slip st in first ch on opposite side of foundation ch, ch 1, sc in each ch across, turn. *You now have* 65 sts.

» **ROW 2:** Ch 1, BLsc in each st across, turn.

» **ROWS 3 AND 4:** Ch 1, sc in each st across, turn.

» **ROW 5:** Ch 1, FLsc in each st across. Fasten off, leaving a length for sewing.

FINISHING

» Fold waistband in half to the outside. Sew in place, leaving a small opening to insert the elastic. Thread the elastic through the band and fasten ends together. Sew back seam of skirt and ends of band. Weave in ends.

Crocheting the Hat

Finished measurements are approximately 11"/28 cm in circumference and 3½"/9 cm deep.

» With larger hook, ch 7.

» **ROW 1:** Sc in 2nd ch from hook and each ch across. *You now have* 6 sc.

» **ROW 2:** Ch 1, BLsc in each sc across, turn.

» Repeat Row 2 for 59 more rows. Holding ends with RS together, sc Row 1 to last row, forming a band. *You now have* 31 ridges.

» Work 1 sc into the last st of every row, join with slip st to first sc. *You now have* 60 sts.

WORKING THE CROWN

» **RND 1:** Ch 1, sc in each st around, join with slip st to first sc.

» **RNDS 2 AND 3:** Repeat Rnd 1.

» **RND 4:** Ch 1, *sc in next 4 sts, sc2tog; repeat from * around, join with slip st in first sc. *You now have* 50 sts.

» **RND 5:** Ch 1, *sc in next 3 sts, sc2tog; repeat from * around, join with slip st in first sc. *You now have* 40 sts.

» **RND 6:** Repeat Rnd 1.

» **RND 7:** Ch 1, *sc in next 2 sts, sc2tog; repeat from * around, join with slip st in first sc. *You now have* 30 sts.

» **RND 8:** Repeat Rnd 1.

» **RND 9:** Ch 1, *sc in next st, sc2tog; repeat from * around, join with slip st in first sc. *You now have* 20 sts.

» **RND 10:** Repeat Rnd 1.

» **RND 11:** Ch 1, *sc2tog; repeat from * around, join with slip st in first sc. *You now have* 10 sts.

» **RND 12:** Repeat Rnd 1.

» **RND 13:** Repeat Rnd 11. *You now have* 5 sts.

» Fasten off, leaving a 6"/15 cm tail. Weave tail through remaining stitches and pull tightly to close. Weave in end.

Crocheting the Vest

Finished measurements are approximately 15"/38 cm in circumference and 6"/15 cm long.

Note: Make two back pieces and omit the fronts for a pullover style.

CROCHETING THE BACK RIBBING

» With larger hook, ch 6.

» **ROW 1:** Sc in 2nd ch from hook and in each ch across, turn. *You now have* 5 sts.

» **ROW 2:** Ch 1, BLsc in each st across, turn.

» **ROWS 3–34:** Repeat Row 2. *You now have* 17 ridges.

» Holding work with the long edge at top, ch 1, sc in the top of each row across. *You now have* 34 sts.

CROCHETING THE BACK

» **ROW 1:** Ch 1, *sc in next st, dc in next st; repeat from * across, turn.

» **ROW 2:** Ch 1, *sc in next dc, dc in next sc; repeat from * across, turn.

» **ROWS 3–10:** Repeat Row 2. Piece measures approximately 3½"/9 cm from bottom of ribbing.

» **ROW 11:** Slip st in first 4 sts, ch 1, *sc in next dc, dc in next sc; repeat from * to last 4 sts, turn, leaving last 4 sts unworked. *You now have* 26 sts.

» **ROW 12:** Ch 1, *sc in next dc, dc in next sc; repeat from * across, turn.

» **ROWS 13–17:** Repeat Row 12.

» **ROW 18:** Ch 1, (sc in next dc, dc in next sc) four times, slip st in next 10 sts, (sc in next dc, dc in next sc) four times, turn.

» **ROW 19:** Ch 1, (sc in next dc, dc in next sc) four times, turn. *You now have* 8 sts.

» **ROWS 20 AND 21:** Repeat Row 19 two times. Fasten off.

» Skipping 10 slipped stitches in the middle for neck, join yarn in unworked sts of last row.

» Repeat Row 19 three times for other shoulder. Fasten off.

continued on next page

CROCHETING THE RIGHT FRONT RIBBING

» With larger hook, ch 6.

» **ROW 1:** Sc in 2nd chain from hook and in each ch across, turn. *You now have* 5 sts.

» **ROW 2:** Ch 1, BLsc in each st across, turn.

» **ROWS 3–16:** Repeat Row 2. *You now have* 8 ridges.

» Holding work with the long edge at top, ch 1, sc in the top of each row across. *You now have* 16 sts.

CROCHETING THE RIGHT FRONT VEST

» **ROW 1 (WS):** Ch 1, *sc in next st, dc in next st; repeat from * across, turn.

» **ROW 2:** Ch 1, *sc in next dc, dc in next sc; repeat from * across, turn.

» **ROWS 3–10:** Repeat Row 1. Piece measures approximately 3½"/9 cm from bottom of ribbing.

» **ROW 11:** Sl st in first 4 sts, ch 1, *sc in next st, dc in next st; repeat from * across. *You now have* 12 sts.

» **ROW 12:** Ch 1, *sc in next dc, dc in next sc; repeat from * across, turn.

» **ROW 13:** Repeat Row 12.

» **ROW 14:** Ch 1, sc2tog, work in pattern to end, turn. *You now have* 11 sts.

» **ROW 15:** Ch 1, *sc in next dc, dc in next sc; repeat from * to last 3 sts, sc in next st, sc2tog, turn. *You now have* 10 sts.

» **ROW 16:** Repeat Row 14. *You now have* 9 sts.

» **ROW 17:** Repeat Row 15. *You now have* 8 sts.

» **ROWS 18–21:** Ch 1, *sc in next dc, dc in next sc; repeat from * across, turn. Fasten off.

CROCHETING THE LEFT FRONT VEST

» Make as for right front vest, using the reverse side as RS.

FINISHING

» Sew side and shoulder seams.

» **SWEATER EDGING:** With RS facing, using larger hook, join yarn at lower right front edge, ch 1, sc evenly spaced up right front, around neck, and down left front, placing 3 sc in each front corner neck st. Fasten off.

» **ARMHOLE EDGING:** With RS facing, using larger hook, join yarn at right underarm, ch 1, sc evenly around armhole, join with slip st in first sc, fasten off. Repeat around left armhole.

Crocheting the Socks

Finished measurements are approximately 3¼"/8.5 cm long and 4"/10 cm in circumference.

Note: If you want matching socks, mark where the color repeat begins, and strand the yarn to that spot to begin the second sock.

WORKING THE TOE AND FOOT

» With smaller hook, ch 24, being careful not to twist chain, join with slip st to form a ring.

» **RND 1:** Ch 1, sc in same ch as join, sc in next 23 ch, join with slip st to first sc. *You now have* 24 sts.

» **RNDS 2–7:** Ch 1, sc in each sc around, join with slip st to first sc.

» **RND 8:** Ch 1, *sc in next 3 sc, sc2tog; repeat from * to last 4 sts, sc in each st to end, join with slip st to first sc. *You now have 20 sts.*

» **RNDS 9–11:** Repeat Rnd 2.

WORKING THE HEEL

» **RND 12:** Ch 2 (counts as dc), dc in next st, hdc in next 2 sts, sc in next 12 sts, hdc in next 2 sts, dc in last 2 sts, join with slip st to top of ch 2.

Note: This is the top of the heel and is at center back of sock.

WORKING THE LEG

» **RND 13:** Ch 1, *sc in next 3 sts, sc2tog; repeat from * around. *You now have 16 sts.*

» **RNDS 14–17:** Ch 1, sc in each st around, join with slip st to first sc.

» **RND 18:** Ch 1, (sc2tog) around, join with slip st to first st. *You now have 8 sts.*

» **RND 19:** Repeat Rnd 14.

» **RND 20:** Repeat Rnd 18. Fasten off, leaving a 6"/15 cm tail. Draw tail through remaining sts to close and fasten off. Weave in ends.

» If desired, dampen sock and slide on doll, allowing to dry overnight to shape the toe and heel to the individual doll.

Rainbow Doll Ensemble

Designed by Gail Tanquary

This adorable sweater and hat set will fit your daughter's favorite 18-inch (45.5 cm) doll — or your own favorite doll! Using only single and double crochet with chain stitches, both pieces are crocheted from the top down.

FINISHED MEASUREMENTS

Sweater: approximately 14"/35.5 cm in circumference

Hat: approximately 11"/28 cm in circumference

YARN

Crystal Palace Sausalito, 80% merino wool/20% nylon, 198 yds (181 m)/1.75 oz (50 g), Color 8101 Prism

CROCHET HOOK

US D/3 (3.25 mm) *or size you need to obtain correct gauge*

GAUGE

20 stitches and 10 rows = 4"/10 cm in double crochet

OTHER SUPPLIES

Yarn needle, two ½"/13 mm buttons

PATTERN ESSENTIALS

Shell (2 dc, ch 2, 2 dc) in 1 stitch or space.

V-st (Dc, ch 2, dc) in 1 space.

Crocheting the Sweater

» Chain 40.

» **ROW 1:** Dc in 3rd ch from hook and in next 2 ch, shell in next ch, (dc in next 9 ch, shell in next ch) three times, dc in last 4 ch, turn. *You now have* 6 dc on each front and 13 dc each on sleeves and back.

» **ROW 2 (RS):** Ch 3 (counts as dc here and throughout), *dc in each dc across to next corner ch-2 space, V-st in next corner space; repeat from * three times, dc in each st across, turn. *You now have* 7 dc on each front and 15 dc each on sleeves and back.

» **ROW 3:** Ch 3, *dc in each dc across to next corner ch-2 space, shell in next corner space; repeat from * three times, dc in each st across, turn. *You now have* 9 dc on front and 19 dc each on sleeves and back.

» **ROWS 4–6:** Repeat Rows 2 and 3 once more, then Row 2 once more. *You now have* 13 dc on each front and 27 dc each on sleeves and back at the end of Row 6.

» **ROW 7:** Ch 4 (counts as dc, ch 1 here and throughout), *(skip 1 dc, dc in next dc, ch 1) to corner space, V-st in corner space, dc in next dc, ch 1; repeat from * three times, (skip 1 dc, dc in next dc, ch 1) to last 2 dc, skip 1 dc, dc in last dc. *You now have* 14 dc on each front and 29 dc each on sleeves and back.

» **ROW 8:** Ch 3, dc in each dc and ch-1 space across to next corner ch-2 space, shell in next corner space; repeat from * three times, dc in each dc and ch-1 space across. *You now have* 16 dc on each front, 33 dc each on sleeves and back. Fasten off.

CROCHETING THE SLEEVES

» **ROW 9:** With WS facing, join yarn with slip st in first corner space, ch 1, sc in first 3 sts, hdc in next 3 sts, dc in each dc to last 6 dc, hdc in next 3 sts, sc in last 3 sts, turn. *You now have* 33 sts.

» **ROWS 10 AND 11:** Ch 1, sc in first 3 sts, hdc in next 3 sts, dc in each dc to last 6 dc, hdc in next 3 sts, sc in last 3 sts, turn.

» **ROW 12:** Ch 3 (counts as dc), dc in next st, dc2tog, dc in each st across to last 4 sts, dc2tog, dc in last 2 sts, turn. *You now have* 31 sts.

» **ROWS 13–16:** Repeat Row 12 four times more. *You now have* 23 sts at the end of Row 16.

» **ROW 17:** Ch 1, sc in next 3 sts, *sc2tog, sc in next 2 sts; repeat from * across, turn. *You now have* 18 sts.

» **ROWS 18 AND 19:** Ch 1, sc in each sc across. Fasten off.

» Work second sleeve in same manner, joining yarn in third corner space with WS facing.

CROCHETING THE BODY

» **ROW 1:** With WS facing, attach yarn to front edge with slip st, ch 3 (counts as dc), dc in each dc to corner space, dc in corner space, skip sleeve sts, dc in next corner space, dc in each dc across back, dc in next corner space, skip sleeve sts, dc in last corner space, dc in each dc to end, turn. *You now have 69 sts.*

» **ROW 2:** Ch 3 (counts as dc), dc in each dc across, turn.

» **ROW 3:** Ch 3 (counts as dc), dc in next 15 dc, 2 dc in next 2 dc, dc in next 30 dc, 2 dc in next 2 dc, dc in each dc to end, turn. *You now have 73 sts.*

» **ROW 4:** Ch 3 (counts as dc), dc in each dc across, turn.

CROCHETING THE BOTTOM BORDER

» **ROW 1:** Ch 1, sc in first dc, *ch 3, skip 3 dc, sc in next dc, ch 7, sc in next dc, ch 3, skip 3 dc, sc in next dc; repeat from * across. *You now have 8 ch-7 spaces.*

» **ROW 2:** Ch 1, sc in first sc, *(6 dc, ch 1, 6 dc) in next ch-7 space, skip next ch-3 space, sc in next sc; repeat from * across. Fasten off.

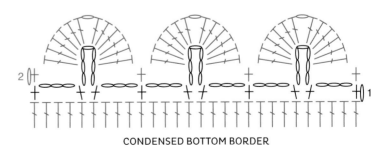

CONDENSED BOTTOM BORDER

81

CROCHETING THE BUTTONHOLE BAND

» **ROW 1:** With RS facing, join yarn with a slip st to last sc above border on right front edge, ch 1, work 24 sc evenly spaced across right front edge, turn.

» **ROW 2:** Ch 1, sc in each sc across, turn.

» **ROW 3 (BUTTONHOLE ROW):** Ch 1, sc in first 12 sc, ch 2, skip 2 sc, sc in next 6 sc, ch 2, skip 2 sc, sc in last 2 sc, turn.

» **ROW 4:** Ch 1, sc in each sc and 2 sc in each ch-2 space across, turn.

» **ROW 5:** Ch 1, sc in each sc across. Fasten off.

CROCHETING THE BUTTON BAND

» **ROW 1:** With RS facing, join yarn with a slip st to corner st at top of left front edge, ch 1, work 24 sc evenly spaced across left front edge to base of bottom border, turn.

» **ROWS 2–5:** Ch 1, sc in each sc across, turn.

CROCHETING THE NECK BAND

» **ROW 1:** With RS facing, join yarn with slip st in corner of right front edge,

» Ch 1, sc in each ch around neck, turn.

» **ROW 2:** Ch 1, sc in each sc across. Fasten off.

FINISHING

» Sew sleeve seams. Weave in ends. Sew buttons opposite buttonholes.

Crocheting the Hat

» Chain 6, join with slip st in first ch to form ring.

» **RND 1:** Ch 3 (counts as dc), 11 dc in ring, join with slip st to top of ch-3. *You now have* 12 dc.

» **RND 2:** Ch 3 (counts as dc), dc in same st, 2 dc in each dc around, join with slip st to top of ch-3. *You now have* 24 dc.

» **RND 3:** Ch 3 (counts as dc), dc in same st, dc in next dc, *2 dc in next dc, dc in next dc; repeat from * around, join with slip st to top of ch-3. *You now have* 36 dc.

» **RND 4:** Ch 3 (counts as dc), dc in same st, dc in next 2 dc, *2 dc in next dc, dc in next 2 dc; repeat from * around, join with slip st to top of ch-3. *You now have* 48 dc.

» **RND 5:** Ch 3 (counts as dc), dc in same st, dc in next 3 dc, * 2 dc in next dc, dc in next 3 dc; repeat from * around, join with slip st to top of ch-3. *You now have* 60 dc.

» **RND 6:** Ch 3 (counts as dc), dc in each dc around, join with slip st to top of ch-3.

» **RND 7:** Ch 4 (counts as dc and ch 1), skip 1 dc, *dc in next dc, ch 1, skip 1 dc; repeat from * around, join with slip st to 3rd ch of ch-4.

» **RND 8:** Ch 3, dc in each dc and ch-1 space around, join with slip st to 3rd ch of ch-4.

» **RND 9:** Ch 3 (counts as dc), dc in each dc around, join with slip st to top of ch-3.

» **RND 10:** Ch 3 (counts as dc), dc in next 13 dc, 2 dc in next dc, (dc in next 14 dc, 2 dc in next dc) three times, join with slip st to top of ch-3. *You now have* 64 dc.

» **RND 11:** Ch 1, sc in same st, *ch 3, skip 3 dc, sc in next dc, ch 7, sc in next dc, ch 3, skip 3 dc, sc in next dc; repeat from * around, omitting last sc, join with slip st to first sc. *You now have* 8 ch-7 spaces.

» **RND 12:** Ch 1, sc in same st, *(6 dc, ch 1, 6 dc) in next ch-7 space, skip next ch-3 space, sc in next sc; repeat from * around, omitting last sc, join with slip st to first sc. Fasten off. Weave in ends.

V-Stitch Sundress

Designed by Tamara Del Sonno

This adorable little sundress adjusts to fit — one side is left open and is closed for wearing with the ribbon. Blocking will lengthen and enhance the lacy pattern in the skirt.

SIZES AND FINISHED MEASUREMENTS

To fit 6–18 months, 20"/51 cm chest circumference

YARN

South West Trading Company Tofutsies, 50% superwash wool/25% Soysilk/22.5% cotton/2.5% chitin, 465 yds (425 m)/3.5 oz (100 g), Color 937 Pina TOElada

CROCHET HOOKS

US B/1 (2.25 mm) *or size you need to obtain correct gauge* and US C/2 (2.75 mm) (one hook size larger) for chain

GAUGE

25 stitches and 6 rows = 4"/10 cm in double crochet; 10 V-stitches and 15 rows = 4"/10 cm in V-st pattern on smaller hook

OTHER SUPPLIES

1 yd (0.9 m) ¼"/6 mm ribbon, yarn needle, sewing needle and coordinating thread

PATTERN ESSENTIALS

Shell (Dtr, ch 1, dtr) two times in same st.

V-st (Dc, ch 1, dc) in same st.

✳ NOTES:

• Chain with the larger hook, then change to smaller hook to work the dress.
• Work all stitches through the back bump of the chain to create smoothly trimmed edges.
• Count the chain at beginning of a row as a stitch.

Crocheting the Shoulder Straps *(make 2)*

- » Chain 13.
- » **ROW 1:** Sc in 2nd ch from hook and in each chain across, turn. *You now have* 12 sc.
- » **ROW 2:** Ch 3 (counts as dc), dc in each st across, turn.
- » Repeat Row 2 until piece measures 6½"/16.5 cm or desired length.
- » **LAST ROW:** Ch 1, sc in each st across. Do not fasten off.

ADDING THE RUFFLE

- » Turn to work along the long side of the strap. Working over the post of each stitch along edge, ch 3 (counts as dc), dc over next row-end dc, *shell over next row-end dc, V-st over next row-end dc; repeat from * across the length of shoulder strap, ending ch 2, sc in last st. Fasten off.

Crocheting the Bodice

- » Chain 124.
- » **ROW 1:** Hdc in 3rd ch from hook and in each ch across. *You now have* 123 hdc.
- » **ROW 2:** Ch 3 (counts as dc), dc in each hdc across, turn.
- » **ROW 3:** Ch 3 (counts as dc), dc in each dc across, turn.
- » **ROWS 4–11:** Repeat Row 3.
- » **ROW 12:** Ch 2 (counts as hdc), hdc in each dc across, turn.

Crocheting the Skirt

- » **ROW 1:** Ch 4 (counts as dc, ch 1 here and throughout), dc in back loop of same st (counts as V-st), V-st in back loop of next hdc, skip 1 hdc, *V-st in back loops of next 2 hdc**, skip next hdc; repeat from * across, ending last repeat at **. *You now have* 82 V-sts.
- » **ROW 2:** Ch 4, dc in center of first V-st (counts as beg V-st), V-st in center of each V-st across, turn.
- » Repeat Row 2 until skirt measures 5½"/14 cm or ½"/13 mm less than desired length, ending with WS row.

ADDING THE RUFFLE

- » **LAST ROW:** Ch 4, dc in center of first V-st, shell in next V-st, *V-st in next V-st, shell in next V-st; repeat from * across. Fasten off.

Finishing

- » Weave in ends. Fold the piece in half to shape the dress, overlapping the edges to make the dress the desired size. Using yarn needle and working from top to bottom, weave ribbon through both layers of bodice and skirt to close the dress. Using yarn needle, weave ribbon under and over pairs of dcs in second row of bodice. Adjust to fit, then cut ribbon, leaving 8"/20.5 cm ends. Tie ends into a bow.
- » Sew shoulder straps equally spaced on either side of center front, with ruffles to outside. Try dress on and pin straps at back to fit. Sew straps to WS of back bodice.

French Toast with Maple Sugar Jacket

Designed by Gwen Steege

Variegated yarn is often best shown off when used in small motifs. Here, two motifs alternate in checkerboard fashion on the asymmetrical jacket front. The sleeves and back are worked in single crochet and half double crochet respectively. This is a cropped jacket with three-quarter length sleeves.

SIZE AND FINISHED MEASUREMENTS

To fit 12-month old, 20"/51 cm chest circumference and 9"/23 cm long

YARN

Kangaroo Dyer's BFL yarn, 75% superwash Bluefaced Leicester/25% nylon, 464 yds (424 m)/3.5 oz (100 g), French Toast with Maple Syrup

CROCHET HOOK

US H/8 (5 mm) *or size you need to obtain correct gauge*

GAUGE

Each motif = approximately 2"/5 cm square; 20 stitches and 12 rows in back pattern = 4"/10 cm

OTHER SUPPLIES

Stitch marker, yarn needle, two ¾"–1"/19–25 mm buttons

Crocheting the Fronts

» Make 10 of each motif.

MOTIF 1

Begin with an adjustable ring (see page 271).

» **RND 1:** Ch 1, 8 sc in ring. *You now have* 8 sc. Place marker at the first st of the round and move it up as you work the rounds.

» **RND 2:** *BLsc in next sc, 3 BLsc in next sc; repeat from * three times, do not join.

» **RND 3:** *BLsc in next 2 sc, 3 BLsc in next sc, BLsc in next sc; repeat from * three more times.

» **RND 4:** *BLsc in next 3 sc, 3 BLsc in next sc, BL sc in next 2 sc; repeat from * three more times.

» **RND 5:** *BLsc in next 4 sc, 3 BLsc in next sc, BLsc in next 3 sc; repeat from * three more times, join with slip st in next sc.

MOTIF 2

Begin with an adjustable ring (see page 271).

» **RND 1:** Ch 1, 3 sc into ring, *ch 3, 3 sc into ring; repeat from * two more times, join with dc to first sc.

» **RND 2:** [Ch 3, 2-dc cluster (see page 273), (ch 3, 3-dc cluster [see page 273]) two times] in space made by joining dc, *[3-dc cluster, (ch 3, 3-dc cluster) two times] in next space; repeat from * two more times, join with slip st to first cluster.

» **RND 3:** Ch 1, sc in same st, *3 sc in next space, sc in next st, picot-3, 3 sc in next space, sc in next 2 sts; repeat from * around, omitting last sc, join to first sc. Fasten off.

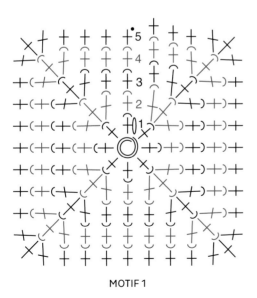

MOTIF 1

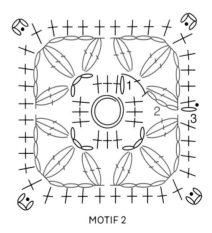

MOTIF 2

> ❊ **NOTE:** These motifs are from Edie Eckman's *Beyond the Square Crochet Motifs* (Storey, 2008). For the swirly pattern (Motif 1), the designer chose to use the WS out to better contrast with the more open, starlike pattern (Motif 2).

Joining the Motifs

» Arrange the completed motifs in the correct order, following the assembly diagram below. Also, note that the WS of Motif 1 is used as the RS in this garment. (You may, of course, choose to keep the RS facing out.) Working on the WS, whipstitch (see page 275) the motifs together, taking up only the back of the stitches of Motif 1 and only half of each stitch of Motif 2. This results in the "frame" of each motif butting against its neighbor in a slightly three-dimensional fashion. Try to allow the picots to pop forward as little accents on the front of the garment.

Crocheting the Back

» **SETUP:** Working with the RS facing, join yarn at the outside of the left shoulder. Ch 1, work 10 sc evenly spaced across the top of the first motif, work 5 sc evenly spaced across the first half of the next motif, ch 20, work 5 sc evenly spaced across the second half of the middle motif on the right front, work 10 sc evenly spaced across the top of the next motif on the right front. *You now have* 50 stitches in all: 15 at the outer edge of each shoulder and 20 chain stitches for the back neck.

» **ROW 1 (WS):** Ch 2 (does not count as st here and throughout), hdc in each st and ch across, turn. *You now have* 50 hdc.

» **ROW 2 (RS):** Ch 2, FLhdc in each st across, turn.

» **ROW 3:** Ch 2, hdc in frontmost loop of each hdc across, turn.

» Repeat Rows 2 and 3 until back measures the same length as front. Fasten off.

1	2	1
2	1	2
1	2	1
2	1	2

RIGHT FRONT

2	1
1	2
2	1
1	2

LEFT FRONT

ASSEMBLY DIAGRAM

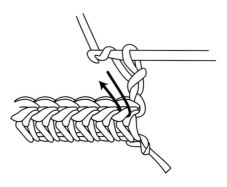

FRONTMOST LOOP OF HDC

Joining the Sides

» Mark the center of sides of fronts and back. Whipstitch the bottom two motifs of each front to the bottom half of the back, taking care to match the centers of the side seams, and leaving the tops open. When joining the motifs, work from the WS and butt the seam without overlap.

Crocheting the Sleeves

» **RND 1:** With RS facing, join yarn at underarm, ch 1, sc 40 sts evenly around the arm opening for the sleeve, do not join, but continue working in the round.

» **RND 2:** Sc in each st around.

» Repeat Rnd 2 until sleeve measures ¾"/19 mm from beg.

» **NEXT RND (DECREASE RND):** *Sc in next 8 sc, sc2tog; repeat from * around. *You now have* 36 stitches.

» **NEXT RNDS:** Sc in each sc around until sleeve measures 2"/5 cm from beginning.

» **NEXT RND (DECREASE RND):** *Sc in next 7 sc, sc2tog; repeat from * around. *You now have* 32 stitches.

» **NEXT RNDS:** Sc in each sc around until sleeve measures 3"/7.5 cm from beginning.

» **SCALLOP BORDER:** *(Sc, ch 3, 3 dc) in next st, skip 3 sts; repeat from * around; join with slip st to first sc. Fasten off.

Crocheting the Border

» **ROW 1:** With RS facing, join yarn at lower left front corner, ch 1, 2 sc in same st, work 18 sc evenly spaced across lower left front edge, 50 sc across back, and 29 sc across right front to corner, 3 sc in corner st, work sc 37 sc evenly spaced up right front edge, 3 sc in corner st, 37 sc around front and back neck edge, 3 sc in corner st, and 37 sc down left front edge, ending with 1 sc in same st as first sc, join with slip st to first sc. *You now have* 220 sts.

» **SCALLOP BORDER:** Ch 1, *(sc, ch 3, 3 dc) in next st, skip 3 sts; repeat from * around to the top of the right front; slip st the last dc into the first sc of the neck stitches. Fasten off.

Finishing

» Sew one button at top neck edge and one at the bottom of the first motif on the left front. Corresponding spaces created by skipping 3 stitches on the Scallop Border are used for buttonholes.

Fine Weight

Fearless Lace Scarf ∗ Pebble Beach Headband ∗ Autumn
Fingerless Gloves ∗ Bohemian Necklaces ∗ Spring Garden
Dress ∗ Eliot-the-Elephant Baby Bib ∗ A Star Is Born
Booties ∗ Lovely Linen Place Mat ∗ Yoga Mat Bag

Fearless Lace Scarf

Designed by Marcia Sommerkamp

Fear lace crochet no more! This scarf features a one-row pattern with an intriguing turn that makes both ends lightly ripple. Better yet, the turning chain does all the work of making a shell-like border with no additional finishing. What more could you ask for?

FINISHED MEASUREMENTS
Approximately 70"/178 cm long and 6"/15 cm wide

YARN
Blue Ridge Yarns Shadow Mini, 100% brushed mohair, 500 yds (458 m)/1.8 oz (52 g), Color 014 Crimson Tide

CROCHET HOOK
US E/4 (3.5 mm) *or size you need to obtain correct gauge*

GAUGE
4 shells and 5 rows = 3"/7.5 cm in pattern; exact gauge is not essential

OTHER SUPPLIES
Yarn needle

Shell (2 dc, ch 1, 2 dc) in next st.

Crocheting the Scarf

» Chain 30.

» **SETUP ROW:** Shell in 4th ch from hook, *skip next 3 ch sts, shell in next ch; repeat from * across to last 2 ch, ch 3, skip 1 ch, sc in last ch, ch 3; rotate work to continue along opposite side of foundation ch, skip 1 ch, shell in next ch at the base of shell, *skip next 3 ch sts, shell in next ch at the base of shell; repeat from * across, turn. *You now have* 7 shells and a turning ch on each row.

» **ROW 1:** Ch 3, *shell in ch-1 space of next shell; repeat from * six times, turn.

» Repeat Row 1 until scarf is desired length. Fasten off.

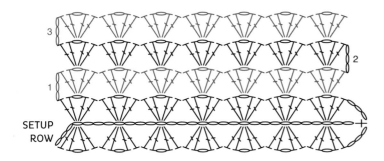

Finishing

» Weave in ends. Block lightly.

Pebble Beach Headband

Designed by Donna Barranti

You can easily adjust the circumference of this highly textured headband by adding or eliminating rows, ensuring the best fit. Elasticity results from working both single crochet and puff stitches in the back loops of the previous rows.

FINISHED MEASUREMENTS
20"/51 cm in circumference and 3"/7.5 cm wide

YARN
Knit Picks Wool of the Andes Sport, 100% Peruvian Highland wool, 137 yds (125 m)/1.75 oz (50 g), Color 25290 Marina

CROCHET HOOK
US F/5 (3.75 mm) *or size you need to obtain correct gauge*

GAUGE
20 stitches and 18 rows = 4"/10 cm in pattern stitch

OTHER SUPPLIES
Yarn needle

PATTERN ESSENTIALS

Puff st Yo, insert hook into next st and pull up a loop, (yo, insert hook into same st and pull up a loop) two times, yo and pull through all 7 loops on hook.

Crocheting the Headband

» Chain 16.

» **ROW 1:** Sc in 2nd ch from hook and in each ch across, turn. *You now have 15 sc.*

» **ROW 2:** Ch 1, BLsc in first sc, *puff st in back loop of next sc, BLsc in next 3 sc; repeat from * across, ending last repeat with BLsc in last sc, turn.

» **ROW 3:** Ch 1, BLsc in each st across, turn.

» **ROW 4:** Ch 1, BLsc in next 3 sts, *puff st in back loop of next sc, BLsc in next 3 sc; repeat from * across.

» **ROW 5:** Repeat Row 3.

» **ROWS 6–90 (or to desired length):** Repeat Rows 2–5. Do not break yarn.

Finishing

» With RS together, seam the two ends of the headband together with a row of sc. Fasten off. Weave in ends.

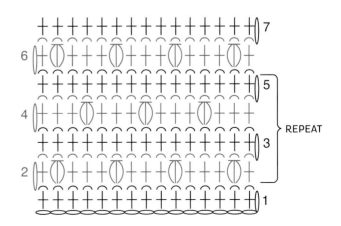

93

Autumn Fingerless Gloves

Designed by Barbara Khouri

These mitts provide just enough warmth for an autumn day when there's a bit of a nip in the air. The gloves are crocheted flat and seamed up the inside edges, leaving openings for thumbs.

FINISHED MEASUREMENTS
7½" (9")/19 (23) cm in circumference; glove shown is 7½"/19 cm

YARN
Classic Elite Fresco, 60% wool/30% baby alpaca/10% angora, 164 yds (150 m)/1.75 oz (50 g), Color 5385 Tandori Spice

CROCHET HOOK
US D/3 (3.25 mm) *or size you need to obtain correct gauge*

GAUGE
2 repeats = 3"/7.5 cm and 14 rows = 4"/10 cm in Shell Net pattern

OTHER SUPPLIES
Yarn needle

PATTERN ESSENTIALS

SHELL NET PATTERN

Chain a multiple of 4 plus 2 sts.

Row 1: Sc in 2nd ch from hook, *ch 4, skip 3 ch, sc in next ch; repeat from * across, turn.

Row 2: Ch 5, *sc in next space, (3 dc, ch 3, 3 dc) in next space — *shell made*, sc in next space**, ch 4; repeat from *, ending last repeat at **, ch 2, dc in last sc, turn.

Row 3: Ch 1, sc in first dc, *ch 4, (sc, ch 4, sc) in center space of next shell, ch 4**, sc in next space; repeat from *, ending last repeat at **, sc in last ch-5 space, turn.

Repeat Rows 2 and 3 for pattern.

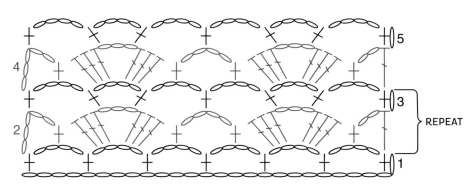

CONDENSED SHELL NET PATTERN

Crocheting the Glove
(make 2)

» Starting at bottom edge, ch 62 (74).

» **ROW 1:** Sc in 2nd ch from hook, *ch 4, skip 3 ch, sc in next ch; repeat from * across, turn. *You now have* 15 (18) ch-4 spaces.

» Beginning with Row 2 of pattern, work Shell Net pattern until piece measures 6½" (7½")/16.5 (19) cm, ending with Row 3 of pattern. Fasten off, leaving a long tail for seaming.

Finishing

» Sew side seam from top edge down ½"/13 mm. Sew side seam from bottom edge up 3" (3½")/7.5 (9) cm, leaving approximately 2½" (3")/6.5 (7.5) cm for thumb opening. Weave in ends.

Bohemian Necklaces

Designed by Julie Blagojevich

Four cords are crocheted and then joined at the top to make a clasp-free necklace, and a small crocheted motif is folded over and joined to form the centerpiece. Both the nylon ribbon and the silk have ample yardage to increase the length, and the silk offers enough yardage for two necklaces.

FINISHED MEASUREMENTS
Motif: 3½"/9 cm square
Necklace: 26"/66 cm in circumference

YARN
Silver necklace: Katia Sevilla, 100% nylon, 153 yds (140 m)/1.75 oz (50 g), Color 08 Gray; copper necklace: Alchemy Yarns of Transformation Silken Straw, 100% silk, 236 yds (216 m)/1.4 oz (40 g), Color 58m Joshua Tree

CROCHET HOOKS
US F/5 (3.75 mm) and US D/3 (3.25 mm) *or size you need to obtain correct gauge*

GAUGE
Motif = 3½"/9 cm square with smaller hook

OTHER SUPPLIES
Locking stitch marker, yarn needle

Crocheting the Cords

» With larger hook, ch 3. Place marker in 2nd ch from hook. Dc in 3rd ch from hook, turn clockwise; dc in 2nd ch made, turn clockwise; *dc under the two diagonal parallel strands as shown below, turn clockwise; repeat from * until cord measures 26"/66 cm. Slip st into the 2 loops you would normally dc in to close off the first cord. (The slip st at the end of the cord puts a necessary bend in the cord before beginning the next cord.) Do not fasten off.

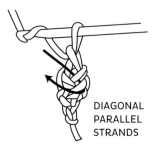

DIAGONAL PARALLEL STRANDS

» Ch 3 and, using the same process, make a second cord that is connected to the first. When the second cord is the same length as the first one, bend in the middle, and join the second cord with a slip st to the first dc of cord 1 (see cord assembly diagram on the next page). Do not fasten off. Ch 3, and make a third cord like the first two cords. When it is the same length as the other two, join with a slip st to beginning of second cord. Do not fasten off. Ch 3, and make a fourth cord, attaching to beginning of previous cord as before. Do not fasten off.

Joining the Cord Ends

» With smaller hook, slip st through ends of all cords, ending at the side of the first cord made. Turn.

» **ROW 1:** Ch 1, work 5 sc evenly spaced across tops of cords, turn. *You now have* 5 sc.

» **ROWS 2–4:** Ch 1, sc in each sc across, turn.

» **ROW 5:** Lay necklace flat, making sure the cords are not twisted. Fold one end on top of the other and then slip st across, catching both ends as you go. Fasten off. Weave in ends.

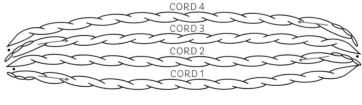

CORD 4
CORD 3
CORD 2
CORD 1

CORD ASSEMBLY

continued on next page

Crocheting the Motif

» With smaller hook, ch 6, join with slip st to form a ring.

» **RND 1:** Ch 3, 2-dc cluster (see page 271) in ring (ch-3 and 2-dc cluster count as 3-dc cluster), ch 1, 3-dc cluster (see page 271) in ring, ch 3, *3-dc cluster in ring, ch 1, 3-dc cluster in ring, ch 3; repeat from * two more times, join with slip st to top of ch-3.

» **RND 2:** Slip st in next space, (ch 3, 2-dc cluster, ch 1, 3-dc cluster) in same space, *ch 3, (dc, ch 3) twice in next space**, (3-dc cluster, ch 1, 3-dc cluster) in next space; repeat from * around, ending last repeat at **, join with slip st to top of ch-3.

» **RND 3:** Slip st in next space, (ch 3, 2-dc cluster, ch 1, 3-dc cluster) in same space, ch 1, *dc in next space, ch 3, (dc, ch 3) twice in corner space, dc in next space, ch 1**, (3-dc cluster, ch 1) twice in next space; repeat from *around, ending last repeat at **, join with slip st to top of ch-3.

» **RND 4:** Slip st in next space, (ch 3, 2-dc cluster, ch 1, 3-dc cluster) in same space, *ch 3, skip next space, dc in next space, ch 3, (dc, ch 3) twice in corner space, dc in next space, ch 3, skip next space**, (3-dc cluster, ch 1, 3-dc cluster) in next space; repeat from * around, ending at **, join with slip st to top of ch-3.

» **RND 5:** Ch 1, sc in same st, sc in each st and ch-1 space, 3 sc in each ch-3 space, and (sc, ch 3, sc) in each corner space around, join with slip st to first sc. Fasten off.

Finishing

» Fold motif over the bottom of the necklace with WS together, making sure all four cords are sandwiched between the two sides of the motif.

» **JOINING ROW:** Join yarn in right-hand corner ch-3 space, working through double thickness of motif and matching sts, ch 1, sc in same space, sc in next st, picot-3, *sc in next two sc, picot-3; repeat from * across, ending with sc in last ch-3 space. Fasten off. Weave in ends.

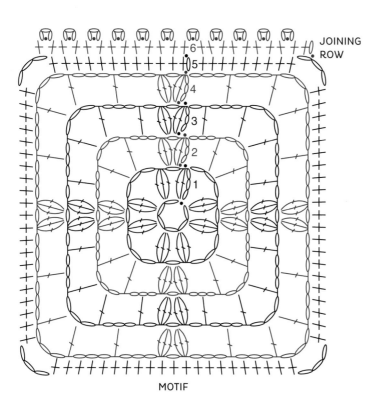

MOTIF

Spring Garden Dress

Designed by Justyna Kacprzak

Yes, that oft-used word adorable comes to mind again when you picture the newborn in your life wearing this dress. Easy to crochet, the dress is worked in the round from the top down.

SIZE AND FINISHED MEASUREMENTS
To fit 0–3 months, approximately 16"/40.5 cm chest circumference and 14"/35.5 cm long with straps

YARN
Red Heart Baby, 100% acrylic, 207 yds (190 m)/1.75 oz (50 g), Color 08508

CROCHET HOOK
US G/6 (4 mm) *or size you need to obtain correct gauge*

GAUGE
18 stitches and 10 rows = 4"/10 cm in double crochet

OTHER SUPPLIES
Yarn needle, two small (³⁄₈"–⅝"/9–16 mm) buttons

PATTERN ESSENTIALS

Shell (2 dc, ch 1, 2 dc) in same st.

V-st (dc, ch 1, dc) in same st.

Crocheting the Dress

» Chain 72, and without twisting ch, join with slip st to first ch.

» **RNDS 1–8:** Ch 2 (counts as dc), dc in each ch around, join with slip st to top of ch-1. *You now have* 72 sts.

» **RND 9:** Ch 2 (counts as dc), dc in next 3 dc, ch 1, skip 2 dc, shell in next dc, ch 1, skip 2 dc, *dc in next 4 dc, ch 1, skip 2 dc, shell in next dc, ch 1, skip 2 dc; repeat from * around, join with slip st to top of ch-2.

» **RNDS 10 AND 11:** Ch 2 (counts as dc), dc in next 3 dc, ch 1, skip 2 dc, shell in next shell space, ch 1, skip 2 dc, *dc in next 4 dc, ch 1, skip 2 dc, shell in next shell space, ch 1, skip 2 dc; repeat from * around, join with slip st to top of ch-2.

» **RNDS 12–16:** Ch 2 (counts as dc), dc in next 3 dc, *ch 2, skip 2 dc, shell in next shell space, ch 2, skip 2 dc**, dc in next 4 dc; repeat from * around, ending last repeat at **, join with slip st to top of ch-2.

» **RND 17:** Slip st in next dc, ch 2 (counts as dc), dc in next dc, *ch 1, skip 1 dc, (2 dc in next dc, ch 1) four times, skip 1 dc**, dc in next 2 dc; repeat from * around, ending last repeat at **, join with slip st to top of ch-2.

» **RND 18:** Ch 2 (counts as dc), dc in next dc, *ch 1, skip 2 dc, shell in next ch-1 space, ch 1, skip 4 dc, shell in next ch-1 space, ch 1, skip 2 dc**, dc in next 2 dc; repeat from * around, ending last repeat at **, join with slip st to top of ch-2.

» **RND 19:** Ch 2 (counts as dc), dc in next dc, *ch 1, skip 2 dc, shell in next shell space, ch 1, sc in next ch-1 space, ch 1, shell in next shell space, ch 1, skip 2 dc**, dc in next 2 dc; repeat from * around, ending last repeat at **, join with slip st to top of ch-2.

» **RND 20:** Ch 2 (counts as dc), dc in next dc, *ch 1, skip 2 dc, shell in next shell space, ch 1, V-st in next sc, ch 1, skip 2 dc, shell in next shell space, ch 1, skip 2 dc**, dc in next 2 dc; repeat from * around, ending last repeat at **, join with slip st to top of ch-2.

» **RND 21:** Ch 2 (counts as dc), dc in next dc, ch 1, *skip 2 dc, shell in next shell space, ch 1, shell in ch-1 space of next V-st, ch 1, shell in next shell space, ch 1, skip 2 dc**, dc in next 2 dc, ch 1; repeat from * around, ending last repeat at **, join with slip st to top of ch-2.

» **RND 22:** Ch 1, dc in next dc (counts as dc2tog) *ch 1, (shell in next shell space, ch 1) three times, skip 2 dc**, dc2tog; repeat from * around, ending last repeat at **, join with slip st to top of ch-2.

» **RNDS 23 AND 24:** Ch 3 (counts as dc and ch 1), *(shell in next shell space, ch 1) three times**, skip 2 dc, dc in next dc, ch 1; repeat from * around, ending last repeat at **, join with slip st to 3rd ch of ch-4.

» **RND 25:** Ch 1, sc in same st, *7 dc in next shell space, (sc in next ch-1 space, 7 dc in next shell space) two times, sc in next dc; repeat from * around, omitting last sc, join with slip st in first sc. Fasten off.

Working the Top Edging

» With RS facing, working across opposite side of foundation ch, join yarn in first ch, ch 1, sc in each ch around, join with slip st to first sc. *You now have* 72 sc. Fasten off.

Making the First Strap

» **ROW 1:** With RS facing, join yarn in 9th sc of the top edging, ch 35, sc in 2nd ch from hook and in each ch across, turn.

» **ROW 2:** Sl st in next 2 sc of the edging, dc in next 32 sc, ch 1, skip 1 sc (for buttonhole), dc in next 2 sc, turn.

» **ROW 3:** Ch 1, sc in next 2 dc, sc in ch-1 space, sc in each dc across, slip st in next sc of edging. Fasten off.

Making the Second Strap

» With WS facing, join yarn in the 60th sc of the edging.

» Repeat Rows 1–3 of first strap. Fasten off. Weave in ends.

Finishing

» Sew the buttons on the front of the dress.

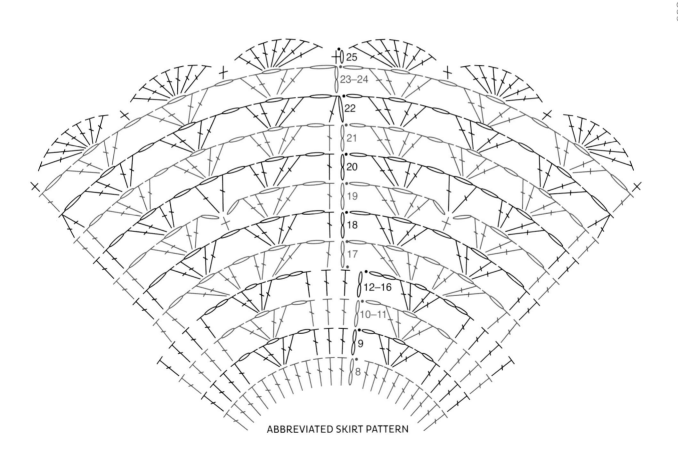

ABBREVIATED SKIRT PATTERN

Eliot-the-Elephant Baby Bib

Designed by Justyna Kacprzak

This quick and easy pattern doesn't require much yarn, making it ideal for a last-minute gift. The little bits that stick out from the bib are ideal for little fingers to fiddle with, and using pink instead of blue will make it girly.

FINISHED MEASUREMENTS

Approximately 7½"/19 cm wide and
  9"/23 cm long excluding ties

YARN

Red Heart Cotton Mix, 50% cotton/50% acrylic,
  164 yds (150 m)/1.75 oz (50 g), Color 06357

CROCHET HOOK

US D/3 (3.25 mm) *or size you need to obtain correct gauge*

GAUGE

20 stitches and 12 rows = 4"/10 cm in double crochet

OTHER SUPPLIES

Two stitch markers, yarn needle, small
  amount of black embroidery floss

PATTERN ESSENTIALS

FLsc2tog (front loop single crochet 2 together)
  (Insert hook into front loop of next st and pull up a loop)
  two times, yo and pull through all 3 loops on hook.

Crocheting the First Leg

» Chain 14.

» **ROW 1:** Dc in 4th ch from hook and in each ch across, turn. *You now have 12 dc.*

» **ROW 2:** Ch 2 (counts as dc), dc in each dc across, turn.

» Fasten off.

Crocheting the Second Leg and Body

» Chain 14.

» **ROW 1:** Dc in 4th ch from hook and in each ch across, turn. *You now have 12 sts.*

» **ROW 2:** Ch 2 (counts as dc), dc in each dc across, turn.

» **ROW 3:** Ch 2 (counts as dc), dc in each dc across, ch 15, dc in each dc across the last row of first leg, turn. *You now have 24 dc and 15 ch.*

» **ROW 4:** Ch 2 (counts as dc), dc in each dc and ch across, turn. *You now have 39 dc.*

» **ROW 5:** Ch 2 (counts as dc), dc in same st, dc in each dc across to last st, 2 dc in last st, turn. *You now have 41 dc.*

» **ROWS 6 AND 7:** Ch 2 (counts as dc), dc in each dc across, turn.

» **ROW 8:** Repeat Row 5. *You now have 43 dc.*

» **ROWS 9–11:** Ch 2 (counts as dc), dc in each dc across, turn.

» **ROW 12 (DECREASE ROW):** Ch 1 (does not count as a st), skip first dc, dc in next dc and in each dc across to last 2 sts, dc2tog, turn. *You now have* 41 sts.

» **ROW 13:** Repeat Row 12. *You now have* 39 sts.

» **ROW 14:** Ch 1, skip first dc, dc in next dc, dc in next 14 dc, FLdc in next 7 sts, dc in next 14 dc, dc2tog, turn. *You now have* 37 sts. Place marker at beginning and end of row for edging.

» **ROW 15:** Repeat Row 12. *You now have* 35 sts.

» **ROW 16:** Ch 1, skip first dc, dc2tog, dc in each dc across to last 4 sts, (dc2tog) twice, turn. *You now have* 31 sts.

» **ROWS 17–19:** Repeat Row 16 three more times. *You now have* 19 sts at the end of Row 19.

» **ROW 20:** Repeat Row 12. *You now have* 17 sts.

» Fasten off.

Crocheting the Edging

» With RS facing, join yarn at right-hand marker. Working toward top of bib, ch 1, 2 sc in end of each row to corner, sc in each sc across top edge, 2 sc in end of each row to marker on left-hand side, turn.

Crocheting the Left Tie

» Ch 1 (does not count as sc).

» **ROW 1:** Ch 1, FLsc2tog, FLsc in next 11 sc, 2 sc in next sc; turn, leaving remaining sts unworked. *You now have* 14 sts.

» **ROW 2:** Ch 1, 2 FLsc in first st, FLsc in next 11 sts, FLsc2tog, turn.

» **ROW 3:** Ch 1, (FLsc2tog) twice, FLsc in each sc across to last st, 2 FLsc in last st, turn. *You now have* 13 sts.

» **ROW 4:** Ch 1, 2 FLsc in first st, FLsc in each sc across to last 2 sts, (FLsc2tog) twice, turn.

» **ROWS 5–11:** Repeat Rows 3 and 4 three times, then repeat Row 3 once. *You now have* 9 sts.

» **ROW 12:** Ch 1, 2 FLsc in first st, FLsc in next 4 sts, (FLsc2tog) twice, turn. *You now have* 8 sts.

» **ROW 13:** Ch 1, skip 1 st, sc in next 6 sts, 2 sc in next st, ch 55.

» **ROW 14:** Slip st in 2nd ch from hook and in each ch across, join with slip st to the last sc from the previous row. Fasten off.

Crocheting the Right Tie

» With RS facing, join yarn in first sc of edging at first marked corner. Repeat Rows 1–14 as for left tie.

Crocheting the Trunk

» With RS facing and ties at bottom, join yarn in the first free loop of the 7 center stitches of Row 14.

» **ROW 1:** Ch 2 (counts as dc here and throughout), dc in free loop of next 6 sts, turn. *You now have* 7 sts.

» **ROW 2:** Ch 2, dc in next 6 dc, turn.

» **ROW 3:** Ch 1, skip first dc, dc in next 4 dc, dc2tog, turn. *You now have* 5 sts.

» **ROWS 4 AND 5:** Ch 2, dc in each dc across, turn.

» **ROW 6:** Ch 1, skip first dc, dc in next 3 dc, 2 dc in last st, turn. *You now have* 5 sts.

» **ROW 7:** Ch 2, dc in same st and in next 2 dc, dc2tog, turn.

» **ROW 8:** Ch 2, dc in next 2 dc, sc in next 2 sts, turn.

» **ROW 9:** Ch 1, sc in same st, dc in next 2 sts, dc2tog, turn. *You now have* 4 sts.

» **ROW 10:** Ch 1, skip 1 st, sc in next 3 sts, turn. *You now have* 3 sts.

» **ROW 11:** Ch 1, skip 1 st, sc in next 2 sts, turn. *You now have* 2 sts.

» **ROW 12:** Ch 1, sc2tog. Fasten off.

Crocheting the Ears *(make 2)*

» **ROW 1:** Ch 3, 6 dc in 3rd ch (first 2 skipped ch count as first dc), turn. *You now have* 7 dc.

» **ROW 2:** Ch 2, dc in same st, 2 dc in next 6 sts, turn. *You now have* 14 dc.

» **ROW 3:** Ch 2, dc in same st, dc in next st, *2 dc in next st, dc in next st, repeat from * across, turn. *You now have* 21 dc.

» **ROW 4:** Ch 2, dc in same st, dc in next 2 dc, *2 dc in next dc, dc in next 2 dc, repeat from * across. *You now have* 28 dc.

» Fasten off, leaving a long tail for sewing.

Finishing

» Sew one ear on each side of the trunk as pictured. Embroider the eyes with black embroidery floss. To make the bib child-safe, tack the bottom of the trunk down.

A Star Is Born Booties

Designed by Anastasia Popova

Those simple booties will be a hit at any baby shower. Depending on color and buttons, they could be great for a boy, a girl, or both. One skein of yarn makes two pairs.

FINISHED MEASUREMENTS
Approximately 4"/10 cm long

YARN
Debbie Bliss Ecobaby, 100% organic cotton, 136 yds (125 m)/1.75 oz (50 g), Color 06 Pea Green

CROCHET HOOK
US D/3 (3.25 mm) *or size you need to obtain correct gauge*

GAUGE
11 stitches and 12 rounds = 2"/5 cm in single crochet

OTHER SUPPLIES
Yarn needle, locking stitch markers, four ½"/13 mm buttons

PATTERN ESSENTIALS

Beg Star st Yo, insert hook in side of hdc just made, yo and draw up loop, insert hook in st at base of last hdc made, yo and draw up loop, (insert hook in next st, yo and draw up loop) twice, yo and draw through all loops on hook, ch 1.

Star st Insert hook under ch-1 just made, yo and draw up loop, insert hook in side of st just made, yo and draw up loop, insert hook in st at base of last st made, yo and draw up loop, (insert hook in next st, yo and draw up loop) twice, yo and draw through all loops on hook, ch 1.

Beg Star st dec Yo, insert hook in side of hdc just made, yo and draw up loop, insert hook in st at base of hdc just made, yo and draw up loop, (insert hook in next st, yo and draw up loop) three times, yo and draw through all loops on hook ch 1.

Star st dec Insert hook under ch-1 just made, yo and draw up loop, insert hook in side of st just made, yo and draw up loop, insert hook in st at base of last st made, yo and draw up loop, (insert hook in next st, yo and draw up loop) three times, yo and draw through all loops on hook.

Crocheting the Bootie *(make 2)*

Note: Bootie is worked in continuous rounds; do not join unless otherwise specified. Place a marker in last stitch of first round and move marker up as work progresses.

» Chain 12.

» **RND 1:** Sc in 2nd ch from hook and in each ch to last ch, 3 sc in last ch; working in opposite side of foundation ch, sc in each ch to last ch (first skipped ch), 3 sc in next ch, do not join. *You now have* 26 sts.

» **RND 2:** Sc in next 5 sts, hdc in next 5 sts, 2 hdc in next st, 3 hdc in next st, 2 hdc in next st, hdc in next 5 sts, sc in next 5 sts, 2 sc in next 3 sts. *You now have* 33 sts.

» **RND 3:** Sc in next 11 sts, (2 sc in next st, sc in next st) three times, sc in next 11 sts, 2 sc in next st, sc in next 2 sts, 2 sc in next st, sc in next st. *You now have* 38 sts.

» **RND 4:** Sc in next 5 sts, hdc in next 6 sts, 2 hdc in next st, hdc in next 2 sts, 2 hdc in next st, hdc in next st, 2 hdc in next st, hdc in next 2 sts, 2 hdc in next st, hdc in next 6 sts, sc in next 5 sts, (2 sc in next st, sc in next 2 sts) twice, 2 sc in next st. *You now have* 45 sts.

» **RND 5:** Sc in next 13 sts, (2 sc in next st, sc in next 4 sts) three times, sc in next 8 sts, (2 sc in next st, sc in next 3 sts) twice, 2 sc in next st. *You now have* 51 sts.

» **RND 6:** Sc in each st around.

» **RND 7:** Sc in next 5 sts, hdc in next st, work beg star st, work 13 star sts, hdc in next st, sc in remaining sts.

» **RND 8:** Sc in next 6 sts, (sc in next ch-1, 2 sc in next ch-1) seven times, sc in last 17 sts.

» **RND 9:** Sc in next 5 sts, hdc in next st, beg star st dec, work 6 star st decs, hdc in next st, sc in next 6 sts, hdc in last 10 sts.

» **RND 10:** Sc in next 6 sts, (2 sc in next ch-1, sc in next ch-1) three times, 2 sc in next ch-1, sc to end. Fasten off.

Making the Straps

» Mark center 13 sts on top edge of heel end of bootie.

» **ROW 1:** Ch 10, with WS facing, sc in center 13 sts on top edge of heel, ch 14, turn.

» **ROW 2:** Hdc in 5th ch from hook and in next 9 chs, hdc in next 13 sc, hdc in next 10 ch sts, ch 4 and slip st to the first ch on the bottom of the strap.

» Fasten off. Weave in ends. Using the photo on page 105 as a guide, sew buttons on booties adjacent to first and last star st in Row 9. Cross straps and button.

Lovely Linen Place Mat

Designed by Judith Durant

Dinner or tea service will look lovely atop this dainty crocheted place mat. The large motifs, based on a motif from The Harmony Guide to Crocheting *edited by Debra Mountford, are joined together at two points on the last rounds, and the filler motifs are added later. Linen yarn provides a nice sheen.*

FINISHED MEASUREMENTS
18"/45.5 cm wide and 13½"/34 cm tall

YARN
Louet Euroflax, 100% wet spun linen, 270 yds (246 m)/3.5 oz (100 g), Color 57 French Blue

CROCHET HOOK
US F/5 (3.75 mm) *or size you need to obtain correct gauge*

GAUGE
One motif = 4½"/11.5 cm in diameter

OTHER SUPPLIES
Yarn needle

Crocheting the First Motif

» Chain 5, join with slip st to form ring.

» **RND 1:** Ch 4 (counts as dc and ch 1), *dc in ring, ch 1; repeat from * six more times, join with slip st to 3rd ch of ch-4.

» **RND 2:** Ch 4 (counts as dc and ch 1), dc in next next ch-1 space, ch 1, *dc in next dc, ch 1, dc in next ch-1 space, ch 1; repeat from * around, join with slip st to 3rd ch of ch-4.

» **RND 3:** Ch 3, 2-dc cluster in same st, ch 2, *3-dc cluster in next dc, ch 2; repeat from * around, join with slip st to top of first cluster.

» **RND 4:** Ch 3 (counts as dc), *3 dc in next space**, dc in next dc; repeat from * around, ending last repeat at **, join with slip st to top of ch-3.

» **RND 5:** Ch 1, sc in same st, skip 1 dc, *(hdc, 3 dc, hdc) in next dc — *shell made*, skip 1 dc**, sc in next dc, skip 1 dc; repeat from * around, ending last repeat at **, join with slip st to top of first sc. Fasten off.

Crocheting the Second Motif

» **RNDS 1–4:** Work as for first motif.

» **RND 5:** Ch 1, sc in same st, skip 1 dc, *(hdc, 3 dc, hdc) in next dc, skip 1 dc, sc in next dc; repeat from * 13 more times, (hdc, 2 dc, slip st in center dc of any shell of previous motif, dc, hdc) in next dc, skip 1 dc, sc in next dc, skip 1 dc, (hdc, 2 dc, slip st in center dc of next shell of previous motif, dc, hdc) in next dc, skip 1 dc, join with slip st to top first sc.

» Work 10 more motifs, joining in this manner to previous motifs as shown on diagram, making a mat that is 4 motifs wide and 3 motifs tall.

Filling in Between the Motifs

» Work Rnd 1 as for the first motif.

» **RND 2:** *Ch 2, join with slip st to the center of a point on large motif, slip st in each of 2 ch just made, slip st same st of Rnd 1, sc in next ch-1 space, slip st in next dc; repeat from * to attach eight points of the large motifs, as shown in diagram.

MOTIF #2

5

5

2

1

3

4

5

MOTIF #1

1

FILLER
MOTIF

5

MOTIF #4

MOTIF #3

Yoga Mat Bag

Designed by Edie Eckman

This openwork bag is plenty big enough for a large yoga mat, or two thinner mats rolled together, but it does take all of one skein. For a slightly smaller bag, work fewer rounds of the Shell and V-Stitch pattern between Rounds 4–21 and Rounds 39–58.

FINISHED MEASUREMENTS
Approximately 14"/35.5 cm in
circumference and 29"/74 cm long

YARN
Kollage Riveting Sport, 100%
recycled yarn made from recycled
blue jeans (95% cotton/5% other),
350 yds (320 m)/3.5 oz (100 g),
Color 7901 Storm Denim

CROCHET HOOK
US 7 (4.5 mm) *or size you need
to obtain correct gauge*

GAUGE
3 repeats = 4¼"/11 cm; 8 rows = 4"/10 cm
in Shell and V-Stitch pattern

OTHER SUPPLIES
Stitch markers, yarn needle,
¾"/19 mm plastic cord lock

PATTERN ESSENTIALS

Reverse sc Working from left to right and keeping hook pointed to the left (for right handers), or working from right to left and keeping hook pointed to the right (for left handers), with RS facing, ch 1, *insert hook in next st, yo and pull up a loop, yo and pull through 2 loops on hook; repeat from *.

Shell (2 dc, ch 1, 2 dc) in same st.

V-st (Dc, ch 1, dc) in same st.

SHELL AND V-ST PATTERN

Rnd 1: Ch 3 (counts as dc), dc in same space, ch 1, *shell in center of next V-st, ch 1; repeat from * around, ending with 2 dc in first space, join with sc to top of ch-3.

Rnd 2: Ch 4 (counts as dc and ch 1), dc in same space, *ch 1, dc in next space, ch 1, V-st in next shell space; repeat from * around, omitting last V-st, join with slip st to 3rd ch of ch-4, slip st in next space.

Repeat Rnds 1 and 2 for Shell and V-st pattern.

Crocheting the Bag

See chart on page 112.

» Chain 6, join with slip st to form ring.

» **RND 1:** Ch 4 (counts as dc and ch 1), dc in ring, (ch 1, dc in ring) 10 times, join with sc to 3rd ch of ch-4. *You now have* 12 dc and 12 spaces.

» **RND 2:** Ch 4 (counts as dc and ch 1), dc in same space — *beg V-st made*, V-st in each space around, join with slip st to 3rd ch of ch-4, slip st in next space.

» **RND 3:** Beg V-st in same space, ch 1, *V-st in next space, ch 1; repeat from * around, join with slip st to 3rd ch of ch-4, slip st in next space. *You now have* 12 V-sts.

» **RNDS 4–21:** Beginning with Rnd 1 of Shell and V-st pattern, work the pattern nine times.

» **RNDS 22–38:** Ch 4 (counts as dc and ch 1), dc in same space, ch 1, skip 1 dc, dc in next dc, ch 1, V-st in next V-st; repeat from * around, omitting last V-st, join with slip st to 3rd ch of ch-4, slip st in next space.

» **RNDS 39–58:** Begin with Rnd 1 of Shell and V-st pattern, work the pattern 10 times.

» **RND 59:** Ch 3 (counts as dc), (2 dc, ch 1, 3 dc) in same space, (3 dc, ch 1, 3 dc) in each V-st around, join with slip st to top of first ch-3. Fasten off.

Crocheting the Strap

» Chain 92.

» **ROW 1:** Sc in 2nd ch from hook and in each ch across, turn.

» **ROWS 2 AND 3:** Ch 1, sc in each sc across, turn.

» **ROW 4:** Ch 1, sc in each sc across. Do not turn.

» **ROW 5:** Ch 1, working from left to right, reverse sc in each st across. Fasten off, leaving a 10"/25.5 cm tail for seaming.

» With RS facing, rejoin yarn at left corner of foundation-ch edge, ch 1, working from left to right, reverse sc in each st across. Fasten off, leaving a 10"/25.5 cm tail for seaming.

Crocheting the Tie

» Chain 76. Sc in 2nd ch from hook and in each ch across. Fasten off.

continued on next page

Finishing

» Insert mat into bag to test fit. Gather top of bag and mark the round of V-sts that meet at top of mat. Weave tie in and out through the center of these V-sts. Insert both ends of tie through hole in cord lock. Tie small overhand knot in each end of tie.

» Sew ends of strap onto Round 3 at bottom of bag and approximately 4"/10 cm from top of bag.

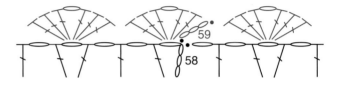

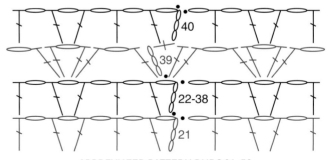

RNDS 41–58: REPEAT RNDS 39 AND 40

ABBREVIATED PATTERN RNDS 21–59

RNDS 6–21: REPEAT RNDS 4 AND 5

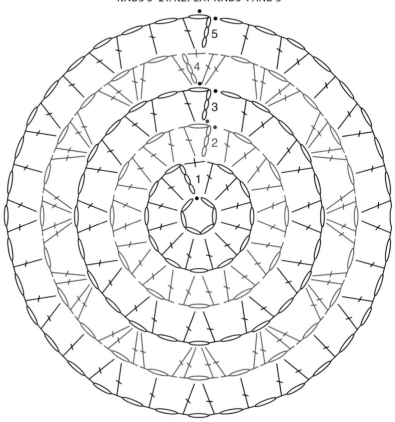

YOGA MAT BAG RNDS 1–5

Light Weight

Diamond-Strike Banded Scarf

Designed by Kristen Stoltzfus

Show off spider web stitches in this fashionable scarf. The edging is worked as you go; add fringe and an optional band for extra wearability and style.

FINISHED MEASUREMENTS

33"/84 cm long, plus 10"/25.5 cm total with fringe, and 6½"/16.5 cm wide

YARN

Kraemer Yarns Tatamy, 55% acrylic/45% cotton, 250 yds (229 m)/3.5 oz (100 g), Loganberry

CROCHET HOOK

US E/4 (3.5 mm) *or size you need to obtain correct gauge*

GAUGE

First complete spider web = 3"/7.5 cm square

OTHER SUPPLIES

Yarn needle

Crocheting the Scarf

See chart on page 116.

» Chain 44.

» **ROW 1:** Dc in 8th ch from hook, work 12 Mesh; *for edging,* ch 3, slip st in ch at base of ending dc, ch 1, turn, (sc, 3 dc, sc) in same ch-3 space, slip st in top of ending dc.

» **ROW 2:** Ch 5 (counts as dc, ch 2 here and throughout), dc in next dc; work 2 Mesh, 2 dc in next space, dc in next dc, work 5 Mesh, 2 dc in next space, dc in next dc, work 3 Mesh; *for edging,* ch 3, slip st in base of ending Mesh dc, ch 1, turn, (sc, 3 dc, sc) in same ch-3 space, slip st in top of ending Mesh dc.

» **ROW 3:** Ch 5, dc in next dc; work 1 Mesh, *2 dc in next space, dc in next dc, ch 7, skip 2 dc, dc in next dc, 2 dc in next space, dc in next dc, work 3 Mesh; repeat from *, omitting last Mesh; work edging.

» **ROW 4:** Ch 5, dc in next dc, *2 dc in next space, dc in next dc, ch 5, sc in ch-7 space, ch 5, skip next 3 dc, dc in next dc, 2 dc in next space, dc in next dc, work 1 Mesh; repeat from * once; work edging.

» **ROW 5:** Ch 3 (counts as dc), *2 dc in space, dc in next dc, ch 5, sc next ch-5 space, sc in next sc, sc in next ch-5 space, ch 5, skip next 3 dc, dc in next dc; repeat from * once, 2 dc in next space, dc in 3rd ch of turning ch; work edging.

» **ROW 6:** Ch 5, skip 2 dc, dc in next dc, *3 dc in ch-5 space, ch 5, skip next sc, sc in next sc, ch 5, 3 dc in ch-5 space, dc in next dc, ch 2, skip 2 dc, dc in next dc; repeat from * once; work edging.

» **ROW 7:** Ch 5, dc in next dc, *ch 2, skip 2 dc, dc in next dc, 3 dc in next ch-5 space, ch 2, 3 dc in next ch-5 space, dc in next dc, work 2 Mesh; repeat from * once; work edging.

» **ROW 8:** Ch 5, dc in next dc, *work 2 Mesh, 2 dc in next space, dc in next dc, work 3 Mesh; repeat from * once; work edging.

» Repeat Rows 3–8 eleven times.

» **LAST ROW:** Ch 5, dc in next dc, work 12 Mesh; work edging. Fasten off and weave in ends. Block if needed.

Finishing

» Cut four 12"/30.5 cm strands for each Mesh space on each end; alternating RS and WS for each knot to make the scarf reversible, pull the center of four strands through a space to form a loop, thread ends through loop, pull up tight. Trim ends.

MAKING THE BAND (optional)

» Ch 35, join with slip st to form ring.

» Ch 3, dc in next 3 ch, 3-dc cluster in next ch, (dc in next 4 chs, 3-dc cluster in next ch) around, join with slip st to first ch 3. Fasten off. Weave in ends.

ABBREVIATED BAND

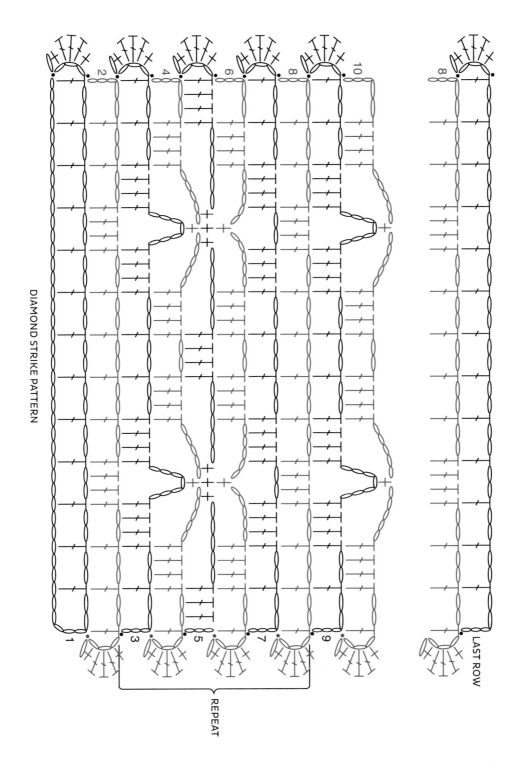

DIAMOND STRIKE PATTERN

REPEAT

LAST ROW

116

Ice-Cold Summer Scarf

Designed by Janet Brani

A cool color and icy sparkles make this an indispensible accessory for summer. With a quick change in color and bead style, this scarf can be modified for any season or event.

FINISHED MEASUREMENTS
Approximately 82"/208 cm long and 2½"/6.5 cm wide

YARN
Cascade Yarns Ultra Pima, 100% pima cotton, 220 yds (200 m)/3.5 oz (100 g), Color 3736 Ice

CROCHET HOOK
US G/6 (4 mm) *or size you need to obtain correct gauge*

GAUGE
16 stitches and 20 rows = 4"/10 cm in single crochet; 14 stitches and 4 rows = 4"/10 cm in pattern

OTHER SUPPLIES
Approximately 2 oz (57 g) size 6° (4 mm) metallic silver round beads, big eye beading needle or dental floss threader

Preparing the Yarn

» Divide yarn into two 50-gram balls (Janet used a kitchen scale). Using a big eye beading needle or floss threader, string half (approximately 1 oz [30 g]) of beads onto each ball of yarn.

Crocheting the Scarf *(make 2 halves)*

Note: Beads are placed in the single crochet stitches at the beginning and end of each half, in the first 3 chains of the turning chain, and in the treble shells in the center of the scarf.

» Chain 13.

» **ROW 1 (RS):** Bsc in 2nd ch from hook and in each ch across, turn. *You now have* 12 Bsc.

» **ROW 2:** Ch 1, Bsc in first 5 sc, ch 2, skip 2 sc, Bsc in next 5 sc, turn.

» **ROW 3:** Bch 3, ch 1 (counts as tr, with beads placed in the first 3 chains here and throughout), 2 tr in same st, skip 4 sc, (3 Btr, ch 2, 3 Btr) in next space, skip 4 sc, 3 tr in last sc, turn.

» **ROW 4:** Bch 3, ch 1, 2 tr in same st, (3 Btr, ch 2, 3 Btr) in next space, 3 tr in top of turning ch, turn.

» **ROWS 5–42:** Repeat Row 4. *You now have* 39 rows of shells.

» **ROW 43:** Bch 3, ch 1, 2 tr in same st, 6 Btr in next ch-space, 3 tr in top of turning ch, turn.

» **ROWS 44–48:** Ch 1, Bsc in each st across. Fasten off.

Finishing

» With RS together, connect foundation rows of each side by slip stitching together. The 5 beaded rows of single crochet form the loose ends.

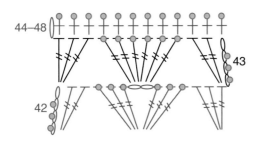

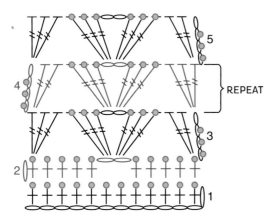

REPEAT

Putting on the Glitz Shrug

Designed by Pam Grushkin

The crossed double crochet pattern shows off variegated yarns very well — changing the order of the stitches mitigates striping and pooling. The pattern's easy to memorize so you don't have to keep referring to the instructions. Throw this shrug over your tank top when the air-conditioning is on or wear it to brighten up any outfit.

FINISHED MEASUREMENTS
Approximately 38"/96.5 cm long and 14"/35.5 cm wide, fully opened

YARN
Blue Heron Rayon Metallic, 88% rayon, 12% metallic, 550 yds (503 m)/8 oz (226 g), Color Water Hyacinth with Copper

CROCHET HOOK
US G/6 (4mm) *or size you need to obtain correct gauge*

GAUGE
16 stitches and 10 rows = 4"/10 cm in pattern

OTHER SUPPLIES
Locking stitch markers, yarn needle

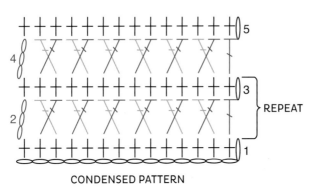

CONDENSED PATTERN

Crocheting the Shrug

» Loosely ch 147.

» **ROW 1:** Sc in 2nd ch from hook and in each ch to end. *You now have* 146 sc.

» **ROW 2:** Ch 3 (counts as dc), *work crossed dc over next 2 sc; repeat from * to last st, dc in last sc, turn.

» **ROW 3:** Ch 1, sc in same st, sc in each st to end, turn.

» Repeat Rows 2 and 3 for pattern until shrug measures 14"/35.5 cm from beginning. Fasten off.

Finishing

» Block shrug by soaking in cool water for 30 minutes. Wrap it in a towel and gently press water from shrug. Lay out on a blocking board or towel and stretch to finished measurements.

» Fold shrug in half lengthwise and pin (using locking stitch markers) approximately 8"/20.5 cm from each edge for sleeves. Try on and adjust sleeve length as desired. Sew or crochet sleeve seams.

» Work 1 round of reverse sc around cuffs and body opening of shrug. Fasten off and weave in ends.

Sunflower Headband

Designed by Birgit Tüchsen

This playful hair band is made with three flower motifs. With the help of a chart, this is a very easy project for the beginning crocheter.

FINISHED MEASUREMENTS
Headband measures 40"/101.5 cm

YARN
Garnstudio DROPS Muskat, 100% Egyptian cotton, 109 yds (100 m)/1.75 oz (50 g), Color 30 Vanilla Yellow

CROCHET HOOK
US G/6 (4 mm) *or size you need to obtain correct gauge*

GAUGE
One flower = approximately 3¾"/9.5 cm in diameter

OTHER SUPPLIES
Yarn needle

Making the First Flower

» Chain 6, join with slip st to first ch to form a ring.

» **RND 1:** Ch 1, *2 sc in ring, ch 7, sc in 5th ch from hook, sc in next 2 ch; repeat from * five times, join with slip st to first sc. *You now have* six rays. Fasten off.

» **RND 2:** Join yarn with slip st in top loop of any ray, ch 1, (sc, 2 hdc, 2 dc, picot-3, 2 dc, 2 hdc, sc, ch 1) in top loop of each ray around, join with slip st to first sc. *You now have* six petals. Fasten off.

Making the Second Flower

» Work as for first flower through Rnd 1.

» **RND 2:** Join yarn with slip st in any top loop of previous rnd, ch 1, (sc, 2 hdc, 2 dc, picot-3, 2 dc, 2 hdc, sc, ch 1) in top loop of first four rays, *(sc, 2 hdc, 2 dc, ch 1, sc in picot of previous flower, ch 1, 2 dc, 2 hdc, sc, ch 1) in next top loop; repeat from * once, join with slip st to first sc.

Making the Third Flower

» Make as for second flower, joining to petals opposite the petals previously joined.

Making the Ties

» Cut six strands of yarn each 46"/117 cm long, three strands for each side. Thread one strand through the tip of outer petal of an end flower; thread the second strand through the other outer petal; thread the third strand through both outer petals. Adjust strands so all six ends are even. Using two strands as one, braid the six strands together; tie an overhand knot to secure end of braid. Repeat tie on the other end.

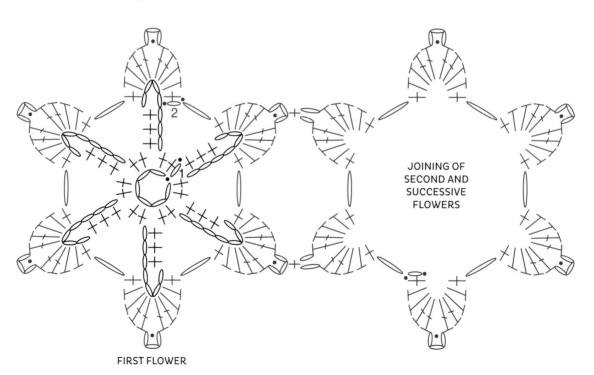

FIRST FLOWER

JOINING OF SECOND AND SUCCESSIVE FLOWERS

Bellisfaire Beanie

Designed by Sarah Grieve

The ever-popular beanie gets a new look with the addition of a picot-edged band. The shell and V-stitch crown makes this a perfect weight for an autumn stroll. Instructions are given for two sizes.

FINISHED MEASUREMENTS
Small (medium) 21" (22½")/53.5 (57) cm circumference

YARN
Cascade Ultra Pima, 100% pima cotton, 220 yds (200 m)/3.5 oz (100 g), Color 3704

CROCHET HOOKS
US F/6 (3.75 mm) and US G/6 (4 mm) *or sizes needed to obtain correct gauge*

GAUGE
17 stitches = 4"/10 cm in single crochet with smaller hook; 4 shells and 8 rows = 4"/10 cm with larger hook, working in shell pattern

OTHER SUPPLIES
Yarn needle

PATTERN ESSENTIALS

Shell (2 dc, ch 1, 2 dc) in same st or space.

V-st (Dc, ch 1, dc) in same st or space.

Crocheting the Hat

» With smaller hook, chain 90 (96). Being careful not to twist ch, join with slip st to first ch.

» **RND 1:** Ch 2, hdc in 2nd ch from hook and in each ch around, join with slip st to top of ch-2. *You now have 90 (96) hdc.*

» **RNDS 2–4:** Ch 2 (counts as hdc), hdc in each hdc around, join with slip st to top of ch-2.

» **RND 5:** Ch 2, hdc in next 7 (10) sts, 2 hdc in next st, *hdc in next 8 (11) sts, 2 hdc in next st; repeat from * to end of rnd, join. *You now have* 100 (104) sts.

» **RND 6:** With larger hook, ch 3 (counts as dc here and throughout), skip 2 hdc, shell in next hdc, *skip 3 hdc, shell in next hdc; repeat from * to last 4 hdc, skip 3 hdc, (2 dc, ch 1, dc) in next hdc; join with slip st to top of ch-3. *You now have* 25 (26) shells.

» **RND 7:** Ch 3, shell in center of each shell around, ending (2 dc, ch 1, dc) in last shell, join with slip st to top of ch-3.

» Repeat Rnd 7 until work measures 7" (7½")/18 (19) cm from beginning.

DECREASING FOR THE CROWN

» **RND 1:** Ch 3, V-st in center of each shell around, join with slip st to top of ch-3. *You now have* 25 (26) V-sts and 1 ch-3.

» **RND 2:** Ch 3, V-st in each V-st around, join with slip st to top of ch-3.

» **RND 3:** Ch 3, dc in each V-st around, join with a slip st to top of ch-3. *You now have* 26 (27) dc.

» **RND 4:** Ch 3, *skip 1 dc, dc in next dc; repeat from * around to last 1 (2) dc, skip last 1 (2) dc, join with a slip st to top of ch-3. *You now have* 13 sts.

» **RND 5:** Ch 2 (counts as hdc), *hdc in next dc, skip 1 dc; repeat from * around, join with slip st to top of ch-2. *You now have* 7 sts.

» **RND 6:** Ch 1, *sc in next hdc, skip 1 hdc; repeat from * to end of rnd, join with slip st to top of first sc. *You now have* 3 sc. Fasten off.

Adding the Picot Edging
(optional)

» Join yarn to bottom edge of hat with a slip st to beginning of round.

» **PICOT RND:** *Slip st in next 3 sts, ch 3, slip st in next st; repeat from * around. Fasten off.

Finishing

» Sew hole at the top of the hat closed with a yarn needle. Weave in ends. Wash and block.

NOTE: FOR MEDIUM ON ROUND 4 SKIP LAST 2 DC.

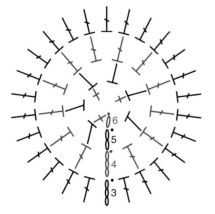

CROWN ROUNDS 3–6

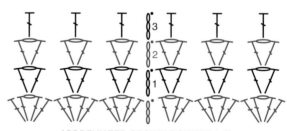

ABBREVIATED CROWN ROUNDS 1–3

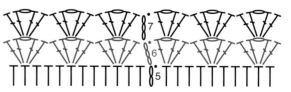

ABBREVIATED HAT ROUNDS 5–7

Blue Sky Dreamin'

Designed by Robin Dykema

With just one skein you can make two pairs of slipper socks — one for you and one for a special little girl in your life. The Big Sister socks fit a woman's U.S. 8 shoe size, and the Little Sister socks fit a girl's U.S. 2 shoe size.

FINISHED MEASUREMENTS

Big Sister: approximately 9½"/24 cm long

Little Sister: approximately 7"/18 cm long

YARN

Bernat Baby Jacquards, 90% acrylic/10% nylon, 346 yds (316 m)/3.5 oz (100 g), Color 06128 Boo Berries

CROCHET HOOK

US E/4 (3.5 mm) *or size you need to obtain correct gauge*

GAUGE

20 stitches and 25 rows = 4"/10 cm in single crochet

OTHER SUPPLIES

Locking stitch markers, yarn needle

PATTERN ESSENTIALS

I-sc dec (invisible single crochet decrease) In the 2 stitches indicated, insert hook through front loop only of first stitch and through back loop only of 2nd stitch, yo and pull up a loop, yo and pull through both loops. This is the primary decrease method in these socks.

✳ **NOTE:** Work is turned at the end of every round to keep the seam straight and the toe flat.

Big Sister Sock *(make 2)*

CROCHETING THE HEEL

» Leaving 6"/15 cm tail, fsc 44 (see page 273). Being careful not to twist work, join with slip st to first fsc.

» **ROW 1:** Ch 1, sc in same st and in next 21 sts, leaving remaining sts unworked, turn. *You now have* 22 sc.

» **ROWS 2–15:** Ch 1, sc in next 22 sc, turn.

» **ROW 16:** Ch 1, sc in next 15 sc, leave remaining sts unworked, turn. *You now have 15 sc.*

» **ROW 17:** Ch 1, sc in next 7 sc, I-sc dec in next 2 sts, turn. *You now have 8 sts.*

» **ROW 18:** Ch 1, sc in next 7 sts, sc2tog over next st and first unworked st from Row 14, turn. *You now have 8 sts.*

» **ROW 19:** Ch 1, sc in next 7 sts, sc2tog next st and first unworked st from Row 15.

» **ROWS 20–29:** Repeat Rows 18 and 19 until no unworked sts remain on either side of heel. *You now have 8 sts.*

CROCHETING THE HEEL GUSSET

» Working toward fsc, work 1 sc in the end of each row up the side of the heel, pm in last st; *skip 1 st of fsc, (sc, ch 1, sc) in next st — *mini-shell made*; repeat from * across fsc; continuing up other side of heel, 1 sc in end of each row, pm in first sc after mini-shells, join with slip st to first sc at bottom of heel, turn. *You now have 8 sc at bottom of heel, 14 sc along each side of heel, and 11 mini-shells over instep.*

CROCHETING THE FOOT

» **RND 1:** Ch 1, sc in each sc to last st before marker, I-sc dec over next st and marked st, move marker up on this and every rnd, (sc, ch 1, sc) in each ch-1 space across instep, I-sc dec in marked st and next st, move marker up on this and every rnd, sc in each sc around, join with slip st to first sc, turn.

» **RNDS 2–14:** Repeat Rnd 1 until you have 22 sc across sole and 11 mini-shells across instep.

» **RND 15:** Ch 1, sc in each sc across sole, work mini-shell in each ch-1 space across top of foot, sc in each remaining sc across sole, join with slip st to first sc, turn.

» Repeat Rnd 15 until sock measures 6¼"/16 cm from top of ankle opening (or length needed to cover the small toe), turn.

CROCHETING THE TOE

Note: If the toe decreases run into the join, slip st 1 st after joining the rounds, before turning. You should then be able to work the decrease as normal.

» **RND 1:** Ch 1, sc in each sc to 2 sts before marked st, I-sc dec over next 2 sts, sc in marked st, sc in next ch-1 space, sc in each sc of next 9 mini-shells, skipping ch-1 spaces, sc in last ch-1 space, sc in marked st, I-sc dec over next 2 sts, sc in each remaining st around, join with slip st to first sc, turn. *You now have 40 sts.*

» **RND 2:** Ch 1, (sc in each sc to 2 sts before marker, I-sc dec over next 2 sts, sc in marked st, I-sc dec over next 2 sts) twice, sc in each remaining st around, join. *You now have 36 sts.*

» **RNDS 3–6:** Repeat Rnd 2 until 16 sts remain. Fasten off, leaving a long tail for sewing. Remove markers. Turn sock inside out, flatten toe to align with heel, and sew toe opening closed. Weave in tail. Using beginning tail, join the bottom edges of fsc (top of sock) together and weave in the tail.

Little Sister Sock *(make 2)*

CROCHETING THE HEEL

» Leaving 6"/15 cm tail, fsc 36 (see page 273). Being careful not to twist work, join with slip st to first fsc.

» **ROW 1:** Ch 1, sc in same st and in next 17 sts, leaving remaining sts unworked, turn. *You now have* 18 sc.

» **ROWS 2–11:** Ch 1, sc in next 18 sc, turn.

» **ROW 12:** Ch 1, sc in next 13 sc, leaving remaining sts unworked, turn.

» **ROW 13:** Ch 1, sc in next 6 sc, I-sc dec in next 2 sts, turn.

» **ROW 14:** Ch 1, turn, 1 sc in each of first 6 sts, sc2tog next st and first unworked st from Row 11.

» **ROW 15:** Ch 1, sc in next 6 sts, sc2tog over next st and first unworked st from Row 12.

» Repeat Rows 14 and 15 until no unworked sts remain. *You now have* 8 sts.

CROCHETING THE HEEL GUSSET

» Working toward fsc, work 1 sc in the end of each row up side of heel, pm in last st; *skip 1 st of fsc, (sc, ch 1, sc) in next st — *mini-shell made*; repeat from * across fsc; continuing up other side of heel, work 1 sc in end of each row, pm in first sc after mini-shells, join with slip st to first sc at bottom of heel, turn. *You now have* 8 sc at bottom of heel, 11 sc along each side of heel, and 9 mini-shells over instep.

CROCHETING THE FOOT

» **RND 1:** Ch 1, sc in each sc to last st before marker, I-sc dec over next st and marked st, move marker up on this and every rnd, (sc, ch 1, sc) in each ch-1 space across instep, I-sc dec in marked st and next st, move marker up on this and every rnd, sc in each sc around, join with slip st to first sc, turn.

» **RNDS 2–5:** Repeat Rnd 1 until you have 18 sc across sole and 9 mini-shells across instep.

» **RND 6:** Ch 1, sc in each sc across sole, mini-shell in each ch-1 space across top of foot, sc in each remaining sc across sole, join with slip st to first sc, turn.

» Repeat Rnd 6 until sock measures 4½"/11.5 cm from top of ankle opening, or length needed to cover the small toe, turn.

CROCHETING THE TOE

Note: If the toe decreases run into the join, slip st 1 st after joining the rounds, before turning. You should then be able to work the decrease as normal.

» **RND 1:** Ch 1, sc in each sc to 2 sts before marked st, I-sc dec over next 2 sts, sc in marked st, sc in next ch-1 space, sc in each sc of next 7 mini-shells, skipping ch-1 spaces, sc in last ch-1 space, sc in marked st, I-sc dec over next 2 sts, sc in each remaining st around, join with slip st to first sc, turn. *You now have* 29 sts.

» **RND 2:** Ch 1, (sc in each sc to 2 sts before marker, I-sc dec over next 2 sts, sc in marked st, I-sc dec over next 2 sts) twice, sc in each remaining st around, join. *You now have* 25 sts.

» **RNDS 3–5:** Repeat Rnd 2 until 13 sts remain. Fasten off, leaving a long tail for sewing. Remove markers. Turn sock inside out, flatten toe to align with heel, and sew toe opening closed. Weave in tail. Using beginning tail, join the bottom edges of fsc (top of sock) together and weave in the tail.

Pixie Hats

Designed by Annelies Baes

This little pixie hat comes in two sizes: baby and toddler. The hat is crocheted in the round, without joining, and is topped with a tassel.

SIZES AND FINISHED MEASUREMENTS
To fit baby (toddler), 13"–15½" (15½"–17½")/33–39.5 (39.5–44.5) cm; finished hat, approximately 15½" (17")/39.5 (43) cm in circumference

YARN
Rico Designs Merino DK, 100% baby merino wool, 131 yds (120 m)/1.75 oz (50 g), Color 19 Mulberry (baby size) or Color 39 Petrol (toddler size)

CROCHET HOOK
US G/6 (4 mm) *or size you need to obtain correct gauge*

GAUGE
20 stitches and 24 rounds = 4"/10 cm in single crochet

OTHER SUPPLIES
Yarn needle, locking stitch markers, small piece of cardboard (for making tassel)

Crocheting the Baby Cap

» **RND 1:** Form an adjustable ring (see page 271), 8 sc in the ring. *Do not join.* Place marker at the first st of the rnd and move it up as you work the rnds.

» **RND 2:** *Sc in next sc, 2 sc in next sc; repeat from * around. *You now have* 12 sts.

» **RND 3:** *Sc in next 2 sc, 2 sc in next sc; repeat from * around. *You now have* 16 sts.

» **RND 4 AND ALL EVEN RNDS THROUGH 16:** Sc in each sc around.

» **RND 5:** *Sc in next 3 sc, 2 sc in next sc; repeat from * around. *You now have* 20 sts.

» **RND 7:** *Sc in next 4 sc, 2 sc in next sc; repeat from * around. *You now have* 24 sts.

» **RND 9:** *Sc in next 2 sc, 2 sc in next sc; repeat from * around. *You now have* 32 sts.

» **RND 11:** *Sc in next 3 sc, 2 sc in next sc; repeat from * around. *You now have* 40 sts.

» **RND 13:** *Sc in next 4 sc, 2 sc in next sc; repeat from * around. *You now have* 48 sts.

» **RND 15:** *Sc in next 5 sc, 2 sc in next sc; repeat from * around. *You now have* 56 sts.

» **RND 17:** *Sc in next 6 sc, 2 sc in next sc; repeat from * around. *You now have* 64 sts.

» **RNDS 18–20:** Sc in each sc around.

» **RND 21:** *Sc in next 7 sc, 2 sc in next sc; repeat from * around. *You now have* 72 sts.

» **RNDS 22–26:** Sc in each sc around.

» **RND 27:** *Sc in next 13 sc, 2 sc in next sc; repeat from * to last 2 sc, sc in last 2 sc. *You now have* 77 sts.

» Work 10 rounds even in sc. Fasten off.

Crocheting the Toddler Cap

» Work as for Baby Cap through Rnd 17.

» **RND 18:** Sc in each sc around.

» **RND 19:** *Sc in next 7 sc, 2 sc in next sc; repeat from * around. *You now have 72 sts.*

» **RNDS 20–22:** Sc in each sc around.

» **RND 23:** *Sc in next 8 sc, 2 sc in next sc; repeat from * around. *You now have 80 sts.*

» **RNDS 24–28:** Sc in each sc around.

» **RND 29:** *Sc in next 15 sc, 2 sc in next sc; repeat from * around. *You now have 85 sts.*

» Work 10 rounds even in sc. Fasten off.

Finishing

» **MAKE A TASSEL AS FOLLOWS:** Cut piece of cardboard 2"–2½"/5–6.5 cm tall. Wind yarn around the cardboard about 25 times. Thread a yarn needle and pass under the loops on one end. Pull up tight and make a double knot around the loops. Cut the other ends of the loops. Remove the tassel from the cardboard. With a second length of yarn, wrap the tassel yarns about ½"/1.3 cm down from the top. Wind a few times around, make a secure knot, and pull both ends (with help of the needle) behind the knot and into the tassel. Trim the tassel if necessary and sew it to the hat.

Five Hair Scrunchies

Designed by Andrea Lyn Van Benschoten

Hair scrunchies are great accessories, and these are quick to make. The best part of this project is that you can make five different versions from one ball of yarn.

FINISHED MEASUREMENTS
To fit 1½"/3.8 cm hair elastics

YARN
Patons Grace, 100% mercerized cotton, 136 yds (125 m)/1.75 oz (50 g), Color 62104 Azure

CROCHET HOOK
US G/6 (4.25 mm) *or size you need to obtain correct gauge*

GAUGE
24 stitches and 20 rows = 4"/10 cm in single crochet; exact gauge is not critical

OTHER SUPPLIES
1½"/3.8 cm hair elastics, yarn needle, stitch marker

Crocheting Scrunchie #1

» **RND 1:** Sc around hair elastic to join yarn to elastic, work 40 more sc around hair elastic, join with slip st to first sc. *You now have* 41 sc.

» **RND 2:** Ch 1, sc in first sc, *ch 3, sc in next sc; repeat from * around, ending ch 1, join with hdc to first sc.

» **RND 3:** Ch 1, sc in same space, ch 3, *sc in next space, ch 3; repeat from * around, join with slip st to first sc. Fasten off. Weave in ends.

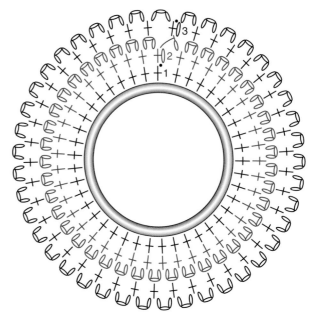

SCRUNCHIE #1

Crocheting Scrunchie #2

» **RND 1:** Sc around hair elastic to join yarn to elastic, work 20 more sc around hair elastic, *ch 20, 2 dc in 4th ch from hook, 3 dc in each remaining ch, (sc around hair elastic) two times; repeat from * twice, work 20 more sc around hair elastic, join with slip st to first sc.

» Fasten off. Weave in ends.

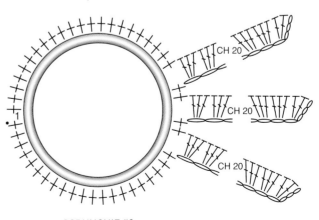

SCRUNCHIE #2

131

Crocheting Scrunchie #3

- » **RND 1:** Sc around hair elastic to join yarn to elastic, work 40 more sc around hair elastic, join with slip st to first sc. *You now have* 41 sc.

- » **RND 2:** Ch 1, 2 sc in each sc around, join with slip st to first sc. *You now have* 82 sc.

- » **RND 3:** Ch 1, *sc in next sc, 2 sc in next sc; repeat from * around, join with slip st to first sc. *You now have* 123 sc.

- » **RND 4:** Ch 1, *sc in next 2 sc, 2 sc in next sc; repeat from * around, join with slip st to first sc. *You now have* 164 sc.

- » Fasten off. Weave in ends.

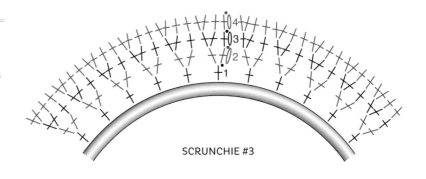

SCRUNCHIE #3

Crocheting Scrunchie #4

- » **RND 1:** Sc around hair elastic to join yarn to elastic, work 40 more sc around hair elastic, join with slip st to first sc. *You now have* 41 sc.

- » **RND 2:** Ch 1, sc in first sc, *ch 15, sc in next sc; repeat from * around, omitting last sc, join with slip st to first sc. Fasten off. Weave in ends.

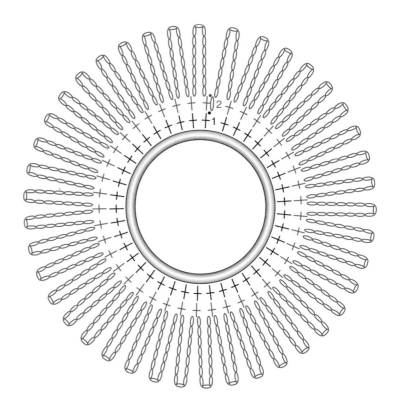

SCRUNCHIE #4

Crocheting
Scrunchie #5

» **RND 1:** Sc around hair elastic to join yarn to elastic, work 45 more sc around hair elastic, join with slip st to first sc, pm in first sc. *Do not fasten off.*

CROCHETING THE FLOWER

» Ch 5, slip st in marked sc to form a ring.

» **RND 1:** (Ch 5, sc in ch-5 ring) four times, ch 5, join with slip st to marked sc. Remove marker.

» **RND 2:** (Sc, hdc, dc, hdc, sc) in each ch-5 space around, join with slip st to first sc. Fasten off. Weave in ends.

FLOWER

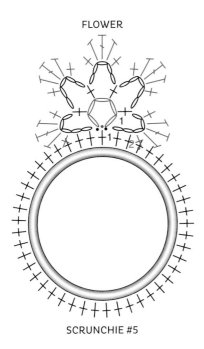

SCRUNCHIE #5

Gerbera Flower Pins

Designed by Jane M. Brown

These little pins will dress up your suit, coat, hat — anything you like. A button adorns the front of flower, and a pin back is sewn to the back for easy wearing.

133

FINISHED MEASUREMENTS
3½"/9 cm in diameter

YARN
Plymouth Yarn Gold
  Rush, 80% viscose/20%
  metallized polyester, 109 yds
  (100 m)/0.88 oz (25 g), shown
  in Colors 92, 61, and 85.

CROCHET HOOKS
US D/3 (3.25 mm) or size you
  need to obtain correct gauge

GAUGE
Rounds 1–4 = 1½"/3.8
  cm in diameter; exact
  gauge is not crucial

OTHER SUPPLIES
Yarn needle, one 1"/2.5 cm
  button, bar pin back

Crocheting the Flower

» Chain 6, leaving a 10"/25.5 cm tail.
Join with slip st to form a ring.

» **RND 1:** Ch 1, 18 sc in ring, join with
slip st to back loop of first sc. *You
now have* 18 sc.

» **RND 2:** Ch 1, BLsc in each st around,
join with slip st to back loop of
first sc.

» **RND 3:** Ch 2 (counts as dc), BLdc in
each st around, join with slip st to
top of ch-2.

» **RND 4:** Ch 1, sc in same st, ch 7, *sc in
next st, ch 7; repeat from * around,
join with slip st to first sc. *You now
have* 18 ch-7 loops.

» **RND 5:** *(2 sc, 2 hdc, 2 dc, 2 tr, 2 dtr, 2
tr, 2 dc, 2 hdc, 2 sc) in next ch-7 space,
slip st in next sc; repeat from *
around, ending last repeat with slip
st in ending slip st of Rnd 4, join
with slip st to first sc. *You now have*
18 petals.

» Fasten off, leaving an 18"/45.5 cm
tail. Overlap the right-hand side of
each petal over the left-hand side
of the adjacent petal. Thread tail
onto yarn needle and sew petals
together.

Finishing

» With the beginning tail, attach button and pin back. Weave in ends.

FLOWER

Sunflower Pillow

Designed by Gwen Steege

Hand-dyed Freia yarn makes only one transition from gold through green, brown, and burgundy to rich purple in a single skein. This pillow makes use of the entire skein to take advantage of the lively palette.

FINISHED MEASUREMENTS
12"/30.5 cm square

YARN
Freia Fine Handpaint Yarns Ombré Sport Wool, 100% wool, 217 yds (200 m)/2.64 oz (75 g), Color Grapevine

CROCHET HOOK
US E/4 (3.5mm) *or size you need to obtain correct gauge*

GAUGE
Rounds 1–6 = 3¾"/9.5 cm

OTHER SUPPLIES
Embroidery needle, perle cotton to match last crocheted round, 13"/33 cm square of fabric to cover pillow back, 12"/30.5 cm square pillow form

135

Crocheting the Pillow Front

See chart on page 138.

» Begin with an adjustable ring (see page 271).

» **RND 1:** Ch 1, 12 sc in ring, join with slip st to first sc. *You now have* 12 sc.

» **RND 2:** Ch 3 (counts as dc here and throughout), dc in same st, 2 dc in each sc around, join with slip st to top of ch-3. *You now have* 24 dc.

» **RND 3:** Ch 3, 2 dc in next dc, *dc in next dc, 2 dc in next dc; repeat from * around, join with slip st to top of ch-3. *You now have* 36 dc.

» **RND 4:** Beg popcorn in first st, 2 sc in next dc, *popcorn in next dc, 2 sc in next dc; repeat from * around, join with slip st to top of beg popcorn. *You now have* 54 sts.

» **RND 5:** Ch 1, starting in first st, *sc in next 8 sts, 2 sc in next st; repeat from * around, join with slip st to first sc. *You now have* 60 dc.

» **RND 6:** Ch 3, dc in each sc around, join with slip st to top of ch-3.

» **RND 7:** Ch 1, sc in each dc around, join with slip st to first sc.

» **RND 8:** Ch 2 (counts as FPdc), FPdc in next 3 sc, 2 FPdc in next sc, *FPdc in next 4 sc, 2 FPdc in next sc; repeat from * around, join with slip st to top of ch-2. *You now have* 72 dc.

» **RND 9:** Ch 1, starting in first st, *sc in next 5 sts, 2 sc in next st; repeat from * around, join with slip st to first sc. *You now have* 84 sc.

» **RND 10:** Ch 2 (counts as FPdc), FPdc in next 12 sc, 2 FPdc in next sc, *FPdc in next 13 sc, 2 FPdc in next sc; repeat from * around, join with slip st to top of ch-2. *You now have* 90 sts.

» **RND 11:** Beg popcorn, sc in next st, 2 sc in next st, *popcorn in next st, sc in next st, 2 sc in next st; repeat from * around, join with slip st to top of beg popcorn. *You now have* 120 sts.

» **RND 12:** Ch 1, sc in each st around, join with slip st to first sc.

» **RND 13:** Ch 2 (counts as hdc), hdc in next 8 sc, 2 hdc in next sc, *hdc in next 9 sc, 2 hdc in next sc; repeat from * around, join with slip st to top of ch-2. *You now have* 132 hdc.

» **RND 14:** Ch 3 (counts as dc), dc in next 9 hdc, 2 dc in next hdc, *dc in next 10 hdc, 2 dc in next hdc; repeat from * around, join with slip st to top of ch-3. *You now have* 144 dc.

» **RND 15:** Ch 1, starting in first st, *sc in next 23 dc, 2 sc in next dc; repeat from * around, join with slip st to first sc. *You now have* 150 sc.

» **RND 16:** Ch 2, FPdc in each st around, join with slip st to top of ch-2.

» **RND 17:** Ch 3, dc in each st around, join with slip st to top of ch-2.

» **RND 18:** Ch 1, sc in each st around, join with slip st to first sc.

» **RND 19:** Ch 2 (counts as hdc), hdc in next 23 sc, 2 hdc in next sc, *hdc in next 24 sc, 2 hdc in next sc; repeat from * around, join with slip st to top of ch-2. *You now have* 156 hdc.

» **RND 20:** Ch 1, sc in first 6 hdc, *hdc in next 6 hdc, dc in next 7 hdc, 3 tr in next hdc, dc in next 7 hdc, hdc in next 6 hdc, sc in next 12 hdc; repeat from * around, omitting last 6 sc, join with slip st to first sc. *You now have* 164 sts.

» **RND 21:** Ch 1, sc in first 6 sc, *hdc in next 6 hdc, dc in next 7 dc, tr in next tr, 3 tr in next tr, tr in next tr, dc in next 7 dc, hdc in next 6 hdc, sc in next 12 sc; repeat from * around, omitting last 6 sc, join with slip st to first sc. *You now have* 172 sts.

» **RND 22:** Ch 1, sc in first 6 sc, *hdc in next 6 hdc, dc in next 7 dc, tr in next 2 tr, 3 tr in next tr, tr in next 2 tr, dc in next 7 dc, hdc in next 6 hdc, sc in next 12 sc; repeat from * around, omitting last 6 sc, join with slip st to first sc. *You now have* 180 sts.

» **RND 23:** Ch 1, sc in first 6 sc, *hdc in next 6 hdc, dc in next 7 dc, tr in next 3 tr, 3 tr in next tr, tr in next 3 tr, dc in next 7 dc, hdc in next 6 hdc, sc in next 12 sc; repeat from * around, omitting last 6 sc, join with slip st to first sc. *You now have* 188 sts.

» **RND 24:** Ch 1, sc in first 6 sc, *hdc in next 6 hdc, dc in next 7 dc, tr in next 4 tr, 3 tr in next tr, tr in next 4 tr, dc in next 7 dc, hdc in next 6 hdc, sc in next 12 sc; repeat from * around, omitting last 6 sc, join with slip st to first sc. *You now have* 196 sts.

» **RND 25:** Ch 2 (counts as hdc), hdc in next 22 sts, 2 hdc in next 3 sts, *hdc in next 46 sts, 2 hdc in next 3 sts; repeat from * two more times, hdc in next 23 sts, join with slip st to top of ch-2. Fasten off.

» Block completed cover to 12"/30.5 cm square.

Making the Fabric Pillow Back

» Fold and press a ½" (1.3 cm) hem on all sides of fabric. Using matching perle cotton and embroidery needle, embroider a line of chain stitches (see box) near the fold line around all four sides of the fabric pillow cover, working 52 chain stitches on each side. Chain stitches should be the same size as hdc stitches in Round 25 of crocheted cover.

Joining Crochet to Fabric

» **RND 1:** Beginning at the corner of one side, attach the crocheted cover to the fabric pillow as follows: Ch 1, sc through each hdc and chain st around, join with slip st to first sc, inserting pillow before completing the fourth side.

» **RND 2:** Ch 1, **(sc, picot-2, sc, picot-3, sc, picot-4, sc, picot-3, sc, picot-2, sc) in corner st, *ch 4, skip 3 sts, (sc, picot-4, sc) in next st; repeat from * across to 4 sts before corner, skip next 3 sts; repeat from ** around, join with slip st in first sc. Fasten off. Weave in ends.

> **EMBROIDERING CHAIN STITCHES ON FABRIC**
> Bring the needle from back to front through the fabric at the starting point and pull all but a short tail through the fabric. Bring the needle from front to back one or two threads away from the starting point and pull the thread through, leaving a small loop of thread on the front. Bring the thread to the front and through the loop at the desired length of your chain stitch. Bring the thread to the back one or two threads away from the last point, catching the loop; pull the thread through to the back, leaving a loop for the next stitch.

ABBREVIATED
PILLOW
PATTERN

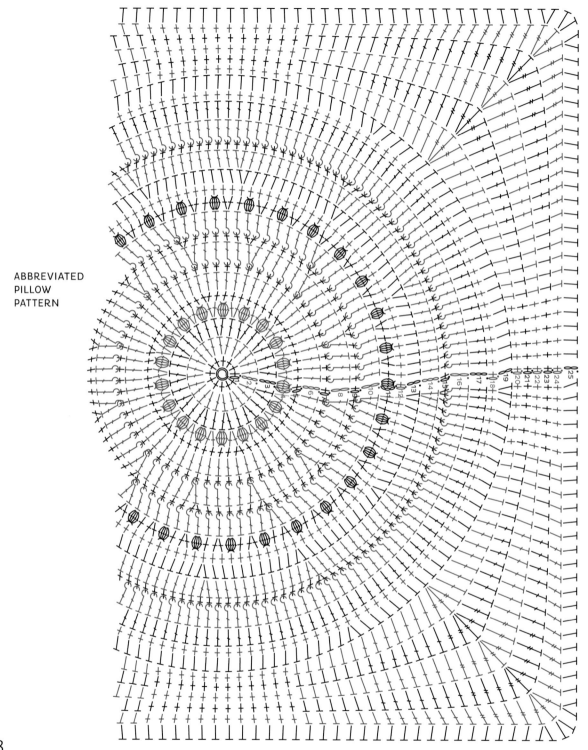

Napkin Rings

Designed by Gwen Steege

Use permanent markers to "handpaint" and color-code these cotton/linen napkin rings so that each person's napkin is easily identifiable.

Crocheting the First Half

See chart on page 140.

» Chain 27, join with slip st to form a ring.

» **RND 1:** Ch 1, sc into back loop of each ch around, join with slip st to first sc. *You now have 27 sc.*

» **RND 2:** Ch 1, *sc in next 2 sc, 2 sc in next sc; repeat from * around, join with slip st to first sc. *You now have 36 sc.*

» **RND 3:** Ch 3 (counts as dc here and throughout), dc in each sc around, join with slip st to top of ch-3. *You now have 36 dc.*

» **RND 4:** Ch 1, (sc, ch 3, 3 dc) in same st, skip 2 sts, *(sc, ch 3, 3 dc) in next st, skip 2 sts; repeat from * around, join with slip st to first ch of ch-4. Fasten off.

FINISHED MEASUREMENTS
2½"/6.5 cm wide and 4½"/11.5 cm in circumference

YARN
Classic Elite Allegoro, 70% organic cotton/30% linen, 152 yds (140 m)/1.75 oz (50 gm), Color 5616 Parchment

CROCHET HOOK
US E/4 (3.5 mm) *or size you need to obtain correct gauge*

GAUGE
24 double crochet = 4"/10 cm

OTHER SUPPLIES
Wide-tip permanent markers in assorted colors

Crocheting the Second Half

» **RND 1:** Working on other side of foundation ch, with RS facing, join yarn with slip st in first ch, ch 1, sc in free loop of each ch around, join with slip st to first sc.

» **RNDS 2–4:** Repeat Rnds 2–4 of first half of napkin ring. Weave in ends.

Coloring the "Buttons"

» Measure about 2 yds (1.8 m) of yarn. Holding the yarn firmly against the tip of a permanent marker, draw the entire length of yarn along the marker tip. You may repeat, if desired, but the yarn doesn't need to be completely covered with color. Color at least three more lengths of yarn, each a different color for each button.

Crocheting the "Buttons"

» Begin with an adjustable ring (see page 271).

» **RND 1:** Ch 1, 12 sc in ring, join with slip st to first sc. *You now have* 12 sc.

» **RND 2:** Ch 3 (counts as dc), 2 dc in next sc, *dc in next sc, 2 dc in next sc; repeat from * to end of rnd, join with slip st to top of ch-3. *You now have* 18 dc. Fasten off.

Finishing

» Weave in outer tails; use beginning tails to sew buttons to center of napkin rings, covering the beginning/ending of each ring with the button.

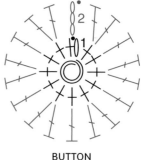

BUTTON

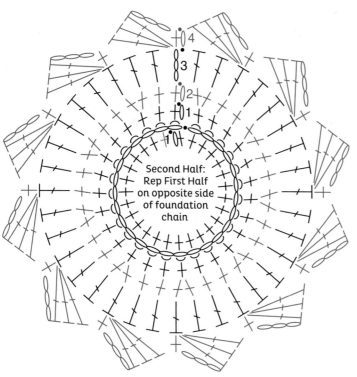

Second Half: Rep First Half on opposite side of foundation chain

NAPKIN RING

Green Water-Bottle Holder

Designed by Pam Thompson

With the protection of a soft crocheted sleeve, recycled glass bottles become portable and practical. And everyone will know the bottle is yours!

FINISHED MEASUREMENTS

3"/7.5 cm in diameter at bottom, sides 6"/15 cm tall, and strap 21"/53.5 cm long

YARN

Rowan Wool Cotton, 50% merino wool/50% cotton, 123 yds (113 m)/1.75 oz (50 g), Color 946 Elf

CROCHET HOOK

US G/6 (4 mm) *or size you need to obtain correct gauge*

GAUGE

First 3 rounds = 3"/7.5 cm in diameter; 16 stitches and 9 rounds = 4"/10 cm in side pattern

OTHER SUPPLIES

Glass water bottle, yarn needle

PATTERN ESSENTIALS

Reverse sc (reverse single crochet) With RS facing, working from left to right and keeping hook pointed to the left (for right-handers), or working from right to left and keeping hook pointed to the right (for left-handers), ch 1, *insert hook in next st, yo and pull up a loop, yo and pull through 2 loops on hook; repeat from *.

✻ **NOTE:** The bottom of this bottle holder is based on the first 3 rows of circular Motif #3 in Edie Eckman's *Beyond the Square Crochet Motifs*. You could use any circular motif you like (and any gauge yarn). As soon as the circular motif is the size of the bottom of your bottle, maintain that number of stitches going up the sides.

Crocheting the Bottom

» Begin with an adjustable ring (see page 271).

» **RND 1:** Ch 3 (counts as dc), 11 dc in ring; join with slip st to top of ch-3. *You now have* 12 sts.

» **RND 2:** Ch 3 (counts as dc), 2 BLdc in same st, ch 2, skip 1 dc, *3 BLdc in next dc, ch 2, skip 1 dc; repeat from * four more times, join with slip st to top of ch-3. *You now have* 6 groups of 3 dc and 6 ch-2 spaces.

» **RND 3:** Ch 3 (counts as dc), BLdc in next 2 dc, 3 dc in next space, *BLdc in next dc, 2 BLdc in next dc, BLdc in next dc, 3 dc in next space*, repeat from * to * once, BLdc in next 3 dc, 3 dc in next space; repeat from * to * twice, join with slip st to top of ch-3. *You now have* 40 sts.

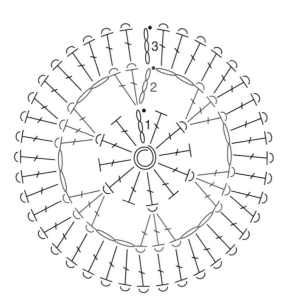

BOTTOM OF WATER-BOTTLE HOLDER

Crocheting the Sides

» **RNDS 4 AND 5:** Ch 3 (counts as dc), BLdc in each st around, join with slip st to top of ch-3.

» **RND 6:** Ch 3 (counts as dc), 2 dc in same st, *ch 1, skip 3 dc, 3 dc in next dc; repeat from * to last 3 sts, ch 1, skip 3 dc, join with slip st to top of ch-3. *You now have* 10 groups of 3 dc and 10 ch-1 spaces.

» Repeat Rnds 4–6 three more times, then work Rnd 4 twice more. Do not fasten off.

Crocheting the Strap

» Chain 80.

» **ROW 1:** Ch 3 (counts as dc), dc in 4th ch from hook and in each ch to end, join with a slip st to bag in second st from starting point. Do not turn.

» **ROW 2:** Ch 1, reverse sc in each dc up the bag strap, ch 3, reverse sc down the remaining edge of the strap, reverse sc in 17 stitches around top of the bag. Line up the 3-ch end of the strap with the next 3 stitches along the top of the bag and join with a reverse sc in each stitch, reverse sc in the remaining dc around the top of the bag, join with slip st to base of strap. Fasten off and weave in ends.

Medium Weight

Fan-Centered Scarf * Three-Round Scarf * Riding the Waves Neck
Warmer * Leyla Cowl * Boutique Weave Scarf * Blushing Erin Neck
Warmer * Pat's Jamaican Bonnet * Montana Hat * Blue Bow Hat *
Hat with Openwork Border * Around-the-Post Hat * Tunisian Croc Rock
Cap * Firebrand Slouch Hat * Peacock Hat * Cozy Ear Warmer *
Dancing Poppies Mini Bolero * Maywood Purse * Spiral Mesh Bag *
Small Brown Bag with Beads * Serrato Purse * Noodles Toddler Beanie *
Openwork Baby Hat * Pinwheel Newsboy Cap * Little Crocheted
and Felted Slippers * Bonnie's Peep Toes * Lullaby Dreams Pillow
Slip * Lullaby Dreams Baby Blanket * Sweet Kitty * Sam the Big-
Bottomed Bunny * Niles the Crocodile * Lucky Dog * Bernie the
Bunny * Robotic * Louis the Lobster * Tunisian Pot Holders *
Entwine Trivets * Lodge Pillow * E-Reader Cover

Fan-Centered Scarf

Designed by Barbara Khouri

Though the pattern in this scarf is very open, the alpaca fiber will provide plenty of warmth. The centered fan motif is flanked by shell stitches, and simple fringe finishes the scarf ends.

FINISHED MEASUREMENTS
40"/102 cm long, exclusive of fringe, and 5"/12.5 cm wide

YARN
Berroco Ultra Alpaca, 50% alpaca/50% wool, 215 yds (197 m)/3.5 oz (100 g), Color 6201 Winter White

CROCHET HOOK
US F/5 (3.75 mm) *or size you need to obtain correct gauge*

GAUGE
24 stitches and 8 rows = 4"/10 cm in pattern stitch

OTHER SUPPLIES
Yarn needle

Crocheting the Scarf

» Chain 30.

» **FOUNDATION ROW:** Dc in 4th ch from hook, ch 2, skip 2 ch, dc in next 3 ch, ch 3, dc in next 3 ch, ch 4, skip 4 ch, (dc, ch 3, dc) in next ch, ch 4, skip 4 ch, dc in next 3 ch, ch 3, dc in next 3 ch, ch 2, skip 2 ch, dc in last ch, turn.

» **ROW 1:** Ch 3, dc in first dc, ch 2, skip next ch-2 space, (3 dc, ch 3, 3 dc) in ch-3 space, ch 3, skip next ch-4 space, 7 dc in center ch-3 space, ch 3, skip next ch-4 space, (3 dc, ch 3, 3 dc) in next ch-3 space, ch 2, skip next (ch-2 space, 1 dc), dc in top of turning ch, turn.

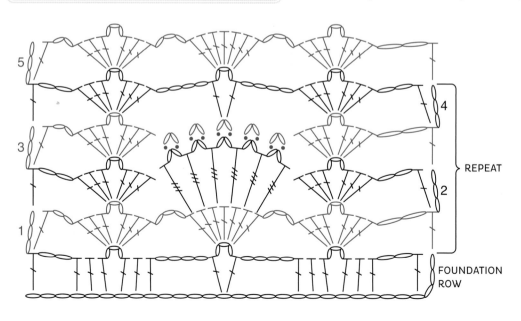

144

» **ROW 2:** Ch 3, dc in first dc, ch 2, skip next ch-2 space, (3 dc, ch 3, 3 dc) in next ch-3 space, skip next ch-3 space, dtr between first 2 dc (of center 7 dc), (ch 2, dtr between next 2 dc) five times, skip next ch-3 space, (3 dc, ch 3, 3 dc) in last ch-3 space, ch 2, skip next (ch-2 space, 1 dc), dc in top of turning ch, turn.

» **ROW 3:** Ch 3, dc in first dc, ch 2, skip next ch-2 space, (3 dc, ch 3, 3 dc) in ch-3 space, (slip st, ch 2, slip st) in each of the next 5 ch-2 spaces, (3 dc, ch 3, 3 dc) in next ch-3 space, ch 2, skip next (ch-2 space, 1 dc), dc in top of turning ch, turn.

» **ROW 4:** Ch 3, dc in first dc, ch 2, skip next ch-2 space, (3 dc, ch 3, 3 dc) in next ch-3 space, ch 4, skip next 2 ch-2 spaces, (dc, ch 3, dc) in center ch-2 space, ch 4, skip next 2 ch-2 spaces, (3 dc, ch 3, 3 dc) in ch-3 space, ch 2, skip next (ch-2 space, 1 dc), dc in top of turning ch, turn.

» Repeat Rows 1–4 until piece measures approximately 40"/102 cm, ending with Row 3. Fasten off. Weave in ends.

Finishing

» Steam lightly. Cut 44 strands of yarn 8"–10"/20.5–25.5 cm long. Using two strands for each fringe, fold the strands in half and pull the fold through a space on the end to form a loop; thread the ends of the strands through the loop and pull up snugly. Repeat to add 11 strands to each end of the scarf.

145

Three-Round Scarf

Designed by Caissa McClinton

A warm and soft scarf is perfect for an autumn stroll, and this one is worked in only three rounds. It's simple to crochet yet looks anything but.

FINISHED MEASUREMENTS

48"/122 cm long and 3¾"/9.5 cm wide

YARN

Berroco Ultra Alpaca, 50% alpaca/50% wool, 215 yds (198 m)/3.5 oz (100 g), Color 6280 Mahogany Mix

CROCHET HOOK

US I/9 (5.5 mm) *or size you need to obtain correct gauge*

GAUGE

14 stitches = 4"/10 cm and 6 rows = 3¾"/9.5 cm in double crochet

OTHER SUPPLIES

Yarn needle

PATTERN ESSENTIALS

Dch (double chain) Beginning with a slip knot on hook, *ch 1, insert hook in the bar on the back of the chain just made, yo and pull up a loop, yo and pull through both loops on hook; repeat from * for desired number of chains.

Shell (2 dc, ch 1, 2 dc) in same st.

Picot-3 Ch 3, slip st in 3rd ch from hook.

Picot shell (2 dc, picot-3, 2 dc) in same st.

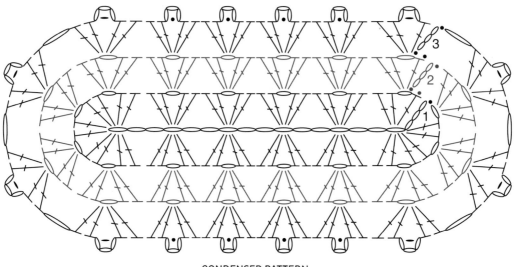

CONDENSED PATTERN

Crocheting the Scarf

» Double chain 150.

» **RND 1:** Ch 3 (counts as dc), (dc, ch 1, 2 dc) in 4th ch from hook — *first shell made*, *skip 2 dch, shell in next dch*; repeat from * to * across to last 3 dch, skip next 2 dch, (2 dc, ch 1) four times in end of foundation ch, 2 dc in same st; working across opposite side of foundation ch, and crocheting in the bottom of existing shells, repeat from * to * across to last 3 dch, skip next 2 dch, (2 dc, ch 1) three times in last ch, join with slip st to 3rd ch of beg ch-3. *You now have* 82 shells and 1 (ch, 2 dc, ch) sequence in each end.

» **RND 2:** Slip st in next dc, slip st in next ch-1 space, ch 3 (counts as dc), (dc, ch 1, 2 dc) in same space, *skip next 4 dc, shell in next shell space; repeat from * around, join with slip st in top of beg ch-3. *You now have 86 shells.*

» **RND 3:** Slip st in next dc, slip st in next ch-1 space, ch 3 (counts as dc), (dc, picot-3, 2 dc) in same space, *picot shell in next shell space*; repeat from * to * 40 times, (ch 1, picot shell in next shell space) three times; repeat from * to * 40 times, (ch 1, picot shell in next shell space) twice, ch 1, join with slip st to top of beg ch-3. Fasten off.

Finishing

» Weave in ends and block.

Riding the Waves Neck Warmer

Designed by Anastasia Popova

Riding the Waves is a simple pattern worked in three main crochet stitches through back and front loops. The neck warmer is made flat in one piece, and buttonholes are created as work progresses. It can easily be made shorter or longer, or wider or narrower, and two sizes are included here. The sample shown is the smaller size.

FINISHED MEASUREMENTS
Small (large), approximately 20" (22½")/51 (57) cm around and 6½"/16.5 cm deep

YARN
Manos del Uruguay Maxima, 100% extrafine merino wool, 219 yds (200 m)/3.5 oz (100 g), Color M6353 Key Lime

CROCHET HOOK
US I/9 (5.50 mm) *or size you need to obtain correct gauge*

GAUGE
16 stitches and 11 rows = 4"/10 cm

OTHER SUPPLIES
Yarn needle, four ¾"/19 mm buttons

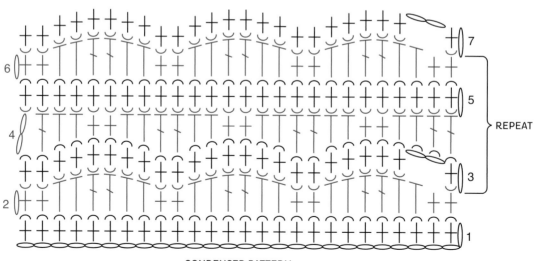

CONDENSED PATTERN

Crocheting the Neck Warmer

» Chain 83 (91) loosely.

» **ROW 1:** Sc in 2nd ch from hook and each ch across, turn. *You now have* 82 (90) sts.

» **ROW 2:** Ch 1 (does not count as st), BLsc in next 2 sc, *BLhdc in next 2 sc, BLdc in next 2 sc, BLhdc in next 2 sc, BLsc in next 2 sc; repeat from * across, turn.

» **ROW 3 (BUTTONHOLE ROW):** Ch 1, FLsc in next st, ch 2, skip next 2 sts, FLsc in each st across, turn.

» **ROW 4:** Ch 2 (counts as dc), BLdc in next st, *BLhdc in next 2 sts, BLsc in next 2 sts, BLhdc in next 2 sts, BLdc in next 2 sts; repeat from * across, turn.

» **ROW 5:** Ch 1, FLsc in each st across, turn.

» **ROW 6:** Ch 1, BLsc in next 2 sts, *BLhdc in next 2 sts, BLdc in next 2 sts, BLhdc in next 2 sts, BLsc in next 2 sts; repeat from * across, turn.

» Repeat Rows 3–6 three more times. Do not fasten off.

Finishing

» **EDGING:** Ch 1, sc evenly all the way around the cowl, working (sc, ch 2, sc) in each corner st. Fasten off. Weave in ends. Block lightly. Sew buttons opposite buttonholes.

Leyla Cowl

Designed by Anastasia Popova

Leyla is a feminine cowl worked in a wool-and-silk blend that is very soft and warm. Worked in the round in one piece, it's fun and easy to make. The main part of the cowl is worked in half double crochet and chains, and the edge is done in a combination of slip stitches, single crochet, and clusters.

FINISHED MEASUREMENTS

Approximately 18"/45.5 cm circumference and 10"/25.5 cm deep

YARN

Cascade Yarns Venezia Worsted, 70% merino wool/30% silk, 219 yds (200 m)/3.5 oz (100 g) Color 101

CROCHET HOOK

US G/6 (4 mm) *or size you need to obtain correct gauge*

GAUGE

18 stitches and 13 rounds = 4"/10 cm in main pattern

OTHER SUPPLIES

Stitch marker, yarn needle

Crocheting the First Border

» **RND 1 (RS):** Fdc 80 (see page 273); being careful not to twist, join with slip st to form a ring.

» **RND 2:** Loosely slip st in each st around.

» **RND 3:** Ch 1, working in tops of sts of Rnd 1, sc in each st around, join with slip st to first st, turn. *You now have 80 sc.*

» **RND 4 (WS):** Ch 1, sc in first sc, *3-dc cluster (see page 271) in next sc**, sc in next 3 sc; repeat from * around, ending last repeat at **, sc in last 2 sc, join with slip st to first sc, turn. *You now have 20 clusters.*

- » **RND 5 (RS):** Ch 1, sc in each st around, join with slip st to first sc.

- » **RND 6:** Loosely slip st in each st around.

- » Use yarn tail to sew beginning and end of base of Rnd 1 together.

Crocheting the Main Pattern

Notes: Do not slip st to join at the end of the round from this point on. Use a marker to keep track of beginning of rounds.

- » **RND 1:** Working in tops of sts of Rnd 5, ch 1, sc in next st, hdc in next 2 sts, ch 1, skip next st, (hdc in next 3 sts, ch 1, skip next st) around.

- » **RND 2:** (Hdc in next 3 hdc, ch 1, skip next space) around.

- » **RNDS 3–25:** Repeat Rnd 2 twenty-three more times.

- » Sc in next st, slip st in next st — *new beginning of round.*

Crocheting the Second Border

- » **RND 1 (RS):** Ch 1, sc in each st around, join with slip st to first sc.

- » **RND 2:** Loosely slip st in each st around.

- » **RND 3:** Ch 1, working in tops of sts of Rnd 1, sc in each st around, slip st into ch-1 to join, turn.

- » **RND 4 (WS):** Ch 1, sc in first sc, *3-dc cluster in next sc**, sc in next 3 sc; repeat from * around, ending last repeat at **, sc in last 2 sc, join with slip st in first sc, turn. *You now have* 20 clusters.

- » **RND 5 (RS):** Ch 1, sc in each st around, join with slip st to first sc.

- » **RND 6:** Loosely slip st in each st around.

- » Fasten off.

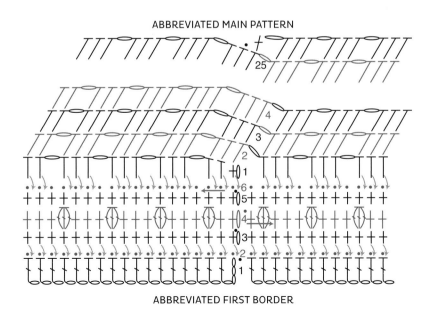

ABBREVIATED MAIN PATTERN

ABBREVIATED FIRST BORDER

151

Boutique Weave Scarf

Designed by Nirmal Kaur Khalsa

With self-striping yarn and basic skills, you can easily create this unique piece. The base is a mesh construction, and chains are woven through the mesh.

FINISHED MEASUREMENTS

Approximately 5"/12.5 cm wide and 40"/102 cm long, excluding fringe

YARN

Red Heart Boutique Treasure, 70% acrylic/30% wool, 151 yds (138 m)/3.5 oz (100 g), Color 1919 Watercolors

CROCHET HOOK

US K/10½ (6.5 mm) *or size you need to obtain correct gauge*

GAUGE

12 stitches and 6 rows = approximately 4"/10 cm in pattern

OTHER SUPPLIES

Two stitch markers

Crocheting the Scarf

Note: Ch-3 at beginning of row counts as a dc.

» Leaving a 6"/15 cm tail, ch 20. Mark 17th ch as corner and leave marker in until fringe is attached. Mark 19th ch as top of turning ch.

» **ROW 1:** Dc in 6th ch from hook, (ch 1, skip 1 ch, dc in next ch) seven times, turn. *You now have 8 ch-1 spaces.*

» **ROW 2:** Ch 4 (counts as dc, ch 1 here and throughout), skip first ch-1 space, dc in next dc, (ch 1, dc in next dc) seven times, ending with last dc in top of turning ch, turn.

» **ROWS 3–59:** Ch 4, skip first ch-1 space, dc in next dc, (ch 1, dc in next dc) seven times, ending with last dc in 3rd ch of ch-4, turn.

» Fasten off, leaving a 6"/15 cm tail.

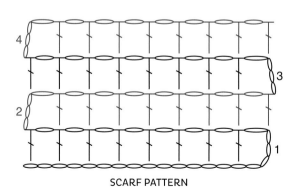

SCARF PATTERN

Weaving through the Crochet

» Leaving a 6"/15 cm tail, form a slip knot and join with slip st to a free ch-1 space on one end of scarf. Make a chain as long as the scarf, adding a few more stitches to be sure you have enough, and fasten off loosely (or put a locking stitch marker in the last stitch), leaving a 6"/15 cm tail. Weave the chain over and under into spaces of scarf. At the end, adjust the length and slip st to ch st on opposite end of scarf.

» Repeat for all spaces, being sure to alternate the over and under of the weaving.

Adding the Fringe

» Cut eighteen 13"/33 cm lengths of yarn. Fold one length in half and bring fold through dc on end to form a loop; thread ends through the loop and pull up snugly. Repeat to attach fringe to each dc at both ends of the scarf, including ch sts that count as double crochets. Trim all fringe to same length.

Blushing Erin Neck Warmer

Designed by Ellen Gormley

A unique neck warmer results from an effective use of basic stitches combined with double treble clusters. Be the first on your block to wear one!

FINISHED MEASUREMENTS
20"/51 cm in circumference and 10"/25.5 cm wide

YARN
Blue Sky Alpaca Worsted Hand Dyes, 50% royal alpaca/50% merino wool, 100 yds (91 m)/3.5 oz (100 g), Color 2026 Petunia

CROCHET HOOK
US J/10 (6 mm) *or size you need to obtain correct gauge*

GAUGE
11 stitches = 4"/10 cm and 8 rounds = 3"/7.5 cm in single crochet pattern

OTHER SUPPLIES
Yarn needle

PATTERN ESSENTIALS

Dtr-cl (double treble cluster) (Yo) three times, insert hook in indicated stitch or space and draw up a loop, (yo and draw through 2 loops on hook) three times; *(yo) three times, insert hook in *same* st or space and draw up a loop, (yo and draw through 2 loops on hook) three times; repeat from * once more, yo and draw through all 4 loops on hook.

154

Crocheting the Cowl

» Fsc 55 (see page 273). Being careful not to twist ch, join with slip st in first ch to form a ring.

» **RND 1 (RS):** Ch 1, FLsc in each st around, join with slip st to first sc. *You now have 55 sc.*

» **RND 2 (RS):** Ch 1, BLsc in each st around, join with slip st to first sc.

» **RNDS 3–8:** Repeat Rnds 1 and 2 three more times.

» Do not fasten off.

Crocheting the Edging

» **RND 1 (RS):** Ch 1, sc in same st, *ch 11, slip st in 5th ch from hook, ch 6, skip 10 sts, sc in next st; repeat from * five times, omitting last sc, join with slip st to first sc.

» **RND 2 (RS):** Ch 5 (counts as first dtr), *skip next ch-6 space, (dtr-cl, ch 5, dtr-cl, ch 5, dtr-cl) in next ch-5 space, dtr in next sc; repeat from * around, omitting last dtr, join with slip st to top of ch-5. Fasten off.

» Working in the underside of the foundation edge with WS facing, join new yarn at the join of the round; repeat Rnds 1 and 2 of edging. ***Note:*** This edging will flip down, and the RS of the edging will show on the front of the cowl; it is now the top of the cowl.

Finishing

» Using yarn needle, weave in all ends. Block lightly.

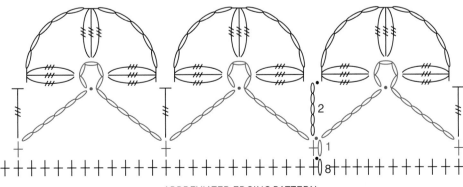

ABBREVIATED EDGING PATTERN

Pat's Jamaican Bonnet

Designed by Marcia Sommerkamp

When a friend who was born in the islands asked Marcia to design a bonnet for her, many hilarious discussions ensued. It finally became apparent that she was referring to a kerchief. You can get more than one out of a skein of yarn, and if you have different-colored skeins, you can mix and match to make a whole wardrobe of kerchiefs. While the eponymous Pat wears hers under a motorcycle helmet, they are also perfect for bad hair days.

FINISHED MEASUREMENTS
Approximately 20"/51 cm along base of triangle, excluding ties, and 8½"/21.5 cm from point to triangle base

YARN
Cascade Yarns Ultra Pima, 100% pima cotton, 220 yds (200 m)/3.5 oz (100 g), Color 3776 Pink Roses

CROCHET HOOK
US I/9 (5.5 mm) *or size you need to obtain correct gauge*

GAUGE
16 stitches and 20 rows = 4"/10 cm in single crochet

OTHER SUPPLIES
Yarn needle

Crocheting the Kerchief

» **ROW 1:** Ch 4, sc in 2nd ch from hook and each remaining ch, turn. *You now have 3 sts.*

» **ROW 2:** Ch 1, 2 sc in first sc, sc to last sc, 2 sc in last sc, turn. *You now have 5 sts.*

» **ROWS 3–35:** Repeat Row 2 until there are 71 sts across long end of triangle. Do not fasten off.

Crocheting the Trim

» Ch 1, sc around, placing 1 sc in end of each row along outside edges of scarf, 3 sc in each corner, and 1 sc in each sc across long end of triangle, join with slip st to first sc.

» **RND 2:** Ch 1, sc in same st, sc in each sc around, placing 3 sc in each corner st, join with slip st to first sc.

» **RND 3 (INCLUDES MAKING THE TIES):** Turn, slip st in last 2 sts made (you should now be in a corner st), turn; ch 61, sc in 2nd ch from hook and each ch to edge of scarf; sc in corner st and in each st to next corner (point), 3 sc in corner st, sc in each st to next corner; ch 61, sc in 2nd ch from hook and each ch across to first corner, join with slip st to sc in corner after tie. Fasten off.

» **EDGING:** With RS facing, join yarn to corner at base of tie. Ch 1, sc in first sc, skip 1 sc, *5 dc in next st, skip 1 sc, sc in next sc, skip 1 sc*; repeat from * to * across to bottom point, sc in corner sc, repeat from * to * to next corner at base of tie, ending with sc in sc at base of tie. Fasten off and weave in ends.

Montana Hat

Designed by Dorian Owen

This hat is worked in one piece without cutting the yarn — only two ends to weave in! The brim is worked in rows and then joined together to form a headband; the crown is then worked in rounds using the edge of the brim as the foundation row.

SIZES AND FINISHED MEASUREMENTS
To fit most adults, 20"/51 cm circumference, unstretched

YARN
Berroco Vintage, 50% acrylic/40% wool/10% nylon,
  217 yds (200 m)/3.5 oz (100 g), Color 5125 Aquae

CROCHET HOOK
US G/6 (4 mm) *or size you need to obtain correct gauge*

GAUGE
20 stitches and 12 rounds = 4"/10 cm in half double
  crochet; 9 rows = 4"/10 cm in brim pattern

OTHER SUPPLIES
Yarn needle

Crocheting the Brim

» Chain 21.

» **ROW 1 (WS):** Sc in 2nd ch from hook and in each ch across, turn. *You now have* 20 sc.

» **ROW 2 (RS):** Ch 3 (counts as dc), (skip next 3 sts, FPtr in next 3 sts; working in front of sts just made, FPtr in 3 skipped sts) three times, dc in last st, turn. *You now have* 18 FPtr and 2 dc.

» **ROW 3:** Ch 2 (counts as first hdc), BPdc in the next 18 sts, hdc in top of ch-3, turn. *You now have* 18 BPdc and 2 hdc.

» **ROW 4:** Ch 2 (counts as dc), FPdc in next 3 sts, (skip next 3 sts, FPtr in next 3 sts; working behind sts just made, FPtr in 3 skipped sts) two times, FPdc in next 3 sts, dc in top of ch-2, turn. *You now have* 6 FPdc, 12 FPtr, and 2 dc.

» **ROW 5:** Repeat Row 3.

» **ROWS 6–52:** Repeat Rows 2–5 eleven more times; then repeat Rows 2–4.

Note: You can add more rows to make the brim larger or eliminate rows to make the brim smaller; end with Row 4 of pattern.

Joining the Brim Ends

» Fold the brim in half with RS facing, ch 1; working through double thickness of last row and foundation ch, slip st in each st across to create a headband. Do not fasten off yarn.

Crocheting the Crown

» Turn brim to work along the ends of the rows on one side.

» **RND 1:** With RS facing, ch 1, work 88 sc evenly spaced around the top of the brim, join with slip st to first sc.

» **RND 2:** Ch 2 (does not count as hdc here and throughout), hdc in same st and in each st around, join with slip st in first hdc.

» **RNDS 3 AND 4:** Repeat Rnd 2 two more times.

» **RND 5:** Ch 2, (hdc in next 9 hdc, hdc2tog) eight times, join with slip st to first hdc. *You now have* 80 sts.

» **RND 6:** Ch 2, (hdc in next 8 hdc, hdc2tog) eight times, join with slip st to first hdc. *You now have* 72 sts.

» **RND 7:** Ch 2, (hdc in next 7 hdc, hdc2tog) eight times, join with slip st to first hdc. *You now have* 64 sts.

» **RND 8:** Ch 2, (hdc in next 6 hdc, hdc2tog) eight times, join with slip st to first hdc. *You now have* 56 sts.

» **RND 9:** Ch 2, (hdc in next 5 hdc, hdc2tog) eight times, join with slip st in first hdc. *You now have* 48 sts.

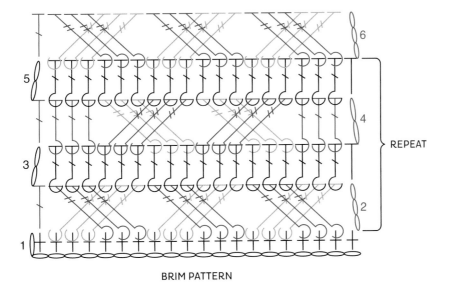

BRIM PATTERN

» **RND 10:** Ch 2, (hdc in next 4 hdc, hdc2tog) eight times, join with slip st to first hdc. *You now have* 40 sts.

» **RND 11:** Ch 2, (hdc in next 3 hdc, hdc2tog) eight times, join with slip st to first hdc. *You now have* 32 sts.

» **RND 12:** Ch 2, (hdc in next 2 hdc, hdc2tog) eight times, join with slip st to first hdc. *You now have* 24 sts.

» **RND 13:** Ch 2, (hdc in next hdc, hdc2tog) eight times, join with slip st to first hdc. *You now have* 16 sts.

» **RND 14:** Ch 2, (hdc2tog) eight times, join with slip st to first st. *You now have* 8 sts.

Finishing

» Break yarn, leaving a long tail, and thread the tail to the inside of the hat. Turn the hat inside out and sew hat closed by using front loops of each st on last round. Pull up tight and weave in ends.

Blue Bow Hat

Designed by Janet M. Spirik

This hat crochets up quickly using single and double crochet. The pattern includes three sizes, making this a go-to pattern for many baby gifts.

SIZES AND FINISHED MEASUREMENTS

To fit baby (toddler, child), approximately 14" (16", 18")/35.5 (40.5, 45.5) cm in circumference

YARN

Red Heart Super Saver Economy, 100% acrylic, 364 yds (333 m)/7 oz (198 g), Color 0505 Aruba Sea

CROCHET HOOK

US G/6 (4 mm) *or size you need to obtain correct gauge*

GAUGE

14 stitches = 4"/10 cm in double crochet; first 2 rounds = 2½"/6.5 cm in diameter

OTHER SUPPLIES

1½"/3.8 cm ribbon measuring 24"/61 cm plus hat circumference, fabric glue (optional)

Crocheting the Crown

» Chain 4, join with slip st to the first ch to form a ring.

» **RND 1:** Ch 3 (counts as dc here and throughout), make 12 dc in ring, join with slip st to top of ch-3. *You now have* 13 dc.

» **RND 2:** Ch 3, dc in same st, 2 dc in each dc around, join with slip st to top of ch-3. *You now have* 26 dc.

» **RND 3:** Ch 3, dc in same st, *dc in next dc, 2 dc in next dc; repeat from * 11 more times, dc in last dc, join with slip st to top of ch-3. *You now have* 39 dc.

BABY HAT ONLY

» **RND 4:** Ch 1, *sc in next 12 dc, 2 sc in next dc; repeat from * around, join with slip st to first sc. *You now have* 42 sc.

» **RND 5:** Ch 3, dc in next 5 sc, 2 dc in next sc, *dc in next 6 sc, 2 dc in next sc; repeat from * around, join with slip st to top of ch-3. *You now have* 48 dc.

» **RND 6:** Ch 1, sc in each dc around, join with slip st to first sc.

» **RND 7:** Ch 3 (counts as dc), dc in each sc around, join with slip st to top of ch-3.

» **RND 8:** Repeat Rnd 6.

» **RND 9 (RIBBON RND):** Ch 5 (counts as tr and ch 1), *skip next sc, tr in next sc, ch 1; repeat from * to last sc, skip next sc, join with slip st to 4th ch of ch-5. *You now have* 24 ch-1 spaces.

» **RND 10:** Ch 1, sc in same st, sc in each ch-space and in each tr around, join with slip st to first sc. *You now have* 48 sc.

» **RND 11:** Repeat Rnd 7.

» **RND 12:** Repeat Rnd 6.

» **RND 13:** Ch 1, sc in same st, *skip 2 sc, 5 dc in next sc— *shell made*, skip 2 sc, sc in next sc; repeat from * around, omitting last sc, join with slip st to first sc. *You now have* 8 shells.

» Fasten off.

TODDLER HAT ONLY

» **RND 4:** Ch 3, dc in same st, *dc in next 2 dc, 2 dc in next st; repeat from * to last 2 sts, dc in last 2 sts, join with slip st to top ch-3. *You now have* 52 dc.

» **RND 5:** Ch 1, 2 sc in same st, *sc in next 12 dc, 2 sc in next dc; repeat from * to last 12 dc, sc in last 12 dc, join with slip st to first sc. *You now have* 56 sc.

» **RND 6:** Ch 3, dc in each sc around, join with slip st to top of ch-3.

» **RND 7:** Ch 1, sc in same st and in each dc around, join with slip st to first sc.

» **RND 8:** Repeat Rnd 6.

» **RND 9:** Repeat Rnd 7.

» **RND 10 (RIBBON RND):** Ch 5 (counts as tr and ch 1), *skip next st, tr in next st, ch 1; repeat from * to last st, skip last st, join with slip st to 4th ch of ch-5. *You now have* 28 ch-1 spaces.

» **RND 11:** Ch 1, sc in same st, sc in each ch-space and in each tr around, join with slip st to first sc. *You now have* 56 sc.

» **RNDS 12 AND 13:** Repeat Rnd 7.

continued on next page

» **RND 14:** Ch 1, sc in same st, *skip 2 sc, 5 dc in next sc — *shell made*, skip 2 sc, sc in next sc; repeat from * to last sc, skip last sc, join with slip st to first sc. *You now have* 9 shells. Fasten off.

CHILD HAT ONLY

» **RND 4:** Ch 3, dc in same st (counts as 2 dc), *dc in next 2 dc, 2 dc in next dc; repeat from * to last 2 dc, dc in last 2 dc, join with slip st to top of ch-3. *You now have* 52 dc.

» **RND 5:** Ch 1, 2 sc in same st, *sc in next 12 dc, 2 sc in next dc; repeat from * to last 12 dc, sc in last 12 dc, join with slip st to first sc. *You now have* 56 sc.

» **RND 6:** Ch 1, 2 sc in same st, *sc in next 7 sc, 2 sc in next sc; repeat from * to last 7 sc, sc in last 7 sc, join with slip st to first sc. *You now have* 63 sc.

» **RND 7:** Ch 3 (counts as 1 dc), dc in each sc around, join with slip st to top of ch-3.

» **RND 8:** Ch 1, sc in same st and in each dc around, join with slip st to first sc.

» **RND 9:** Repeat Rnd 7.

» **RND 10:** Repeat Rnd 8.

» **RND 11:** Repeat Rnd 7.

» **RND 12:** Ch 1, 2 sc in same st, dc in each sc around, join with slip st to first sc. *You now have* 64 sts.

» **RND 13 (RIBBON RND):** Ch 5 (counts as tr and ch 1), *skip next sc, tr in next sc, ch 1; repeat from * to last sc, skip last sc, join with slip st to 4th ch of ch-5. *You now have* 32 ch-1 spaces.

» **RND 14:** Ch 1, sc in same st, [sc in next ch-1 space, sc in next tr] 14 times, sc in next ch-1 space, sc2tog, [sc in next tr, sc in next ch-1 space] 15 times, sc2tog, join with slip st to first sc. *You now have* 62 sts.

» **RNDS 15 AND 16:** Repeat Rnd 7.

» **RND 17:** Ch 1, sc in same st, (skip 2 sc, 5 dc in next sc — *shell made*, skip 2 sc, sc in next sc) nine times, skip 3 sc, shell in next sc, skip 3 sc, join with slip st to first sc. *You now have* 10 shells. Fasten off.

Finishing

» Cut ribbon 24"/61 cm plus circumference of hat. Weave the ribbon in and out of the openings in the Ribbon Round. Tie a bow with the ends. You can either glue the ends of the ribbon so it does not unravel, or you can sew a hem in them.

Hat with Openwork Border

Designed by Jane M. Brown

A simple openwork stitch makes a delicate border for this single crochet hat, and the buttoned flower dresses it up. The pattern is given in two sizes.

FINISHED MEASUREMENTS

17½" (20")/44.5 (51) cm
  in circumference

YARN

Kraemer Yarns Tatamy Tweed
  DK, 55% acrylic/45% cotton,
  250 yds (229 m)/3.5 oz (100 g),
  Color Y1227 It's a Boy

CROCHET HOOK

US F/5 (3.75 mm) *or size you need
  to obtain correct gauge*

GAUGE

20 stitches and 21 rounds =
  4"/10 cm in single crochet

OTHER SUPPLIES

Yarn needle, one decorative button

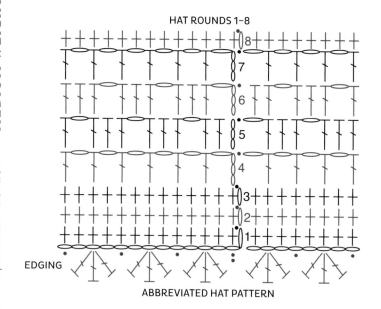

HAT ROUNDS 1–8

EDGING

ABBREVIATED HAT PATTERN

Crocheting the Hat

» Chain 88 (100); join with slip st to first ch.

» **RND 1:** Ch 1, sc in each ch around, join with slip st to first sc. *You now have* 88 (100) sc.

» **RNDS 2 AND 3:** Ch 1, sc in each sc around, join with slip st to first sc.

» **RND 4:** Ch 4 (counts as dc and ch 1), skip 1 sc, (dc in next sc, ch 1, skip 1 sc) around, join with slip st to top of ch-3. *You now have* 44 (50) ch-1 spaces.

» **RND 5:** Ch 3 (counts as dc), *dc in next space, dc in next dc, ch 1, skip 1 space**, dc in next dc; repeat from * around, ending last repeat at **, join with slip st to top of ch-3. *You now have* 22 (25) ch-1 spaces.

» **RND 6:** Ch 4 (counts as dc and ch 1), *skip 1 dc, dc in next dc, dc in next space**, dc in next dc, ch 1; repeat from * around, ending last repeat at **, join with slip st to 3rd ch of ch-4. *You now have* 22 (25) ch-1 spaces.

» **RND 7:** Ch 4 (counts as dc and ch 1), skip 1 space, (dc in next dc, ch 1, skip 1 st or space) around, join with slip st to 3rd ch of ch-4. *You now have* 44 (50) ch-1 spaces.

» **RND 8:** Sc in each st and ch-1 space around. Do not join. *You now have* 88 (100) sts.

» Repeat Rnd 8 until hat measures 4½"/11.5 cm or desired length to beginning of crown shaping.

Decreasing the Crown

» **RND 1:** Sc in next 4 (0) sts, *sc2tog, sc in next 10 (8) sc; repeat from * around. *You now have* 81 (90) sts.

» **RNDS 2, 4, 6, AND 8:** Sc in each sc around.

» **RND 3:** *Sc2tog, sc in next 7 sc; repeat from * around. *You now have* 72 (80) sts.

» **RND 5:** *Sc2tog, sc in next 6 sc; repeat from * around. *You now have* 63 (70) sts.

» **RND 7:** *Sc2tog, sc in next 5 sc; repeat from * around. *You now have* 54 (60) sts.

» **RND 9:** *Sc2tog, sc in next 4 sc; repeat from * around. *You now have* 45 (50) sts.

» **RND 10:** *Sc2tog, sc in next 3 sc; repeat from * around. *You now have* 36 (40) sts.

» **RND 11:** **Sc2tog, sc in next 2 sc; repeat from * around. *You now have* 27 (30) sts.

» **RND 12:** *Sc2togs, sc in next sc; repeat from * around. *You now have 18 (20) sts.*

» **RND 13:** (Sc2tog) around. *You now have 9 (10) sts.*

» **RND 14:** Sc in next 1 (0) sc, (sc2tog) around. *You now have 5 sts.*

» Cut yarn, leaving an 8"/20.5 cm tail. Thread tail onto yarn needle and pass through remaining 5 sts. Gather tightly and secure. Fasten off. Weave in ends.

Edging the Brim

» With RS facing, join yarn with slip st in any ch on brim, working across opposite side of foundation ch, (skip 1 ch, 3 dc in next ch, skip 1 ch, slip st in next ch) around, ending with last slip st in first slip st. *You now have 22 (25) shells. Fasten off. Weave in ends.*

Crocheting the Flower

» Chain 6, leaving an 8"/20.5 cm tail; join with slip st to form a ring.

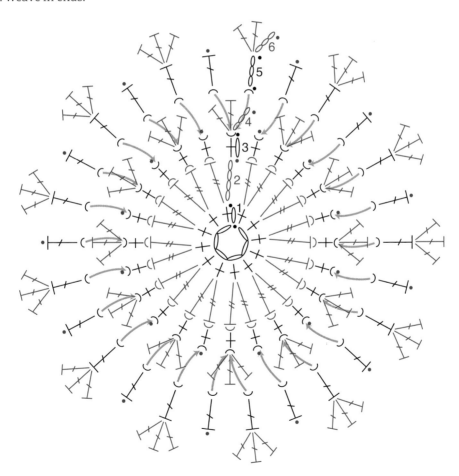

FLOWER

» **RND 1:** Ch 1, 12 sc in ring; join with slip st to first sc. *You now have* 12 sc.

» **RND 2:** Ch 4 (counts as tr), tr in same st, 2 tr in each st around, join with slip st to top of ch-4. *You now have* 24 tr.

» **RND 3:** Ch 1, sc in same st, BLsc in each st around, join with slip st to first sc.

» **RND 4:** *Working in front loops only,* ch 3 (counts as dc), 2 dc in same st, *slip st in next st**, 3 dc in next st; repeat from * around, ending last repeat at **, join with slip st to top of ch-3. *You now have* 12 petals.

» **RND 5:** *Working in back loops of Rnd 3,* turn petals down, slip st in back loop of first sc in Rnd 3, ch 3, dc in same st — *increase made,* dc in next 11 sts, 2 dc in next st, dc in next 11 sts, join with slip st to top of ch-2. *You now have* 26 dc.

» **RND 6:** Ch 3 (counts as dc), 2 dc in same st, *slip st in next st**, 3 dc in next st; repeat from * around, ending last repeat at **, join with slip st to top of ch-3. *You now have* 13 shells. Fasten off.

Finishing

» Using tail at center of flower, sew button to flower and sew flower to hat.

Around-the-Post Hat

Designed by Deb Swinski

This around-the-post double crochet ribbed hat is modeled after a hat Deb's mother crocheted over 30 years ago. The style is classic and suits both men and women.

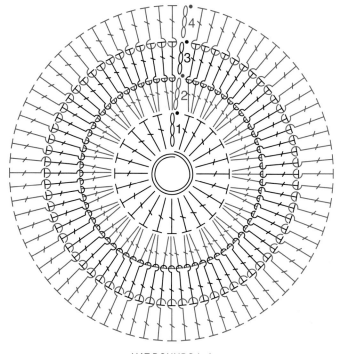

FINISHED MEASUREMENTS

Approximately 20"/51 cm circumference, unstretched, and 8"/20.5 cm tall

YARN

Berroco Vintage, 50% acrylic/40% wool/10% nylon, 217 yds (198 m)/3.5 oz (100 g), Color 5183 Lilacs

CROCHET HOOK

US H/8 (5 mm) *or size you need to obtain correct gauge*

GAUGE

14 post stitches and 12 rows = 4"/10 cm in pattern, relaxed

OTHER SUPPLIES

Yarn needle

HAT ROUNDS 1–4

Crocheting the Hat

» Begin with an adjustable ring (see page 271).

» **RND 1:** Ch 3 (counts as dc), 23 dc into ring, join with slip st to top of ch-3. *You now have* 24 sts.

» **RND 2:** Ch 3 (counts as dc), 2 dc in same st, 3 dc in each st around, join with slip st to top of ch-3. *You now have* 72 sts.

» **RND 3:** Ch 2 (counts as FPdc), FPdc in next 2 sts, BPdc in next 3 sts, *FPdc in next 3 sts, BPdc in next 3 sts; repeat from * around, join with slip st to top of first FPdc.

» **RNDS 4–25:** Repeat Rnd 3 twenty-two times.

» Fasten off.

Finishing

» Weave in ends.

Tunisian Croc Rock Cap

Designed by Yvonne Cherry

Tunisian crochet makes the deep brim of this cap, and when it's folded up not quite in half we get to see both sides — one side that looks like knitted garter stitch, and the other that looks woven. The handsome brim is topped off with a crown of half double crochet. Bonus: There's enough yarn left over to make a matching scarf.

FINISHED MEASUREMENTS

20"/51 cm in circumference and 10"/25.5 cm deep before turning up the brim

YARN

Lorna's Laces Fisherman, 100% wool, 500 yds (457 m)/3.5 oz (100 g), Verve

CROCHET HOOK

US H/8 (5 mm) afghan hook *or size you need to obtain correct gauge*

GAUGE

20 stitches and 18 rows = 4"/10 cm in Tunisian simple stitch; 16 stitches and 12 rounds = 4"/10 cm in half double crochet

OTHER SUPPLIES

Yarn needle

Crocheting the Band

» Using afghan hook, ch 25.

» Work even in Tunisian simple stitch (see page 274) until piece is 19"/48.5 cm long or length to comfortably, yet a bit snugly, fit around the wearer's head.

» **LAST ROW:** Sc in each vertical bar across. Fold band in half and with RS together, working through double thickness of previous row and foundation ch, sc in each st across to seam ends of band together. Fasten off.

Crocheting the Crown

» **RND 1:** Join yarn in any row-end st on either edge of the band, ch 1, work 96 sc evenly spaced around, join with slip st to first sc. *You now have 96 sc.*

» **RND 2:** Sc in back loops only of each sc around, join with slip st to first sc.

» **RND 3:** Ch 2 (counts as hdc here and throughout), hdc in next 3 sts, hdc2tog, *hdc in next 4 sts, hdc2tog; repeat from * around, join with slip st to top of ch-2. *You now have 80 sts.*

» **RND 4:** Ch 2, hdc in next 2 sts, hdc2tog, *hdc in next 3 sts, hdc2tog; repeat from * around, join with slip st to top of ch-2. *You now have 64 sts.*

- » **RND 5:** Ch 2, hdc in each st around, join with slip st to top of ch-2.

- » **RND 6:** Ch 2, hdc in next 5 sts, hdc-2tog, *hdc in next 6 sts, hdc2tog; repeat from * around, join with slip st to top of ch-2. *You now have* 56 sts.

- » **RNDS 7 AND 8:** Repeat Rnd 5.

- » **RND 9:** Ch 2 (counts as hdc), hdc in next st, hdc2tog, *hdc in next 2 sts, hdc2tog, repeat from * around, join with slip st to top of ch-2. *You now have* 42 sts.

- » **RND 10:** Repeat Rnd 5.

- » **RND 11:** Ch 2 (counts as hdc), hdc in next 3 sts, hdc2tog, *hdc in next 4 sts, hdc2tog; repeat from * around, join with slip st to top of ch-2. *You now have* 35 sts.

- » **RND 12:** Repeat Rnd 4. *You now have* 28 sts.

- » **RND 13:** Ch 1, sc in each st around, join with slip st to first sc.

- » **RND 14:** Ch 1, (sc2tog in next 2 sts) around, join with slip st to first sc. *You now have* 14 sts.

Finishing

- » Turn hat inside out; fold top of hat in half and slip st remaining sts together to form a seam at the top. Fasten off.

- » With RS facing, join yarn at lower edge of band, ch 1, sc in each row-end st around, join with slip st to first sc. Fasten off. Weave in ends. Fold up band.

Firebrand Slouch Hat

Designed by Brenda K. B. Anderson

This super-quick hat features an easy-to-memorize shell-and-post-stitch lace pattern. The ribbing band is worked back and forth in rows and then slipstitched to form a tube. The body of the hat is then worked in a spiral from the ribbing up to the top.

SIZES AND FINISHED MEASUREMENTS

Approximately 18" (20)"/45.5 (51) cm in circumference at ribbed edge, unstretched, and 9"/23 cm tall; will stretch to fit 19½"–21½" (21"–23")/49.5–54.5 (53.5–58.5) cm head. Hat shown is 20"/51 cm.

YARN

Araucania Toconao Multy, 100% merino wool, 139 yds (127 m)/3.5 oz (100 g), Color 410 Orange, Wine. *Note:* It may be necessary to unravel your gauge swatch in order to have enough yarn for the hat.

CROCHET HOOKS

US J/10 (6 mm) and US G/6 (4 mm) *or size you need to obtain correct gauge*

GAUGE

16 stitches and 12 rows = 4"/10 cm in pattern on smaller hook
Note: Follow swatching instructions at right and measure swatch.

OTHER SUPPLIES

Stitch markers, yarn needle

PATTERN ESSENTIALS

Working into the back of chain With the WS of chain facing, insert hook into the bumps on the back of the chain. (The RS of the chain is a series of Vs.)

Swatching the Pattern Stitch

Note: Your gauge swatch should measure 4"/10 cm across, not including the dc on each end (just measure from the first post stitch to the last post stitch). The swatch should also measure 4"/10 cm in length. Please note that this gauge swatch was made flat, in turned rows, and the hat will be made in joined rounds with

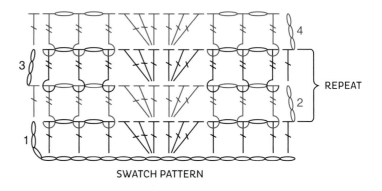

SWATCH PATTERN

the RS always facing you. There will be a slight difference in the gauge of the stitch pattern depending on whether it was made in the round or flat, but if your gauge swatch matches these measurements, your gauge for the hat (in the round) will be right. The gauge of this stitch pattern (when crocheted in the round) is 3"/7.5 cm wide per pattern repeat, and 6¼ rounds per 4"/10 cm.

» With larger hook, ch 20.

» **ROW 1 (WS):** Dc in 4th ch from hook, (ch 1, skip 1 ch, dc in next ch) twice, skip 2 ch, 3 dc in next 2 ch, skip 2 ch, (dc in next ch, ch 1, skip 1 ch) twice, dc in next 2 ch, turn.

» **ROW 2:** Ch 3 (counts as dc), turn, FPtr in next dc, ch 1, BPtr in next dc, ch 1, FPtr in next st, skip 2 dc, 3 dc in next 2 dc, skip 2 dc, FPtr in next dc, ch 1, BPtr in next dc, ch 1, FPtr in next st, dc in top of turning ch, turn.

» **ROW 3:** Ch 3 (counts as dc), BPtr in next st, ch 1, FPtr in next st, ch 1, BPtr in next st, skip 2 dc, 3 dc in next 2 dc, skip 2 dc, BPtr in next st, ch 1, FPtr in next st, ch 1, BPtr in next st, dc in top of turning ch.

» **ROWS 4–6:** Repeat Rows 2 and 3 once more, then work Row 2 once more.

Crocheting the Ribbing

» Using smaller hook, ch 6.

» **ROW 1:** Sc in 2nd ch from hook and in each ch across, turn. *You now have* 5 sts.

» **ROW 2:** Ch 1, BLsc in each st across, turn.

» **ROWS 3–55 (61):** Repeat Row 2.

» Fold the ribbing in half. Working through double thickness of foundation ch and last row, and working in back loops only, slip st in each st across. *Do not fasten off.*

Crocheting the Body

» Turn ribbing so that the seam is on the inside. Use stitch markers to mark four equal sections on the top edge.

» **RND 1:** Ch 1, working across side edge of ribbing, 88 sc evenly around (22 sts between each set of markers), join with slip st to first sc. *You now have 88 sts.*

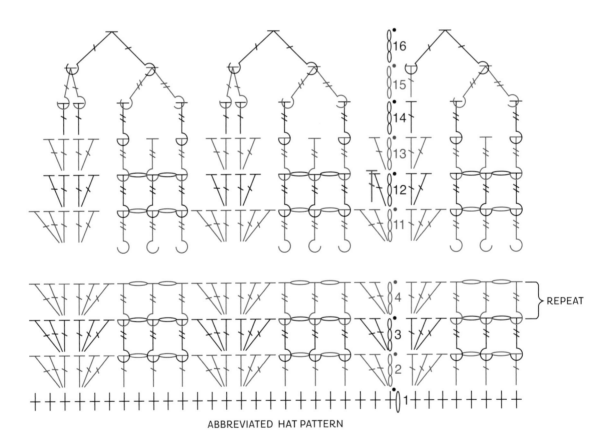

ABBREVIATED HAT PATTERN

REPEAT

» **RND 2:** Change to larger hook, ch 3 (counts as dc), 2 dc in same st, skip 2 sc, *(dc in next st, ch 1, skip 1 sc) twice, dc in next st, skip 2 sc**, 3 dc in next 2 sc, skip 2 sts; repeat from * around, ending last repeat at **, 3 dc in next st, join with slip st to top of ch-3.

» **RND 3:** Ch 3 (counts as dc), 2 dc in same st, skip 2 dc, *FPtr in next dc, ch 1, BPtr in next dc, ch 1, FPtr in next dc, skip 2 dc**, 3 dc in next 2 dc, skip 2 dc; repeat from * around, ending last repeat at **, 3 dc in next st, join with slip st to top of ch-3.

» **RND 4:** Ch 3 (counts as dc), 2 dc in same st, skip 2 dc, *FPtr in next st, ch 1, BPtr in next st, ch 1, FPtr in next st, skip 2 dc**, 3 dc in next 2 dc, skip 2 dc; repeat from * around, ending last repeat at **, 3 dc in next dc, join with slip st to top of ch-3.

» **RNDS 5–11:** Repeat Rnd 4 seven more times.

» **RND 12:** Ch 3 (counts as dc), dc in same st, skip 2 dc, *FPtr in next st, ch 1, BPtr in next st, ch 1, FPtr in next st, skip 2 dc**, 2 dc in next 2 dc, skip 2 dc; repeat from * around, ending last repeat at **, 2 dc in next dc, join with slip st to top of ch-3. *You now have* 72 sts.

» **RND 13:** Ch 3 (counts as dc), dc in same st, skip 1 st, *FPtr in next st, BPtr in next st, FPtr in next st, skip 1 dc**, 2 dc in next 2 dc, skip 1 dc; repeat from * around, ending last repeat at **, 2 dc in next dc, join with slip st in top of ch-3. *You now have* 56 sts.

» **RND 14:** Ch 3 (counts as dc), skip 1 dc, *FPtr in next st, skip 1 st, FPtr in next st, skip 1 dc**, dc in next 2 dc, skip 1 dc; repeat from * around, ending last repeat at **, dc in next dc, join with slip st to top of ch-3. *You now have* 32 sts.

» **RND 15:** Ch 3, *FPtr2tog, dc2tog; repeat from * seven more times, FPtr2tog, dc in next st, join with slip st in 3rd ch. *You now have* 17 sts.

» **RND 16:** Ch 3, dc2tog eight times, join with slip st to top of ch-3. *You now have* 9 sts.

Finishing

» Use yarn needle to weave tail through the front loop of remaining 8 sts, pull snugly to close top of hat. Weave in ends.

Peacock Hat

Designed by Brenda K. B. Anderson

This charming hat, worked with an open fan stitch, will keep you warm and allow for ventilation at the same time. The brim is edged with back loop single crochet.

FINISHED MEASUREMENTS
20"/51 cm circumference, stretches to 22"/56 cm

YARN
Red Heart Stitch Nation by Debbie Stoller Full o' Sheep, 100% Peruvian wool, 155 yds (142 m)/3.5 oz (100 g), Color 2529 Mediterranean

CROCHET HOOK
US H/8 (5 mm) *or size you need to obtain correct gauge*

GAUGE
Each 9 double crochet fan stitch = 2"/5 cm in width and 1½"/3.8 cm in height

OTHER SUPPLIES
Yarn needle

PATTERN ESSENTIALS

V-st (Dc, ch 1, dc) in same st.

Crocheting the Hat

See chart on page 176.

» Make an adjustable ring (see page 271).

» **RND 1:** 6 sc in ring, join with slip st to first sc, pull on beginning yarn tail to tighten loop. *You now have* 6 sts.

» **RND 2:** Ch 1, 2 sc in each st around, join with slip st to first sc. *You now have* 12 sts.

» **RND 3:** Ch 1, (sc in next st, skip 1 st, 9 dc in next st, skip 1 st) three times, join with slip st to first sc. *You now have* 3 sc and 3 fan sts.

» **RND 4:** Ch 4 (counts as dc and ch 1 here and throughout), (dc, ch 2, dc, ch 1, dc) in same st as join, [ch 5, skip next 9-dc fan, (dc, ch 1, dc, ch 2, dc, ch 1, dc) in next sc] twice, ch 5, join with slip st in 3rd ch of ch-4.

» **RND 5:** Slip st in next ch-1 space, ch 3 (counts as dc here and throughout), 3 dc in same space, sc in next space, 7 dc in next space, (sc over next ch-5 loop in center dc of 9-dc fan, 7 dc in next space, sc in next space, 7 dc in next space) twice, sc over next ch-5 loop in center dc of next 9-dc fan, 3 dc in first ch-space of rnd to complete fan, join with slip st to top of ch-3. *You now have* 6-dc fans and 6 sc.

» **RND 6:** Ch 3, [V-st in next sc, ch 5, (dc, ch 1, dc, ch 2, dc, ch 1, dc) in next sc, ch 5] twice, V-st in next sc, ch 5, (dc, ch 1, dc, ch 2, dc, ch 1, dc) in next sc, ch 2, join with slip st to first ch of rnd.

» **RND 7:** Ch 1 (counts as sc), skip ch-3 space, *(9 dc in center of next V-st, sc over next ch-5 loop in center dc of next 7-dc fan, 7 dc in next space, sc in next space, 7 dc in next space**, sc over next ch-5 loop in center dc of next fan) twice; repeat from * to **, join with slip st to first ch. *You now have* three 9-dc fans, six 7-dc fans, and 9 scs.

» **RND 8:** Ch 4, 1 dc in same st as join (counts as first V-st), (ch 5, V-st in next sc) eight times, ch 5, join with slip st in 3rd ch of ch-4.

» **RND 9:** Slip st in ch-1 space, ch 3, 4 dc in same st as join, (sc over next ch-5 loop in center dc of next fan, 9 dc in next ch-1 space) eight times, sc over next ch-5 loop in center dc of next fan, 4 dc in same st as join to complete fan, join with slip st to top of ch-3. *You now have* nine 9-dc fans and 9 scs.

» **RND 10:** Ch 3, (V-st in next sc, skip next 9-dc shell, ch 5) eight times, V-st in next sc, ch 2, join with slip st to first ch of rnd.

» **RND 11:** Ch 1, (9 dc in next ch-1 space, sc over next ch-5 loop in center dc of next fan) eight times, 9 dc in next ch-1 space, join with slip st to first ch of rnd.

» **RNDS 12–15:** Repeat Rnds 8–11.

» **RNDS 16 AND 17:** Repeat Rnds 8 and 9.

» **RND 18:** Ch 1, sc in same st, (ch 2, V-st in next sc, ch 2, sc in center dc of next fan, ch 2) eight times, V-st in next sc, ch 2, join with slip st in first sc. *You now have* 72 sts.

» **RNDS 19–22:** Ch 1, BLsc in each st around, join with slip st to first sc of rnd.

Finishing

» Fasten off. Weave in ends. Block if desired.

continued on next page

PEACOCK HAT ROUNDS 1–11

Cozy Ear Warmer

Designed by Jane M Brown

This lovely headband is easy to wear — it's shaped for maximum ear protection, and the narrow ends button together at the back. Search through your mother's button box for the perfect accent.

SIZE AND FINISHED MEASUREMENTS

To fit a child or small woman, approximately 18"/45.5 cm circumference and 5¾"/14.5 cm at widest point

YARN

Berroco Ultra Alpaca, 50% alpaca/50% wool, 215 yds (198 m)/3.5 oz (100 g), Color 6283 Lavender Mix

CROCHET HOOK

US H/8 (5 mm) *or size you need to obtain correct gauge*

GAUGE

16 stitches and 20 rows = 4"/10 cm in single crochet

OTHER SUPPLIES

Stitch marker, yarn needle, one ¾"/19 mm button for closure, one 1"/2.5 cm decorative button (optional)

Crocheting the Ear Warmer

» Chain 4.

» **ROW 1 (RS):** Sc in 2nd ch from hook, 3 sc in next st, sc in next sc, turn. *You now have* 5 sts.

» **ROW 2 (WS):** Ch 1, sc in each sc across, turn.

» **ROW 3:** Ch 1, sc in first 2 sc, 3 sc in next sc, pm in 2nd sc of 3-sc group (center st), sc in next 2 sc, turn. *You now have* 7 sts. Move marker up in each row.

» **ROW 4:** Ch 1, sc in each sc across, turn.

» **ROW 5:** Ch 1, sc in each sc across to marker, 3 sc in next sc, sc in each sc across, turn. *You now have* 9 sts.

» **ROWS 6–17:** Repeat Rows 4 and 5 six times. *You now have* 21 sts.

» **ROW 18:** Ch 1, sc in each sc across, turn.

» Repeat Row 18 until piece measures 14½"/37 cm, or 3½"/9 cm less than desired length, ending with a WS row.

» Begin decreasing for the second side as follows.

» **ROW 1 (RS):** Ch 1, sc in next 9 sc, sc3tog, sc in next 9 sc, turn. *You now have* 19 sts.

» **ROW 2 (WS):** Ch 1, sc in each sc across, turn.

» **ROW 3:** Ch 1, sc in each sc across to 2 sts before marker, sc3tog, sc in each sc across, turn. *You now have* 17 sts.

» **ROWS 4–17:** Repeat Rows 2 and 3 seven times. *You now have* 3 sts. Do not fasten off.

Crocheting the Edging

» **RND 1:** Ch 1, working across side edge, sc in every other row-end st across to opposite end, 3 sc in end st, work sc in every other row-end st to beginning end, ch 5 for buttonhole, join with slip st to first sc.

» **RND 2:** Ch 1, sc in each sc around, ending with 5 sc in ch-5 buttonhole loop, join with slip st to first sc. Fasten off. Weave in ends.

Crocheting the Flower (optional)

» Leaving a 10"/25.5 cm tail, ch 6, join with slip st to form a ring.

» **RND 1:** Ch 1, 10 sc in ring, join with slip st to first sc. *You now have* 10 sts.

» **RND 2:** Working in back loops only, ch 3 (counts as dc), dc in same st, 2 dc in each st around, join with slip st to top of ch-3. *You now have* 20 sts.

» **RND 3:** Ch 1, sc in first st, ch 5, skip next 3 dc, (sc in next dc, ch 5, skip next 3 sts) around; join with slip st to first sc. *You now have* 5 ch-5 spaces.

» **RND 4:** *(Sc, hdc, 2 dc, 2 tr, 2 dc, hdc, sc) in ch-5 space, slip st in next sc; repeat from * around. *You now have* five petals.

» **RND 5:** *Skip next sc, sc in next 8 sts, skip next sc, slip st in next slip st, repeat from * around.

» **RND 6:** Working behind petals and into back loops of Rnd 2 sts, sc in next 3 dc, *ch 5, skip next 3 dc, sc in next dc, repeat from * around. (Second round of petals will alternate behind front petals in Rnd 4.) *You now have* 5 ch-5 spaces.

» **RND 7:** (Sc, hdc, 2 dc, 2 tr, 2 dc, hdc, sc) in each ch-5 space around. *You now have* five petals.

» **RND 8:** *Skip next sc, sc in next 8 sts, skip next sc, slip st between petals, repeat from * around.

» Fasten off leaving a 10"/25.5 cm tail.

Finishing

» Sew closure button to end of band opposite buttonhole, adjusting as necessary for proper fit. Position flower as desired and stitch to ear warmer with center tail, sewing button to center. Use outer yarn tail to tack down second round of petals. Weave in ends.

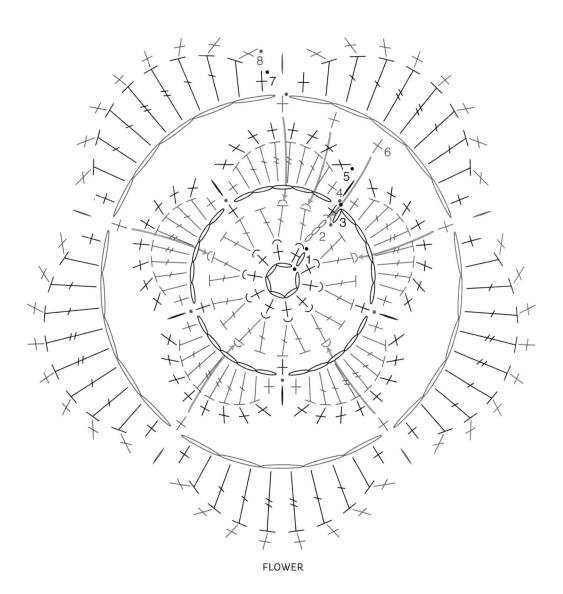

FLOWER

Dancing Poppies Mini Bolero

Designed by Sylvie Damey

This baby bolero is worked seamlessly from the top down and has two mesh rows at the bottom leading to a lovely edging of poppies. It closes with pretty crocheted ties rather than buttons.

FINISHED MEASUREMENTS

17"/43 cm chest circumference and 7½"/19 cm length, excluding poppies

YARN

Cascade Yarns Cascade 220, 100% Peruvian Highland wool, 220 yds (200 m)/3.5 oz (100 g), Color 8415

CROCHET HOOK

US I/9 (5.5 mm) *or size you need to obtain correct gauge*

GAUGE

17½ stitches and 9 rows = 4"/10 cm in double crochet

OTHER SUPPLIES

Yarn needle

✳ **NOTE:** The cardigan is worked from the top down, starting with neckline.

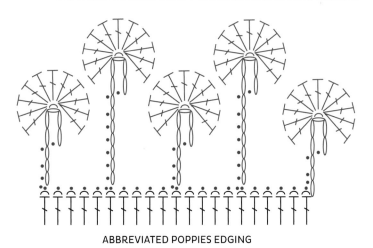

ABBREVIATED POPPIES EDGING

Crocheting the Bolero

» Chain 63.

» **ROW 1 (RS):** Dc in 4th chain from hook, dc in next ch, *(2 dc in next ch), dc in next 2 ch; repeat from * to last ch, 2 dc in last ch, turn. *You now have 81 dc.*

» **ROW 2 (WS MESH ROW):** Ch 4 (counts as dc and ch 1), skip next dc, dc in next dc, *ch 1, skip next dc, dc in next dc; repeat from * across, turn. *You now have 40 ch-1 spaces.*

» **ROW 3:** Ch 3 (counts as dc here and throughout), BLdc in each ch and dc across, turn. *You now have 81 sts.*

» **ROW 4 (INCREASE ROW):** Ch 3 (counts as dc), *FLdc in next 3 sts, 2 FLdc in next st; repeat from * to last 4 sts, FLdc in last 4 sts, turn. *You now have 100 sts.*

» **ROWS 5 AND 6:** Ch 3, FLdc in each st across, turn.

» **ROW 7 (INCREASE ROW):** Ch 3, FLdc in next st, *2 FLdc in next st, FLdc in next 3 sts; repeat from * to last 2 sts, 2 FLdc in next st, FLdc in last st, turn. *You now have 125 sts.*

» **ROW 8:** Ch 3, FLdc in each st across, turn.

DIVIDING FOR THE SLEEVES

» **ROW 9:** Ch 3, FLdc in next 18 sts, skip 25 sts — *first sleeve opening made*, FLdc in next 37 sts, skip 25 sts — *second sleeve opening made*, FLdc in last 19 sts. *You now have* 75 sts.

» **ROWS 10–14:** Ch 3, FLdc in each st across, turn.

Note: Work in both loops for next 2 rows.

» **ROW 15 (MESH ROW):** Ch 4 (counts as dc and ch 1), skip next dc, dc in next st, *ch 1, skip next dc, dc in next dc; repeat from * across, turn.

» **ROW 16:** Ch 3 (counts as dc), dc in each dc and ch-1 space across, turn.

Crocheting the Poppies Edging

» With RS facing, *ch 8, slip st in 5th ch from hook, 11 dc in back loop of 3rd ch from hook, (center ch of 5-ch ring), slip st in same ch as first slip st to join circle, slip st in next 2 ch of ch-8, slip st in same st of Row 16 — *short poppy made*; slip st in back loop of next 5 dc; ch 12, slip st in 5th ch from hook, 11 dc in back loop of 3rd ch from hook, slip st in same ch as first slip st to join circle, slip st in next 6 ch of ch-8, slip

181

st in same st of Row 16 — *long poppy made***; slip st in back loop of next 5 dc; repeat from * across lower edge of sweater, ending last repeat at **, sc evenly up right front edge to top Mesh Row.

Crocheting the Tie Closure

» *Ch 17, 12 dc in back loop of 3rd ch from hook, slip st in 5th ch from hook, skip 2 ch, slip st in next ch to join circle, slip st in next 11 ch, slip st in same st of edging row**, sc evenly along edge to corner of neck, place 3 sc in corner st, sc evenly across neck edge, place 3 sc in corner st, sc evenly to Mesh Row; repeat from * to ** once, sc evenly down left front edge to beginning of round, join with slip st to base of first poppy. Fasten off.

Finishing

» Weave in ends. Block, opening each poppy.

Maywood Purse

Designed by Brenda K. B. Anderson

This felted purse with appliquéd leaves is easy to make — in other words, don't worry if you've never felted before. The use of a purse frame and the leaf embellishments put this in the "I can't believe you made that" category.

FINISHED MEASUREMENTS

11"/28 cm in diameter before felting; 18"/45.5 cm around and 7"/18 cm tall after felting

YARN

Patons Classic Wool, 100% pure new wool, 210 yds (192 m)/3.5 oz (100 g), Color 77208 Jade Heather

CROCHET HOOK

US J/10 (6 mm) *or size you need to obtain correct gauge*

GAUGE

13 stitches and 17 rounds = 4"/10 cm in single crochet

OTHER SUPPLIES

Stitch marker, yarn needle, one 6"/15 cm half-round metal purse frame, sewing needle, coordinating thread, embroidery needle, one 8.7 yds (8 m) package embroidery floss (sample used DMC 25 in color #400), 72"/183 cm copper chain, two copper jump rings

Crocheting the Purse

» **RND 1:** Make an adjustable ring (see page 271), 6 sc into loop. Do not join but work in a spiral. *You now have* 6 sts.

» **RND 2:** 2 sc in each sc around. *You now have 12 sts;* pm in last st of rnd and move marker up at end of each rnd.

- » **RND 3:** (Sc in next sc, 2 sc in next sc) six times. *You now have* 18 sts.

- » **RND 4:** (Sc in next st, 2 sc in next st, sc in next st) six times. *You now have* 24 sts.

- » **RND 5:** (2 sc in next st, sc in next 3 sts) six times. *You now have* 30 sts.

- » **RNDS 6–18:** Continue making 6 increases each round as established. Try to place the increased stitches in a different place on each round so that they are not all concentrated in one line. *You now have* 108 sts at the end of Rnd 18.

- » **RNDS 19–21:** Sc in each st around.

- » **RND 22:** Ch 30, skip next 30 sts, sc in next 78 sts.

- » **RNDS 23 AND 24:** Sc in each st and ch around. *You now have* 108 sts.

- » **RND 25:** (Sc in next 16 sts, sc2tog) six times. *You now have* 102 sts.

- » **RND 26:** (Sc in next 6 sts, sc2tog, sc in next 9 sts) six times. *You now have* 96 sts.

- » **RND 27:** (Sc in next 10 sts, sc2tog, sc in next 4 sts) six times. *You now have* 90 sts.

- » **RNDS 28–41:** Continue decreasing 6 sts evenly spaced in each round. Try to place the decreased stitches in a different place each round so that they are not all concentrated in one line. *You now have* 6 sts at the end of Rnd 41.

» Cut yarn, leaving an 8"/20.5 cm tail; thread tail onto yarn needle and pass through the remaining 6 sts; pull tight and weave in ends.

Crocheting Fabric for Leaves

Note: Leaf fabric measures approximately 9¼" × 6½"/23.5 × 16.5 cm before felting.

» Chain 31.

» **ROW 1:** Sc in 2nd ch from hook and in each ch across, turn. *You now have* 30 sts.

» **ROW 2:** Ch 1, sc in each sc across.

» Repeat Row 2 for 26 rows, or until you run out of yarn. Fasten off.

Finishing

» Felt the purse and leaves (see page 275), checking periodically to see if the opening of the purse is approximately the same size as your purse frame opening. If the opening of the purse is about an inch longer, you can ease the extra fabric in the length of the frame, creating a more bulbous shape at the top of the purse (this is how the sample was constructed). If the purse opening is the same as the size of the frame, the purse will be flatter at the top. If the opening of the purse accidentally gets too small to accommodate the purse frame, you can very carefully snip the corners to lengthen the opening. Shape the purse with your hands while it is still wet.

» When the purse is almost dry, use a needle and thread to stitch the top edge of the purse to the purse frame. Stuff the purse with paper to help keep the desired shape while it dries completely — this may take a couple of days. When dry, cut several leaves from the leaf fabric and stitch them to the purse. Use an embroidery needle and floss to create veins and stems.

» Fold the chain in half and use jump rings to attach the chain to the purse.

Spiral Mesh Bag

Designed by Kennita Tully

This market bag has an asymmetrical closure — slip the long strap through the short strap to close the top of the bag, and you still have a long strap for carrying. The Mesh Stitch is somewhat stretchy, so you can carry more in there than you may think.

FINISHED MEASUREMENTS
Approximately 26"/66 cm in
  circumference and 12"/30.5 cm high

YARN
Dream in Color Classy, 100%
  superfine Australian merino,
  250 yds (229 m)/4oz (113 g),
  Color VM370 Cloud Jungle

CROCHET HOOKS
US I/9 (5.5 mm) and US G/6 (4 mm) *or
  size you need to obtain correct gauge*

GAUGE
18 stitches and 12 rows = 4"/10 cm
  in Mesh Stitch on larger hook

OTHER SUPPLIES
Locking stitch marker
  (optional), yarn needle

PATTERN ESSENTIALS

LINEN STITCH

Worked on an odd number of stitches.

Rnd 1: *Sc in next BLsc, BLsc in next sc; repeat from * around, end sc in last BLsc.

Rnd 2: *BLsc in next sc, sc in next BLsc; repeat from * around, end BLsc in last sc.

Repeat Rnds 1 and 2 for pattern. *Note:* BLsc stitches will be staggered. In this project, Linen Stitch is worked in spiral rounds.

MESH STITCH (FOR GAUGE SWATCH ONLY)

With the larger hook, chain 19.

Row 1: Hdc in 3rd ch from hook, *ch 1, skip 1 st, hdc in next ch; repeat from * across, turn. *You now have 18 sts.*

Row 2: Ch 2 (counts as hdc), *hdc in next ch-1 space, ch 1, skip 1 hdc; repeat from * across, ending with hdc in top of ch-2, turn.

Rows 3–12: Repeat Row 2.

Gauge swatch should measure 4" × 4"/10 × 10 cm.

✳ **NOTES:**
• The bag is worked in a spiral without joining rounds.
• While it's not necessary to mark rounds, a removable stitch marker can be placed at the beginning of the round and moved up as the work progresses.

Crocheting the Straps

» With smaller hook, ch 141; join with slip st to first ch, being careful not to twist sts.

» **SETUP RND 1:** Sc in each ch around.

» **SETUP RND 2:** *BLsc in next sc, sc in next sc; repeat from * around, end BLsc in last sc.

» Begin with Rnd 1 of Linen St pattern and continue until piece measures approximately 1½"/3.8 cm from beginning.

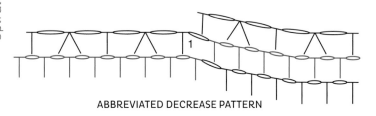

ABBREVIATED DECREASE PATTERN

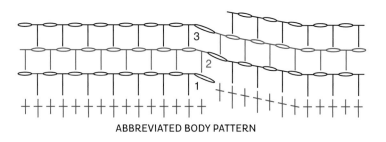

ABBREVIATED BODY PATTERN

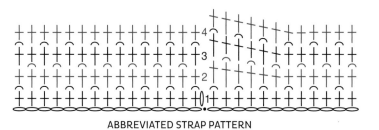

ABBREVIATED STRAP PATTERN

» **NEXT RND:** Continuing in Linen St, work 12 sts in pattern, ch 20, skip 20 sts, work 25 sts in pattern, ch 21, skip 71 sts, work remaining 13 sts in pattern. *You now have* 91 sts.

» **NEXT RND:** Continue in Linen St, working sc in each ch st for this round only.

» Work in Linen St pattern for another 1½"/3.8 cm from beginning of opening.

Crocheting the Body

» **RND 1:** Change to larger hook, *ch 1, skip 1 st, hdc in next st; repeat from * around — first Mesh St round.

» Repeat Rnd 1, working into ch-spaces, until body measures approximately 11"/28 cm from beginning of Mesh St pattern, ending with hdc.

Crocheting the Bottom

» **RND 1:** *Ch 1, hdc in next ch-1 space, ch 1, skip 1 st, hdc2tog over next 2 ch-1 spaces; repeat from * around.

» Repeat Rnd 1, decreasing until only a small opening remains, ending with an hdc or hdc2tog. Fasten off, leaving a 6"/15 cm tail. Thread tail onto yarn needle and weave through remaining sts. Gather tightly and secure. Weave in ends.

Small Brown Bag with Beads

Designed by Nancy Brown

This small brown bag is the perfect size for quick trips around town when all you need is your wallet, sunglasses, and car keys. Wooden beads provide a casual accent.

FINISHED MEASUREMENTS
7"/18 cm wide and 7½"/19 cm tall, excluding bead fringe

YARN
Cascade 220, 100% Peruvian Highland wool, 220 yds (201 m)/ 3.5 oz (100 g), Color 1208

CROCHET HOOKS
US J/10 (6 mm) *or size you need to obtain correct gauge* and US H/8 (5 mm)

GAUGE
16 stitches and 14 rounds = 4"/10 cm in pattern with larger hook

OTHER SUPPLIES
Stitch marker, twenty-six 10 mm wooden crow beads, yarn needle

Crocheting the Bag

» With larger hook, ch 54, and without twisting ch, join with slip st in first ch to form a ring.

» **RND 1:** Ch 2 (counts as hdc), hdc in each ch around. *You now have* 54 sts. *Do not join.* Place marker at the first stitch of the round and move it up as you work the rounds.

» **RND 2:** Work 1 sc in each st around.

» **RND 3:** Work 1 hdc in each st around.

» Repeat Rnds 2 and 3 until piece measures approximately 7½"/19 cm from beginning, ending with Rnd 2 of pattern.

Working the Top Edging

» With smaller hook, *sc in each of next 3 sts, tight picot-3; repeat from * around, join with slip st in first sc. Fasten off.

Working the Bottom Edging

» String 26 beads on yarn. Flatten bag. With smaller hook and working through both thicknesses of bag, join yarn with sc in corner on bottom of bag.

» *Beaded tight picot-3, sc in each of next 3 sts; repeat from * across, beaded tight picot-3, sc in last st. Fasten off.

Crocheting the Shoulder Strap

» With larger hook join two strands of yarn (one with beads and one without beads) at one side edge.

» (Ch 3, sc in 3rd ch from hook) three times, *Bch, (ch 3, sc in 3rd ch from hook) three times; repeat from * until strap measures approx 36"/91 cm or desired length. Join with slip st on opposite side of bag. Fasten off. Weave in all ends.

Serrato Purse

Designed by Akua Lezli Hope

Named for its serrated appearance, which is achieved with a technique known as crocodile stitch, this small bag can be dressed up or down by the chosen yarn.

FINISHED MEASUREMENTS

Approximately 7"/18 cm wide and 8"/20.5 cm tall excluding strap

YARN

Plymouth Yarn Galway Colornep, 90% wool, 10% polyester neps, 210 yds (183 m)/3.5 oz (100 g), Color 509 Black

CROCHET HOOK

US I/9 (5.5 mm) *or size you need to obtain correct gauge*

GAUGE

2 pattern repeats and 8 rows = approximately 4"/10 cm in body pattern; exact gauge is not crucial to project

OTHER SUPPLIES

Yarn needle, paper for making lining pattern, ½ yd/45.5 cm of fabric for lining, sewing needle, and thread to coordinate with lining

PATTERN ESSENTIALS

V-st (Dc, ch 1, dc) in same st.

✳ **NOTES:**
• The body is worked flat and seamed with slip stitch, then the circular bottom is crocheted.
• The top flap is made as a separate piece and attached to the body.

189

Crocheting the Body

» Chain 38.

» **ROW 1 (WS):** Sc in 2nd ch from hook, *ch 2, skip 2 ch, V-st in next ch, ch 2, skip 2 ch, sc in next ch; repeat from * across, turn. *You now have 6 V-sts.*

» **ROW 2:** Ch 1, sc in first sc, *work (tr, 5 dc, ch 1) around first dc of next V-st; turn so that point of V is facing right and second dc of V-st is horizontal; work (5 dc, tr) around second dc of V-st, sc into next sc; repeat from * across, turn. *You now have* six petals.

» **ROW 3:** Ch 1, sc in first sc, ch 2, *sc in ch-1 space of next V-st from Row 1, ch 2**, V-st in next sc, ch 2; repeat from * across, ending last repeat at **, sc in last sc, turn. *You now have* 5 V-sts.

» **ROW 4:** Ch 2, sc in first st, ch 2, sc in next sc, *work (tr, 5 dc, ch 1) around first dc of next V-st; turn so that point of V is facing right and second dc of V-st is horizontal; work (5 dc, tr) around second dc of V-st, sc into next sc; repeat from * across, ch 2, sc in last sc, turn. *You now have* five petals.

» **ROW 5:** Ch 1, sc in first st, *ch 2, V-st in next sc, ch 2**, sc in ch-1 space of next V-st from Row 3; repeat from * across, ending last repeat at **, sc in last sc. *You now have* 6 V-sts.

» **ROWS 6–13:** Repeat Rows 2–5 two times.

» **ROWS 14–16:** Repeat Rows 2–4 once. Do not fasten off.

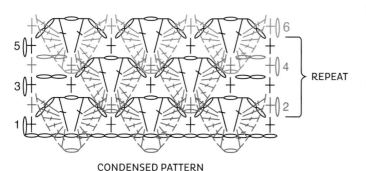

5
3
1
6
4
2

REPEAT

CONDENSED PATTERN

Joining the Side Seam

» Trace the bag shape onto paper to make a pattern for the lining.

» Fold bag with RS together. Matching sts, ch 1, slip st sides together matching row-end sts. Fasten off. Turn body right side out.

Crocheting the Bottom

Note: The bottom is worked in the round along the bottom edge of the bag body.

» **RND 1:** Join yarn with slip st to foundation ch, ch 2 (counts as hdc), 2 hdc in each ch-2 space, and 1 hdc in ch at base of each sc and V-st around, join with slip st to top of ch-2. *You now have* 38 hdc.

» **RND 2:** Ch 2 (counts as hdc here and throughout), hdc in next 16 sts, hdc2tog, hdc in next 17 sts, hdc2tog, join with slip st to top of ch-2. *You now have* 36 hdc.

» **RND 3:** Ch 2, *hdc in next 5 hdc, hdc2tog; repeat from * around, join with slip st to top of ch-2. *You now have* 31 sts.

» **RND 4:** Ch 2, *hdc in next 4 hdc, hdc2tog; repeat from * around, join with slip st to top of ch-2. *You now have* 26 sts.

» **RND 5:** Ch 2, hdc in next st, *hdc2tog, hdc in next 2 hdc; repeat from * around, join with slip st to top of ch-2. *You now have* 20 sts.

» **RND 6:** Ch 2, hdc in next hdc, (hdc2tog) around, join with slip st to top of ch-2. *You now have* 11 sts.

» **RND 7:** Ch 1, sc in same st, (sc2tog) around. *You now have* 6 sts.

» **RND 8:** Ch 1, (sc2tog) around. *You now have* 3 sts.

» Fasten off, leaving a 6"/15 cm tail. Weave tail through last round, gather tightly, and secure. Weave in ends. Measure bottom circle to make a pattern for the lining.

Crocheting the Flap

» Chain 21.

» **ROWS 1–10:** Work same as Rows 1–10 of body, working three petals in Rows 2, 6, and 10, and two petals in Rows 4 and 8.

» **ROW 11:** Ch 2, (3 hdc in side of next tr, hdc in next ch-1 space of petal, 3 hdc in side of next tr) three times, hdc in last sc. Fasten off. *You now have* 23 hdc.

Edging the Body

» **ROW 1:** With RS of bag body facing, join yarn at beginning of round, repeat Row 11 of flap across first three petals. Do not fasten off. *You now have* 23 hdc.

Finishing

» With RS of flap and body together, working through double thickness of bottom edge of flap and edging row on top of body, slip st in each st across to join flap to body. Fasten off. Weave in ends. Assemble the lining, slip into bag, and whipstitch (see page 275) to top edge of bag.

Crocheting the Shoulder Strap

» Leaving a 6"/15 cm sewing length, ch 2.

» **ROW 1:** Sc in 2nd ch from hook, turn.

» **ROW 2:** *Sc in both loops on the back of the stitch just made, turn.

» Repeat Row 2 until strap measures 27"/69 cm or desired length. Fasten off, leaving a 6"/15 cm sewing length. Sew strap to top corners of bag.

Noodles Toddler Beanie

Designed by Sandy Scoville

This is a great hat to stitch if you don't know the toddler's head size — it's very stretchy and will fit most children. The fabric is an open mesh, and the yarn choice makes it downright funky!

SIZE AND FINISHED MEASUREMENTS
To fit 12–24 months; 17½"/44.5 cm in circumference, relaxed; will stretch easily to 20"/51 cm

YARN
Crystal Palace Bunny Hop, 50% microacrylic/42% micronylon/8% rabbit angora, 113 yds (103 m)/1.75 oz (50 g), Color 9575 Circus

CROCHET HOOK
US G/6 (4 mm) *or size you need to obtain correct gauge*

GAUGE
16 stitches and 9 rounds = 4"/10 cm in brim pattern, relaxed

OTHER SUPPLIES
Yarn needle

❋ **NOTE:** Draw up first loop of each stitch about ½"/13 mm to obtain proper stitch height. Row gauge is important.

Crocheting the Brim

» Chain 70, join with slip st to first ch to form a ring.

» **RND 1:** Ch 2 (counts as dc), dc in each ch around, join with slip st in top of ch-2. *You now have 70 dc.*

» **RND 2:** Ch 2 (counts as dc), FPdc in first dc, *dc in next dc, FPdc in next dc; repeat from * around, join with slip st to top of ch-2. *You now have 35 dc and 35 FPdc.*

» **RNDS 3 AND 4:** Repeat Rnd 2.

Crocheting the Body

» **RND 5:** Slip st in next st, ch 1 loosely, FPtr in first st, ch 1, skip 1 st, *FPtr in next st, ch 1, skip 1 st; repeat from * around, join with slip st to first FPtr. *You now have 35 FPtr and 35 ch-1 spaces.*

» **RND 6:** Ch 1 loosely, FPtr around first st, ch 1, skip next ch-1 space, *FPtr around next st, ch 1, skip next ch-1 space; repeat from * around, join with slip st to first FPtr.

» **RNDS 7–12:** Repeat Rnd 6.

Crocheting the Crown

» **RND 13:** Ch 1 loosely, FPtr around first st, FPtr around each FPtr, join with slip st to first FPtr. *You now have 35 FPtr.*

» **RND 14:** Ch 1 loosely, FPtr around first FPtr, (FPtr2tog) around, join with slip st to first FPtr. *You now have 18 sts.*

» **RND 15:** Ch 1 loosely, (FPtr2tog) around, join with slip st to first FPtr. *You now have 9 sts.*

» Fasten off, leaving a 6"/15 cm tail.

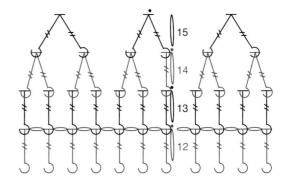

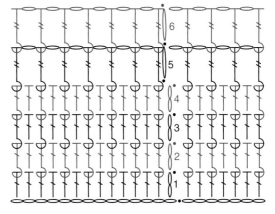

ABBREVIATED PATTERN

Crocheting the Noodles

» Ch 7, sc in 2nd ch from hook and in next 5 chs — *first noodle made;* *ch 7, sc in 2nd ch from hook and in next 5 chs, slip st in unused loop of first ch at bottom of first noodle; repeat from * 10 times more — *12 joined noodles made.* Fasten off, leaving a 6"/15 cm tail.

Finishing

» With yarn needle, draw 6"/15 cm tail through 9 remaining sts at top of beanie, gather tightly, draw end to WS. Place noodles at top of beanie and draw ends to WS. Using ends, secure noodles to top of beanie. Weave in ends.

Openwork Baby Cap

Designed by Sandy Scoville

This soft openwork cap is perfect for baby boys and girls. It uses less than 90 yards, so almost any single skein of sport-weight yarn can be used. Easily worked by most beginners, an optional crocheted flower is included for baby girls.

SIZE AND FINISHED MEASUREMENTS
To fit 6–12 months, approximately 16"/40.5 cm in circumference

YARN
Crystal Palace Bamboozle, 55% bamboo/24% cotton/21% elastic nylon, 90 yds (83 m)/1.75 oz (50 g), Color 1240 Limeade

CROCHET HOOK
US G/6 (4 mm) *or size you need to obtain correct gauge*

GAUGE
16 stitches = 4"/10 cm in double crochet

OTHER SUPPLIES
Yarn needle

Crocheting the Cap

See chart on page 196.

» Ch 64, and without twisting ch, join with slip st in first ch to form a ring.

» **RND 1 (RS):** Ch 1, sc in each ch around, join with slip st in first sc. *You now have 64 sc.*

» **RND 2:** Ch 1, BLsc in first sc, BLdc in next sc, *BLsc in next sc, BLdc in next sc, repeat from * around, join with slip st in both loops of first sc.

» **RND 3:** Slip st in back loop of first sc, ch 2 (counts as a dc), BLsc in next dc, *BLdc in next sc, BLsc in next dc; repeat from * around, join with slip st to top of ch-2.

» **RND 4:** Ch 3 (counts as dc and ch 1), skip 1 st, *BLdc in next st, ch 1, skip 1 st, repeat from * around, join with slip st in 2nd ch of ch-3. *You now have 32 dc and 32 ch-1 spaces.*

» **RND 5:** Ch 1, sc in first st, dc in next ch, *BLsc in next dc, dc in next ch, repeat from * around, join with slip st in both loops of first sc.

» **RND 6:** Slip st in back loop of first sc, ch 2 (counts as a dc), BLsc in next dc, *BLdc in next sc, BLsc in next dc, repeat from * around, join with slip st to 2nd ch of ch-2.

» **RNDS 7–9:** Repeat Rnds 4–6.

» **RND 10 (DECREASE RND):** Ch 2 (counts as a dc), skip next st, BLdc in next st, ch 1, skip next st, *BLdc in next st, skip next st, BLdc in next st, ch 1, skip next st, repeat from * around, join with slip st in 2nd ch of beg ch-2. *You now have* 32 dc and 16 ch-1 spaces.

» **RND 11:** Ch 1, sc in joining ch, BLdc in next dc, *BLsc in next st, BLdc in next st, repeat from * around, join with slip st in first sc. *You now have* 48 sts.

» **RND 12:** Repeat Rnd 6.

» **RND 13 (DECREASE RND):** Repeat Rnd 10. *You now have* 24 dc and 12 ch-1 spaces.

» **RND 14 (DECREASE RND):** Slip st in back loop of beg ch-2, ch 1, BLdc in next dc — *first dec made,* *insert hook in back loop of next st and draw up a loop, yo, insert hook in back loop of next st and draw up a loop, (yo, draw through 2 loops on hook) 3 times – dec made; repeat from * around, join with slip st in first dc. *You now have* 18 sts.

» **RND 15 (DECREASE RND):** Slip st in back loop of first dc, ch 1, BLdc in next st — *first dec made,* decrease as for Rnd 14 around, join with slip st in first dc. *You now have* 9 sts.

» **RND 16 (DECREASE RND):** Slip st in back loop of first dc, ch 1, BLdc — *first dec made,* decrease as for Rnd 14 three more times, dc in next st, join with slip st in first dc. *You now have* 5 sts. Fasten off, leaving a 6"/15 cm tail.

continued on next page

ABBREVIATED BABY CAP PATTERN

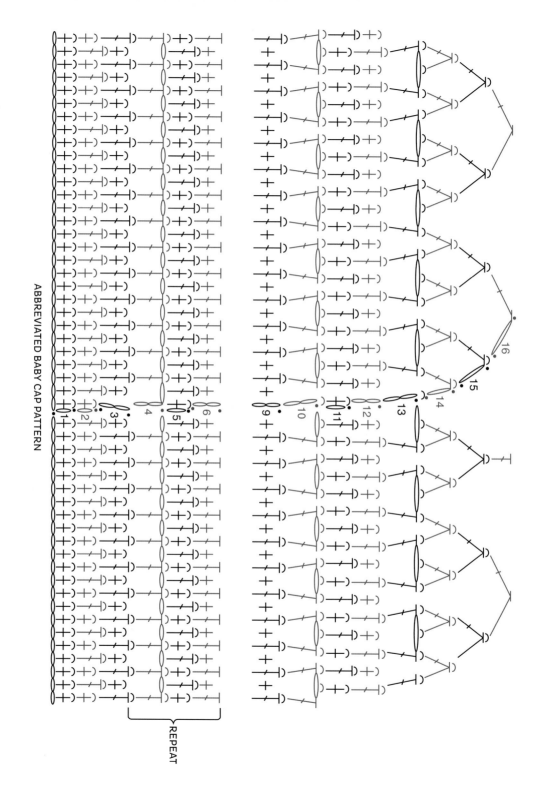

REPEAT

FLOWER

Crocheting the Flower
(optional)

» Ch 4, join with slip st to first ch to form a ring.

» **RND 1 (RS):** Ch 1, 10 sc in ring, join with slip st to first sc.

» **RND 2:** Slip st in back loop of first sc, ch 1, BLsc in same sc, 5 BLdc in next sc, *BLsc in next sc, 5 BLdc in next sc; repeat from * around, join to first sc. *You now have* five petals. Fasten off, leaving a 6"/15 cm tail.

Finishing

» With yarn needle and ends, sew flower to cap. Weave in ends.

Pinwheel Newsboy Cap

Designed by Jenny Allbritain

Read all about it! This cotton cap has a small visor in front to keep the sun out of baby's eyes. A quick crochet, this cap is great for newsgirls, too.

197

SIZES AND FINISHED MEASUREMENTS

To fit baby (toddler, child, adult), approximately 14" (16", 18", 20½")/35.5 (40.5, 45.5, 52) cm in circumference; sample shown is toddler size

YARN

Hobby Lobby I Love This Cotton, 100% cotton, 180 yds (165 m)/3.5 oz (100 g), Color 302 Washed Denim

CROCHET HOOK

US J/10 (6 mm) *or size you need to obtain correct gauge*

GAUGE

14 stitches and 11 rows = 4"/10 cm in body pattern; first 5 rounds = 4"/10 cm in diameter

OTHER SUPPLIES

Yarn needle

PATTERN ESSENTIALS

Spike st Insert hook into the st in the row below next st, yo and pull up a loop to the height of the current row, yo and pull through 2 loops on hook to complete st.

Crocheting the Cap

See charts on pages 200–203.

» Start with an adjustable ring (see page 271).

» **RND 1:** Ch 2 (does not count as a st here and throughout), work 8 hdc into ring, join with slip st to first hdc. Pull on tail to close ring. *You now have* 8 sts.

» **RND 2:** Ch 2, hdc in same st, *FPdc around next st, hdc in same st behind dc; repeat from * around, ending with FPdc around first hdc of previous rnd, join with slip st to top of first hdc. *You now have* 16 sts.

» **RND 3:** Ch 2, hdc in same st, *FPdc in next dc, hdc in same st behind dc **, hdc in next st; repeat from * around, ending last repeat at **, join with slip st to first hdc. *You now have* 24 sts.

» **RND 4:** Ch 2, hdc in same st, *FPdc around next dc, hdc in same st behind dc, skip next hdc**, FPdc around next hdc, hdc in same st behind dc; repeat from * around, ending last repeat at **, FPdc around first hdc of previous rnd, join with slip st to first hdc. *You now have* 32 sts.

» **RND 5:** Ch 2, hdc in same st, *FPdc around next dc, hdc in same st behind dc, skip next hdc, FPdc around next dc, hdc in same st behind dc **, hdc in next st; repeat from * around, ending last repeat at **, join with slip st to first hdc. *You now have* 40 sts.

» **RND 6:** Ch 2, hdc in same st, *(FPdc around next dc, hdc in same st behind dc, skip next hdc) two times**, FPdc around next hdc, hdc in same st behind dc; repeat from * around, ending last repeat at **, FPdc around first hdc of previous rnd, join with slip st to first hdc. *You now have* 48 sts.

TODDLER SIZE ONLY

» **RND 7:** Ch 2, hdc in same st, *(FPdc around next dc, hdc in same st behind dc, skip next hdc) five times, FPdc around next dc, hdc in same st behind dc **, hdc in next st; repeat from * around, ending last repeat at **, join with slip st to first hdc. *You now have* 52 sts.

» **RND 8:** Ch 2, hdc in same st, *(FPdc around next dc, hdc in same st behind dc, skip next hdc) six times**, FPdc around next hdc, hdc in same st behind dc; repeat from * around, ending last repeat at **, FPdc around first hdc of previous rnd, join with slip st to first hdc. *You now have* 56 sts.

CHILD AND ADULT SIZES ONLY

» **RND 7:** Ch 2, hdc in same st, *(FPdc around next dc, hdc in same st behind dc, skip next hdc) two times, FPdc around next dc, hdc in same st behind dc **, hdc in next st; repeat from * around, ending last repeat at **, join with slip st to first hdc. *You now have 56 sts.*

» **RND 8:** Ch 2, hdc in same st, *(FPdc around next dc, hdc in same st behind dc, skip next hdc) three times**, FPdc around next hdc, hdc in same st behind dc; repeat from * around, ending last repeat at **, FPdc around first hdc of previous rnd, join with slip st to first hdc. *You now have 64 sts.*

ADULT SIZE ONLY

» **RND 9:** Ch 2, hdc in same st, *(FPdc around next dc, hdc in same st behind dc, skip next hdc) seven times, FPdc around next dc; hdc in same st behind dc **, hdc in next st; repeat from * around, ending last repeat at **, join with slip st to first hdc. *You now have 68 sts.*

» **RND 10:** Ch 2, hdc in same st, *(FPdc around next dc, hdc in same st behind dc, skip next hdc) eight times**, FPdc around next hdc, hdc in same st behind dc; repeat from * around, ending last repeat at **, FPdc around first hdc of previous rnd, join with slip st to first hdc. *You now have 72 sts.*

ALL SIZES

» **RNDS 7–13 (9–16, 9–19, 11–22):** Ch 2, *FPdc around next dc, hdc in same st behind dc**, skip next hdc; repeat from * around, ending last repeat at **, join with slip st to first st. *You now have 48 (56, 64, 72) sts.*

Note: If hat fits comfortably, eliminate decreases in the next round and simply sc in every st.

» **RND 14 (17, 20, 23):** Ch 1, *sc in next 4 (5, 6, 7) sts, sc2tog; repeat from * around; join with slip st to first sc. *You now have 40 (48, 56, 64) sts.*

BABY AND TODDLER SIZES ONLY

» **RND 15 (18):** Ch 1, sc in each st around, join with slip st to first sc.

» Turn. Follow visor directions from here.

CHILD AND ADULT SIZES ONLY

» **RNDS 21 AND 22 (24 AND 25):** Ch 1, sc in each st around, join with slip st to first sc. *You now have 56 (64) sts.*

» Turn. Follow visor directions from here.

Crocheting the Visor

» **ROW 1 (WS):** Ch 1, sc in next 13 (15, 17, 19) sts, slip st in next st, turn.

» **ROW 2 (RS):** Ch 1, 2 spike st in first st, 1 spike st in next st, 2 spike st in next st, [1 spike st in next 3 (4, 5, 6) sts, 2 spike st in next st] two times, 1 spike st in next st, 2 spike st in next st, sc in side of visor, slip st in left bottom corner of visor, turn. *You now have 19 (21, 23, 25) sts.*

» **ROW 3:** Ch 1, sc in each st across, sc in side of visor, slip st in right bottom corner of visor, turn. *You now have 20 (22, 24, 26) sts.*

continued on next page

BABY AND TODDLER SIZES ONLY

» **ROW 4:** Ch 1, 1 spike st in each st across, sc in side of visor, sc in left bottom corner of visor. Do not turn.

CHILD AND ADULT SIZES ONLY

» **ROW 4:** Ch 1, 1 spike st in each st, sc in side of visor, slip st in left bottom corner of visor, turn. *You now have* 25 (27) sts.

» **ROW 5:** Ch 1, sc in each st across, sc in side of visor, slip st in right bottom corner of visor, turn. *You now have* 26 (28) sts.

» **ROW 6:** Ch 1, spike st in each st across, sc in side of visor, sc in left bottom corner of visor. Do not turn.

VISOR

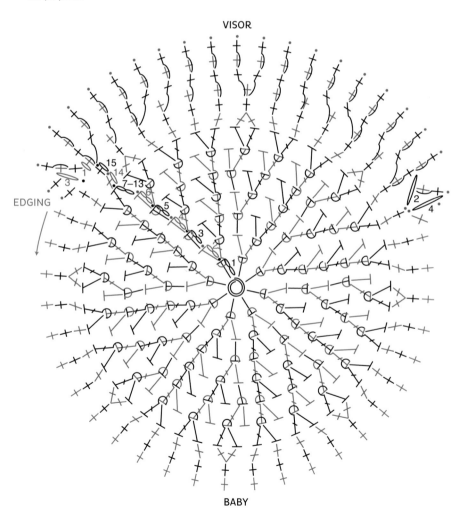

BABY

Crocheting the Edging

» Sc in each of the remaining sts of the hat, sc in bottom corner of the visor, slip st across each st of visor. Fasten off. Weave in ends.

VISOR

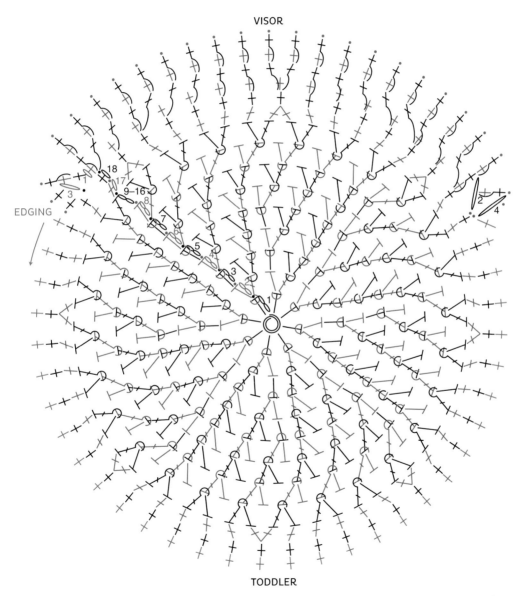

EDGING

TODDLER

continued on next page

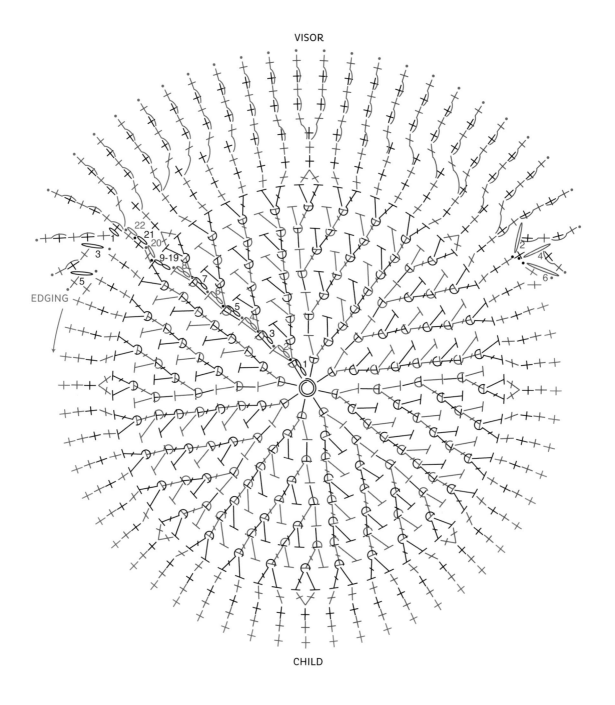

VISOR

EDGING

CHILD

VISOR

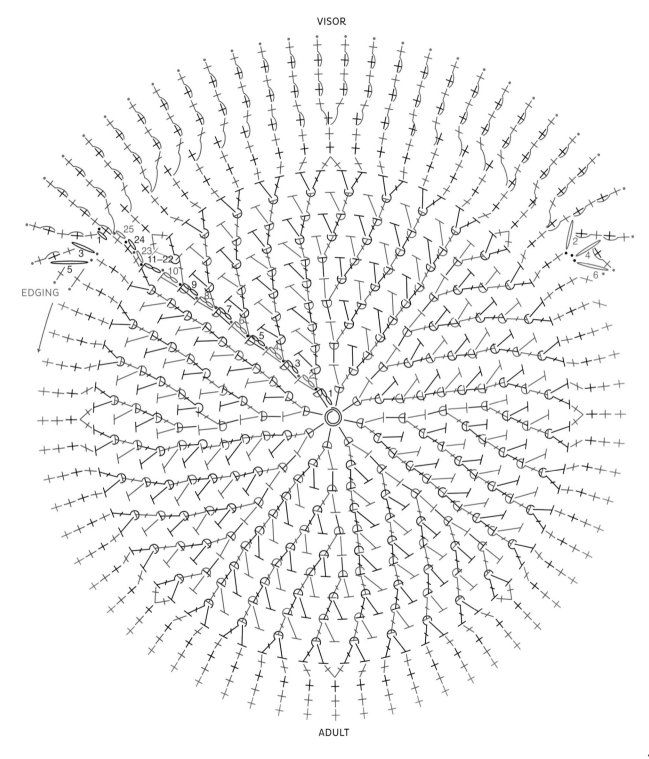

EDGING

ADULT

Little Crocheted and Felted Slippers

Designed by Adrienne Hopkins

These crocheted and felted slippers are great for boys and girls; a change of color and/or embellishments can make the distinction! Add an extra round at the toe or row at the heel, or both, to alter the size. Liquid latex rug backing applied to the sole makes them skid-resistant.

SIZES AND FINISHED MEASUREMENTS
To fit a 3- to 4-year-old, approximately
6½"-7"/16.5-18 cm long

YARN
Valley Yarns Northampton, 100% wool, 247
yd (226 m)/3.5 oz (100 g), Color Azure

CROCHET HOOK
US K/10½ (6.5 mm) *or size you need to obtain correct gauge*

GAUGE
14 stitches and 8 rows = 4"/10 cm in double crochet before felting

OTHER SUPPLIES
Buttons, crocheted flowers, or other embellishments (optional); liquid latex for skid-resistance (optional)

Crocheting the Toe

» Chain 4.

» **RND 1:** 7 dc in 4th ch from hook (3 chs count as dc), join with slip st to top of first dc. *You now have* 8 dc.

» **RND 2:** Ch 3 (counts as dc), dc in same st, 2 dc in each dc around, join with slip st in top of ch-3. *You now have* 16 dc.

» **RND 3:** Ch 3 (counts as dc), 2 dc in next dc, * 1 dc in next dc, 2 dc in next dc; repeat from * around; join with slip st in top of ch-3. *You now have* 24 dc.

» **RND 4:** Ch 3 (counts as dc), 1 dc in next dc, 2 dc in next dc, * 1 dc in next 2 dc, 2 dc in next dc; repeat from * around; join with slip st in top of ch-3. *You now have* 32 dc.

» **RNDS 5-8:** Ch 3 (counts as dc), 1 dc in each dc around; join with slip st in top of ch-3.

Crocheting the Foot

» **ROW 9:** Ch 2 (counts as hdc), 1 hdc in next dc, 1 dc in next 14 dc, 1 hdc in next 2 dc, turn.

» **ROW 10:** Ch 2 (counts as hdc), 1 hdc in next hdc, 1 dc in next 14 dc, 1 hdc in next 2 hdc, turn.

» **ROWS 11-18:** Repeat Row 10.

» **ROW 19:** Ch 2 (counts as hdc), 1 hdc in next hdc, 1 dc in next 6 dc, 1 sc in next 2 dc, 1 dc in next 6 dc, 1 hdc in next 2 hdc.

Crocheting the Heel

» Fold in half with RS together to make heel. Ch 1, slip st halves together, working in the back loop only on the front half and the front loop only on the back half. Fasten off.

Crocheting around the Opening

» **RND 1:** With RS facing, join yarn on top edge of opening at heel, ch 3 (counts as dc), work 15 dc evenly spaced to corner; working across top of foot, (dc in next 2 dc, skip 1 dc) four times, dc in next 2 dc, work 16 dc evenly spaced to end; join with slip st to top of ch-3. *You now have* 42 dc.

» **RND 2:** Ch 3 (counts as dc), dc in each dc around; join with slip st to top of ch-3.

» **RND 3:** Ch 1, * sc in next 5 dc, skip 1 dc; repeat from * around, join with slip st to top of first sc. *You now have* 35 sc.

» Fasten off, weave in all ends, and turn slipper RS out. Repeat all steps to make a second slipper.

Finishing

» Felt (see page 275) slippers to desired size. Once desired length is achieved, run the slippers under cold water, squeeze out excess water, and then roll in a towel to remove more water. Slippers can now be formed to feet and shaped for drying. Let air dry.

» After slippers have dried, add the embellishments and liquid latex to soles, if desired.

BEFORE FELTING

205

Bonnie's Peep Toes

Designed by Marcia Sommerkamp

Easy enough for a beginner to stitch, this charming flip-flop decoration is a real attention getter. The stitching resembles medallions or yo-yos, and the ribbon yarn is soft and comfortable to wear.

FINISHED MEASUREMENTS
To fit any woman's size flip-flop

YARN
Knit One Crochet Too Tartelette, 50% cotton/50% nylon, 75 yds (69 m)/1.75 oz (50 g), Color 278 Hollyhock

CROCHET HOOK
US J/10 (6 mm) *or size you need to obtain correct gauge*

GAUGE
3 (5-dc shells, 1 sc) repeats = 4"/10 cm; exact gauge is not crucial to pattern

OTHER SUPPLIES
Flip-flops of your choice (woman's size), buttons or charms for embellishment (optional), needle and thread to sew on embellishments (optional)

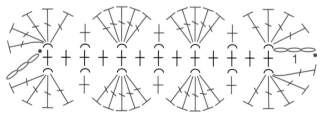

CONDENSED PATTERN

Crocheting the Flip-Flop

» Using a single strand of yarn, work 17 sc around first strap of flip-flop, sc in toe thong, work 17 sc around other strap, turn. **Note:** If crochet loops do not fill the thong area, change to a larger size hook, or use any multiple of 4 plus 3 sts.

» **RND 1:** Ch 3 (counts as dc), 4 BLdc in same st, *skip 1 sc, BLsc in next sc, skip 1 sc, 5 BLdc in next sc — *shell made*; repeat from * to * across to last sc, slip st to last st, turn, working along opposite edge of foundation row in free loops, ch 3 (counts as dc), 4 BLdc in same st, repeat from * to * across to last sc, working shells in same sts as shells on opposite side of strap. Fasten off.

Finishing

» Weave in ends. Attach buttons or charms as desired.

Lullaby Dreams Pillow Slip

Designed by Sharon Ballsmith

This pretty ruffled pillow will add a sweet touch anywhere you place it. And it's worked in the round with no seams to sew!

SIZE AND FINISHED MEASUREMENTS

12" × 20"/30.5 × 51 cm, to fit a 12" × 16"/30.5 × 40.5 cm pillow

YARN

Lion Brand Pound of Love, 100% acrylic, 1020 yds (932 m)/16 oz (454 g), Color 100 White

CROCHET HOOK

US K/10½ (6.5 mm) *or size you need to obtain correct gauge*

GAUGE

4 shells and 8 rows = approximately 4"/10 cm

OTHER SUPPLIES

Yarn needle, 12" × 16"/30.5 × 40.5 cm pillow

PATTERN ESSENTIALS

Back bar The horizontal loop on the back side of a ch st.

Shell (2 dc, ch 2, sc) in same st or space.

MAKING A GAUGE SWATCH

Row 1: Ch 12, shell in back bar of 3rd ch from hook, *skip next 2 chs, shell in back bar of next ch, repeat from * across, turn. *You now have* 4 shells.

Rows 2–8: Ch 2, shell in ch-2 space of each shell across, turn. *You now have* 4 shells. Fasten off and measure. Swatch should measure 4" x 4"/10 x 10 cm. Adjust hook size if necessary.

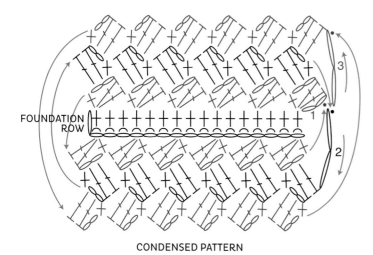

FOUNDATION ROW

CONDENSED PATTERN

Crocheting the Pillow Slip

Note: Pillow slip is worked in the round from the bottom to the ruffled edge.

» **FOUNDATION ROW:** Ch 41, sc in back bar of 2nd ch from hook, sc in back bar of each ch across, turn. *You now have 40 sc.*

» **RND 1:** Ch 2 (not a st; counts as turning ch and joining ch only, now and throughout), shell in first sc, *(skip next 2 sts, shell in next st) 13 times across**; working in unworked loops on opposite side of foundation ch, shell in first st; repeat from * to **; join with slip st in top of beg ch-2, turn. *You now have 28 shells.*

» **RND 2:** Ch 2, shell in ch-2 space of each shell around; join with slip st in top of beg ch-2, turn.

» **RNDS 3–36:** Repeat Rnd 2.

Crocheting the Ruffle

» **RND 37:** Ch 2, shell in ch-2 space of first shell, *skip next dc of same shell, shell in last dc of same shell**, shell in ch-2 space of next shell; repeat from * around, ending last repeat at **, join with slip st in top of beg ch-2, turn. *You now have 56 shells.*

» **RNDS 38–43:** Repeat Rnd 2. *You now have 56 shells.*

» **RND 44:** Ch 1, 4 sc in ch-2 space of first shell, *slip st in each next 2 dc of same shell**, 4 sc in ch-2 space of next shell; repeat from * around, ending last repeat at **; join with slip st in first sc.

Finishing

» Fasten off. Weave in ends.

Lullaby Dreams Baby Blanket

Designed by Sharon Ballsmith

This sweet little blanket has ribbing at the top, a ruffle at the bottom, and a pretty shell edging along the sides that are formed along with the blanket. Pair this with the Lullaby Dreams Pillow Slip on page 207.

FINISHED MEASUREMENTS
Approximately 28"/71 cm wide and 38"/96.5 cm long

YARN
Lion Brand Pound of Love, 100% acrylic, 1020 yds (932 m)/16 oz (454 g), Color 100 White

CROCHET HOOK
US K/10½ (6.5 mm) *or size you need to obtain correct gauge*

GAUGE
4 shells and 8 rows = approximately 4"/10 cm

OTHER SUPPLIES
Yarn needle

PATTERN ESSENTIALS

Back bar The horizontal loop on the back side of a ch st.

Shell (2 dc, ch 2, sc) in same st or space.

MAKING A GAUGE SWATCH (see page 208)

Crocheting the Ribbing

Note: Blanket is worked from the top ribbing down to the ruffled bottom.

» **ROW 1:** Ch 10, sc in back bar of 2nd ch from hook, sc in back bar of each next ch across, turn. *You now have 9 sc.*

» **ROW 2:** Ch 1, BLsc in each sc across, turn.

» **ROWS 3–99:** Repeat Row 2.

» Pivot top ribbing and work across long edge of ribbing as follows.

» **FOUNDATION ROW:** Ch 1, sc in sc just worked and in each row-end st across, turn. *You now have 100 sc.*

Crocheting the Main Body

» **ROW 1:** Ch 2 (not a stitch; counts as a turning ch, now and throughout pattern), shell in first sc, *skip next 2 sc, shell in next sc; repeat from * across, turn. *You now have 34 shells.*

» **ROW 2:** Ch 2, shell in ch-2 space of each shell across, turn.

» **ROWS 3–68:** Repeat Row 2.

Crocheting the Ruffle

» **ROW 69:** Ch 2, shell in ch-2 space of first shell, *shell in ch-2 space of next shell**, skip next dc of same shell, shell in last dc of same shell; repeat from * across, ending last repeat at **. *You now have 66 shells.*

» **ROWS 70–75:** Repeat Row 2 of main body. *You now have 66 shells.*

» **ROW 76:** Ch 1, 4 sc in ch-2 space of first shell, *slip st in each next 2 dc of same shell**, 4 sc in ch-2 space of next shell; repeat from * across, ending last repeat at **. Fasten off. Weave in ends.

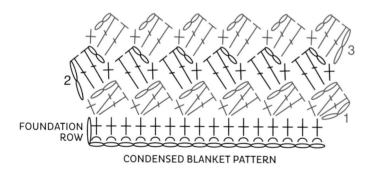

FOUNDATION ROW

CONDENSED BLANKET PATTERN

MAKING AMIGURUMI TOYS

On the following pages you'll find instructions for seven crocheted and stuffed toys. These are also known as *amigurumi*, from the Japanese words *ami* (crocheted or knitted) and *nuigurumi* (stuffed toy). If the projects are intended for babies, please take these safety precautions:

✳ Use carefully hidden knots when joining new yarns. Secure the knot and weave it to the inside of the toy.

✳ Stuff toys with fiberfill, not poly-pellets, which can come through the fabric and become a choking hazard.

✳ Use safety eyes when possible. If using regular buttons, be extra-sure that they are sewn so firmly that you couldn't pry them off if you wanted to.

Notes on Construction

✳ Start with a "ch 2, work in the 2nd ch from hook" or an adjustable ring (see page 271) when instructed to work in a ring, whichever you prefer.

✳ Do not turn at the end of each round unless directed to; work in rounds, moving a stitch marker at the end of each round.

✳ Firmly stuff as you work and overstuff slightly before finishing the part you're working on; this will allow the stuffing to fill out the shape after the crocheting is done.

Sweet Kitty

Designed by Deb Richey

Who would not love to see a kitty like this one sitting on the couch? She's completely child safe, and the best part is that she doesn't shed!

FINISHED MEASUREMENTS
Approximately 8"/20.5 cm tall

YARN
Red Heart Stripes, 100% acrylic, 170 yds (155 m)/3.5 oz (100 g), Color 0938 Sonoma Stripes

CROCHET HOOK
US G/6 (4 mm) *or size you need to obtain correct gauge*

GAUGE
17 and 19 rounds = 4"/10 cm in single crochet (*Note:* Exact gauge is not crucial for this project; however, the tighter you crochet, the less stuffing you'll see through the stitches.)

OTHER SUPPLIES
Locking stitch marker; two 12 mm cat safety eyes (optional); fiberfill for stuffing; yarn needle; embroidery floss or yarn for making eyes, nose, and mouth (optional); buttons for eyes (optional)

❄ **SEE MAKING AMIGURUMI TOYS ON PAGE 211.**

Crocheting the Head

» Starting at front of head, begin with your choice of ring.

» **RND 1:** Work 6 sc in ring. *You now have* 6 sts. Place marker on the first st of the round and move it up as you work the rounds.

» **RND 2:** 2 sc in each sc around. *You now have* 12 sts.

» **RND 3:** (Sc in next sc, 2 sc in next sc) around. *You now have* 18 sts.

» **RND 4:** (2 sc in next sc, sc in next 2 sc) around. *You now have* 24 sts.

» **RND 5:** Sc in each sc around.

» **RND 6:** (Sc in next 3 sc, 2 sc in next sc) around. *You now have* 30 sts.

» **RND 7:** Sc in each sc around.

» **RND 8:** (Sc in next 2 sc, 2 sc in next sc) six times, sc in next 12 sc. *You now have* 36 sts. **Note:** Increases will be at top of head.

» **RNDS 9–17:** Sc in each sc around. If using safety eyes, insert them between Rnds 7 and 8 with 6 sts between them. Begin to stuff with fiberfill, and continue stuffing as remaining rounds are worked.

» **RND 18:** Sc in next 2 sc, (sc2tog, sc in next 4 sc) five times, sc2tog, sc in next 2 sc. *You now have* 30 sts.

» **RND 19:** (Sc in next 3 sc, sc2tog) around. *You now have* 24 sts.

» **RND 20:** (Sc2tog, sc in next 2 sc) around. *You now have* 18 sts.

» **RND 21:** (Sc in next sc, sc2tog) around. *You now have* 12 sts.

» **RND 22:** Sc2tog around, join with slip st to next st. *You now have* 6 sts. Fasten off, leaving a long length for sewing. Sew hole closed.

Crocheting the Body

» Starting at bottom, begin with your choice of ring.

» **RND 1:** Work 6 sc in ring. *You now have* 6 sts. Place marker at the first st of the round and move it up as you work the rounds.

» **RND 2:** 2 sc in each sc around. *You now have* 12 sts.

» **RND 3:** (Sc in next sc, 2 sc in next sc) around. *You now have* 18 sts.

» **RND 4:** (2 sc in next sc, sc in next 2 sc) around. *You now have* 24 sts.

» **RND 5:** (Sc in next 3 sc, 2 sc in next sc) around. *You now have* 30 sts.

» **RND 6:** Sc in next 2 sc, (2 sc in next sc, sc in next 4 sc) five times, 2 sc in next sc, sc in next 2 sc. *You now have* 36 sts.

- » **RND 7:** (Sc in next 5 sc, 2 sc in next sc) around. *You now have* 42 sts.

- » **RNDS 8–15:** Sc in each sc around.

- » **RND 16:** (Sc2tog, sc in next 4 sc) three times, sc2tog, sc in next 22 sc. *You now have* 38 sts.

- » **RND 17:** Sc in each sc around.

- » **RND 18:** (Sc in next 2 sc, sc2tog) four times, sc in next 22 sc. *You now have* 34 sts.

- » **RND 19:** Sc in each sc around.

- » **RND 20:** Sc in next sc, (sc2tog, sc in next 2 sc) three times, sc2tog, sc in next 19 sc. *You now have* 30 sts.

- » **RND 21:** Sc in each sc around.

- » **RND 22:** (Sc in next sc, sc2tog) four times, sc in next 18 sc. *You now have* 26 sts.

- » **RND 23:** Sc in each sc around.

- » **RND 24:** (Sc in next 11 sc, sc2tog) twice. *You now have* 24 sts.

- » **RND 25:** Sc in each sc around.

- » **RND 26:** (Sc in next 10 sc, sc2tog) twice. *You now have* 22 sts.

- » **RND 27:** Sc in each sc around.

- » **RND 28:** Sc in next 11 sc. Join and fasten off, leaving remaining stitches unworked and a long length of yarn for sewing.

Crocheting the Front Legs *(make 2)*

- » Starting at bottom, begin with your choice of ring.

- » **RND 1:** Work 6 sc in ring. *You now have* 6 sts. Place marker at the first st of the round and move it up as you work the rounds.

- » **RND 2:** 2 sc in each sc around. *You now have* 12 sts.

- » **RND 3:** (Sc in next sc, 2 sc in next sc) around. *You now have* 18 sts.

- » **RNDS 4–6:** Sc in each sc around.

- » **RND 7:** Sc in next 5 sc, (sc2tog) four times, sc in next 5 sc. *You now have* 14 sts. **Note:** Decreases will be at front of leg.

- » **RND 8:** Sc in each sc around.

- » **RND 9:** Sc in next 3 sc, sc2tog, sc in next 4 sc, sc2tog, sc in next 3 sc. *You now have* 12 sts.

- » **RNDS 10 AND 11:** Sc in each sc around. Begin to stuff the leg and continue as remaining rounds are worked.

- » **RND 12:** (Sc in next 4 sc, sc2tog) twice. *You now have* 10 sts.

- » **RNDS 13–18:** Sc in each sc around.

- » **RND 19:** Sc2tog around, join with slip st to next st. *You now have* 5 sts. Fasten off, leaving a long length for sewing. Sew hole closed.

Crocheting the Back Legs *(make 2)*

- » Starting at bottom, begin with your choice of ring.

213

» **RND 1:** Work 6 sc in ring. *You now have* 6 sts. Place marker at the first st of the round and move it up as you work the rounds.

» **RND 2:** 2 sc in each sc around. *You now have* 12 sts.

» **RND 3:** (Sc in next sc, 2 sc in next sc) around. *You now have* 18 sts.

» **RNDS 4–6:** Sc in each sc around.

» **RND 7:** Sc in next 5 sc, (sc2tog) four times, sc in next 5 sc. *You now have* 14 sts. **Note:** Decreases will be at front of leg.

» **RND 8:** Sc in next 3 sc, sc2tog, sc in next 4 sc, sc2tog, sc in next 3 sc. *You now have* 12 sts.

» **RND 9:** Sc in each sc around, join with slip st to next st. Fasten off, leaving a long length for sewing. Sew hole closed.

Crocheting the Tail

» Starting at end, begin with your choice of ring.

» **RND 1:** Work 6 sc in ring. *You now have* 6 sts. Place marker at the first st of the round and move up as you work the rounds.

» **RND 2:** (2 sc in next 2 sc, sc in next sc) twice. *You now have* 10 sts.

» **RND 3:** (Sc in next 4 sc, 2 sc in next sc) twice. *You now have* 12 sts.

» **RNDS 4–6:** Sc in each sc around. Begin to stuff the tail and continue as you work the remaining rounds.

» **RNDS 7–24:** Hdc in next 6 sc, sc in next 6 sc.

» **RNDS 25–29:** Sc in each st around.

» **RND 30:** Sc2tog around, join with slip st to next st. *You now have* 6 sts. Fasten off, leaving a long length for sewing. Sew hole closed.

Crocheting the Ears (make 2)

» Starting at top, begin with your choice of ring.

» **RND 1:** Work 6 sc in ring. *You now have* 6 sts. Place marker at the first st of the round and move it up as you work the rounds.

» **RND 2:** (Sc in next 2 sc, 2 sc in next sc) twice. *You now have* 8 sts.

» **RND 3:** (Sc in next 3 sc, 2 sc in next sc) twice. *You now have* 10 sts.

» **RND 4:** (Sc in next 4 sc, 2 sc in next sc) twice. *You now have* 12 sts.

» **RND 5:** (Sc in next 5 sc, 2 sc in next sc) twice. *You now have* 14 sts.

» **RND 6:** (Sc in next 6 sc, 2 sc in next sc) twice, join with slip st to next st. *You now have* 16 sts. Fasten off, leaving a long length for sewing.

Finishing

» Stuff the body. Sew the head to the body. The body will slope outward to the back. If you did not use safety eyes, embroider or sew buttons on for eyes now. Embroider a mouth and nose if desired. Flatten the ears so that the 2-sc increases are on the sides, then sew them to the top of the head over Rnds 13–15.

» Sew the legs to the front of the body so that the bottoms of the feet are even with the bottom of the body. Stuff, then sew the back legs to the sides of the body so that the bottom of the legs will be even with the bottom of the body.

» Sew the tail on the back of the body so that it curves around to the front of the body. Weave in ends.

Sam the Big-Bottomed Bunny

Designed by Laura Biondi

This bunny works up in a few short hours, so it's perfect for last-minute gift giving! The adjustable ring method of starting makes the beginning hole very small.

FINISHED MEASUREMENTS
6"/15 cm tall

YARN
Caron Naturally Caron Country, 75% microdenier acrylic/25% merino wool, 185 yds (170 m)/3 oz (85 g), Color 0005 Ocean Spray

CROCHET HOOK
US H/8 (5 mm) *or size you need to obtain correct gauge*

GAUGE
18 stitches and 20 rounds = 4"/10 cm in single crochet

OTHER SUPPLIES
Stitch markers, fiberfill for stuffing, yarn needle, two 6 mm black safety eyes (optional), small amount of black embroidery floss (optional), embroidery needle (optional), 18"/45.5 cm of ½" (13 mm) ribbon for bow (optional)

※ **SEE MAKING AMIGURUMI TOYS ON PAGE 211.**

Crocheting the Body

Note: See page 211, Notes for Making Amigurumi.

» Begin with your choice of ring.

» **RND 1:** Work 6 sc in ring. *You now have* 6 sts. Place marker at the first st of the round and move it up as you work the rounds.

» **RND 2:** 2 sc in each sc around. *You now have* 12 sts.

» **RND 3:** (Sc in next sc, 2 sc in next sc) around. *You now have* 18 sts.

» **RND 4:** (Sc in next 2 sts, 2 sc in next st) around. *You now have* 24 sts.

» **RND 5:** (Sc in next 3 sts, 2 sc in next st) around. *You now have* 30 sts.

» **RND 6:** (Sc in next 4 sc, 2 sc in next sc) around. *You now have* 36 sc.

» **RND 7:** (Sc in next 5 sc, 2 sc in next sc) around. *You now have* 42 sc.

» **RNDS 8–10:** Sc in each sc around.

» **RND 11:** (Sc in next 5 sc, sc2tog) around. *You now have* 36 sc.

» **RNDS 12 AND 13:** Sc in each sc around.

» **RND 14:** (Sc in next 4 sc, sc2tog) around. *You now have* 30 sc.

» **RNDS 15 AND 16:** Sc in each sc around.

» **RND 17:** (Sc in next 3 sc, sc2tog) around. *You now have* 24 sc.

» **RNDS 18 AND 19:** Sc in each sc around.

» Stuff body lightly.

» **RND 20:** (Sc in next 2 sc, sc2tog) around. *You now have* 18 sc.

» **RND 21:** Sc2tog around. *You now have* 9 sts.

» Fasten off.

Crocheting the Head

» Begin with your choice of ring.

» **RND 1:** Work 6 sc in ring. *You now have* 6 sts. Place marker at the first st of the round and move it up as you work the rounds.

» **RND 2:** 2 sc in each sc around. *You now have* 12 sts.

» **RND 3:** (Sc in next sc, 2 sc in next sc) around. *You now have* 18 sts.

» **RND 4:** (Sc in next 2 sc, 2 sc in next sc) around. *You now have* 24 sts.

» **RND 5:** (Sc in next 3 sc, 2 sc in next sc) around. *You now have* 30 sts.

» **RND 6:** (Sc in next 4 sc, 2 sc in next sc) around. *You now have* 36 sc.

» **RNDS 7–11:** Sc in each sc around.

» **RND 12:** (Sc in next 4 sc, sc2tog) around. *You now have* 30 sc.

» **RND 13:** (Sc in next 3 sc, sc2tog) around. *You now have* 24 sc.

» Stuff head lightly.

» **RND 14:** *(Sc in next 2 sc, sc2tog) around. *You now have* 18 sc.

» **RND 15:** Sc2tog around. *You now have* 9 sc.

» Fasten off, leaving a long tail to sew the head to the body.

Crocheting the Arms
(make 2)

» Begin with your choice of ring.

» **RND 1:** Work 6 sc in ring. *You now have* 6 sts. Place marker at the first st of the round and move it up as you work the rounds.

» **RND 2:** 2 sc in each sc around. *You now have* 12 sts.

» **RND 3–13:** Sc in each sc around.

» Fasten off, leaving a long tail to sew the arm to the body.

» Make two small balls of stuffing and push these firmly into the bunny's arms to form hands. The rest of the arms are not stuffed.

Crocheting the Ears
(make 2)

» Begin with your choice of ring.

» **RND 1:** Work 6 sc in ring. *You now have* 6 sts. Place marker at the first st of the round and move it up as you work the rounds.

» **RND 2:** 2 sc in each sc around. *You now have* 12 sts.

» **RND 3–15:** Sc in each sc around.

» **RND 16:** (Sc in next 2 sc, sc2tog in next 2 sts) around. *You now have* 9 sts.

» **RND 17:** Sc in each sc around.

» Fasten off, leaving a long tail to sew the ear to the head.

Crocheting the Tail

» Begin with your choice of ring.

» **RND 1:** Work 6 sc in ring. *You now have* 6 sts. Place marker at the first st of the round and move it up as you work the rounds.

» **RND 2:** 2 sc in each sc around. *You now have* 12 sts.

» **RND 3–5:** Sc in each sc around.

» **RND 6:** Sc2tog around. *You now have* 6 sts.

» Fasten off, leaving a long tail to sew the tail to the body.

Assembling the Bunny

» Decide which is the front and back of your bunny's head and body (you can use stitch markers to help you remember). Thread the yarn tail from the head onto a yarn needle and sew the head to the body, matching up the two openings. Add more stuffing to the body as you go so it can support the head. Flatten tops of arms and sew the arms right up against the neck. Flatten tops of ears and sew the ears about 2 rows down from the top of the head. Sew the tail in back; if positioned correctly it can help your bunny stand. Use buttons or embroidery floss for the features, tie on the bow, and your bunny is finished!

Niles the Crocodile

Designed by Deb Richey

How could something so cute represent a large and devious reptile that lies in wait to ambush its prey? This crocheted version is adorable and harmless.

FINISHED MEASUREMENTS

Approximately 14"/35.5 cm long

YARN

Berroco Comfort, 50% nylon/50% acrylic, 210 yds (192 m)/3.5 oz (100 g), Color 9740 Seedling

CROCHET HOOK

US G/6 (4 mm) *or size you need to obtain correct gauge*

GAUGE

20 stitches and 22 rounds = 4"/10 cm in single crochet (*Note:* Exact gauge is not crucial for this project; however, the tighter you crochet, the less stuffing you'll see through the stitches.)

OTHER SUPPLIES

Stitch markers, fiberfill for stuffing, yarn needle, two 18 mm black safety eyes

❋ **SEE MAKING AMIGURUMI TOYS ON PAGE 211.**

Crocheting the Head

» Starting at front of head, ch 4.

» **RND 1:** 3 sc in 2nd ch from hook, sc in next ch, 3 sc in last ch; working on opposite side of foundation ch, sc in next ch. *You now have 8 sc.* Place marker at the first st of the round and move it up as you work the rounds.

» **RND 2:** (2 sc in next 3 sc, sc in next sc) twice. *You now have 14 sts.*

» **RND 3:** *(Sc in next sc, 2 sc in next sc) three times, sc in next sc; repeat from * once more. *You now have 20 sts.*

» **RND 4:** *(2 sc in next sc, sc in next 2 sc) three times, sc in next sc; repeat from * once more. *You now have 26 sts.*

» **RNDS 5–8:** Sc in each sc around.

» **RND 9:** Sc in next sc, (sc2tog, sc in next 3 sc) around. *You now have 21 sts.*

» **RNDS 10–14:** Sc in each sc around. Begin stuffing the head and continue as you work the remaining rounds.

» **RND 15:** Sc in next 6, (2 sc in next sc, sc in next sc) four times, 2 sc in next sc, sc in next 6 sc. *You now have 26 sts.*

» **RND 16:** Sc in each sc around.

» **RND 17:** Sc in next 7 sc, (2 sc in next sc, sc in next 2 sc) four times, 2 sc in next sc, sc in next 6 sc. *You now have 31 sts.*

» **RND 18:** Sc in each sc around.

» **RND 19:** Sc in next 7 sc, 2 sc in next sc, sc in next 2 sc, 2 sc in next sc, sc in next 12 sc, 2 sc in next sc, sc in next 2 sc, 2 sc in next sc, sc in next 4 sc. *You now have* 35 sts.

» **RNDS 20–25:** Sc in each sc around.

» **RND 26:** Sc in next 2 sc, (sc2tog, sc in next 5 sc) four times, sc2tog, sc in next 3 sc. *You now have* 30 sts.

» **RND 27:** (Sc in next 3 sc, sc2tog) around. *You now have* 24 sts.

» **RND 28:** (Sc2tog, sc in next 2 sc) around. *You now have* 18 sts.

» **RND 29:** (Sc in next sc, sc2tog) around. *You now have* 12 sts.

» **RND 30:** Sc2tog around, join with slip st in next st. *You now have* 6 sts. Fasten off, leaving a long length for sewing. Sew hole closed.

Crocheting the Body

» Starting at tail, begin with your choice of ring.

» **RND 1:** Work 5 sc in ring. *You now have* 5 sts. Place marker at the first st of the round and move it up as you work the rounds.

» **RND 2:** Sc in next sc, hdc in next 3 sc, sc in next sc.

» **RND 3:** Sc in next 2 sts, 2 hdc in next st, sc in next 2 sts. *You now have* 6 sts.

» **RND 4:** Sc in next 2 sc, 2 hdc in next 2 hdc, sc in next 2 sc. *You now have* 8 sts.

219

» **RND 8:** Sc in next 4 sts, hdc in next 4 sts, sc in next 4 sts.

» **RND 9:** Sc in next 4 sts, hdc in next st, 2 hdc in next 2 sts, hdc in next st, sc in next 4 sts. *You now have* 14 sts.

» **RND 10:** Sc in next 5 sts, hdc in next 4 sts, sc in next 5 sts.

» **RND 11:** Sc in next 5 sts, hdc in next st, 2 hdc in next 2 sts, hdc in next st, sc in next 5 sts. *You now have* 16 sts.

» **RND 12:** Sc in next 5 sts, hdc in next 6 sts, sc in next 5 sts.

» **RND 13:** Sc in next 6 sts, hdc in next st, 2 hdc in next 2 sts, hdc in next st, sc in next 6 sts. *You now have* 18 sts.

» **RND 14:** Sc in next 6 sts, hdc in next 6 sts, sc in next 6 sts.

» **RND 15:** Sc in next 6 sts, hdc in next 2 sts, 2 hdc in next 2 sts, hdc in next 2 sts, sc in next 6 sts. *You now have* 20 sts.

» **RND 16:** Sc in next 6 sts, hdc in next 8 sc, sc in next 6 sc.

» **RND 17:** Sc in next 6 sts, hdc in next 3 sts, 2 hdc in next 2 sts, hdc in next 3 sts, sc in next 6 sts. *You now have* 22 sts.

» **RND 18:** Sc in next 7 sts, hdc in next 8 sts, sc in next 7 sts.

» **RNDS 19–22:** Sc in each st around.

» **RND 23:** Sc in next 5 sts, 2 sc in next st, sc in next 10 sts, 2 sc in next st, sc in next 5 sts. *You now have* 24 sts.

» **RNDS 24–27:** Sc in each st around.

» **RND 5:** Sc in next 3 sts, 2 hdc in next 2 sts, sc in next 3 sts. *You now have* 10 sts.

» **RND 6:** Sc in next 3 sts, hdc in next 4 sts, sc in next 3 sts. *You now have* 10 sts.

» **RND 7:** Sc in next 3 sts, hdc in next st, 2 hdc in next 2 sts, hdc in next st, sc in next 3 sts. *You now have* 12 sts. Begin and continue to stuff the body.

» **RND 28:** Sc in next 6 sts, 2 sc in next st, sc in next 10 sts, 2 sc in next st, sc in next 6 sts. *You now have* 26 sts.

» **RNDS 29–32:** Sc in each st around.

» **RND 33:** Sc in next 5 sts, 2 sc in next st, sc in next 2 sc, 2 sc in next st, sc in next 8 sts, 2 sc in next st, sc in next 2 sts, 2 sc in next st, sc in next 5 sts. *You now have* 30 sts.

» **RND 34:** Sc in each st around.

» **RND 35:** Sc in next 6 sts, 2 sc in next st, sc in next 2 sts, 2 sc in next st, sc in next 10 sts, 2 sc in next st, sc in next 2 sts, 2 sc in next st, sc in next 6 sts. *You now have* 34 sts.

» **RND 36:** Sc in each st around.

» **RND 37:** Sc in next 12 sc, 2 sc in next st, sc in next 17 sts, 2 sc in next st, sc in next 3 sts. *You now have* 36 sts.

» **RND 38:** Sc in each st around.

» **RND 39:** Sc in next 11 sts, 2 sc in next st, sc in next 2 sts, 2 sc in next st, sc in next 15 sts, (2 sc in next st, sc in next 2 sts) twice. *You now have* 40 sts.

» **RNDS 40–47:** Sc in each st around.

» **RND 48:** Sc in next 12 sts, sc2tog, sc in next 2 sts, sc2tog, sc in next 14 sts, (sc2tog, sc in next 2 sts) twice. *You now have* 36 sts.

» **RND 49:** Sc in each st around.

» **RND 50:** Sc in next 8 sts, sc2tog, sc in next 2 sts, sc2tog, sc in next 13 sts, sc2tog, sc in next 2 sts, sc2tog, sc in next 3 sts. *You now have* 32 sts.

» **RND 51:** Sc in each st around.

» **RND 52:** Sc in next 9 sts, sc2tog, sc in next 2 sts, sc2tog, sc in next 10 sts, sc2tog, sc in next 2 sts, sc2tog, sc in next st. *You now have* 28 sts.

» **RND 53:** Sc in each st around.

» **RND 54:** (Sc in next 8 sts, sc2tog, sc in next 2 sts, sc2tog) twice. *You now have* 24 sts.

» **RND 55:** Sc in each st around.

» **RND 56:** (Sc in next 4 sts, sc2tog) around. *You now have* 20 sts.

» **RNDS 57–59:** Sc in each st around. At the end of Rnd 59, join with slip st in next st. Fasten off, leaving a length for sewing.

Crocheting the Legs
(make 4)

» Begin with your choice of ring.

» **RND 1:** Work 6 sc in ring. *You now have* 6 sts.

» **RND 2:** 2 sc in each sc around. *You now have* 12 sts.

» **RND 3:** (Sc in next sc, 2 sc in next sc) around. *You now have* 18 sts.

» **RND 4:** (2 sc in next sc, sc in next 2 sc) around. *You now have* 24 sts.

» **RND 5:** Working in back loops only, sc in each sc around.

» **RNDS 6 AND 7:** Sc in each sc around.

» **RND 8:** Sc in next 8 sc, (sc2tog) four times, sc in next 8 sc. *You now have* 20 sts.

» **RND 9:** Sc in each sc around.

» **RND 10:** Sc in next 6 sc, (sc2tog) four times, sc in next 6 sc. *You now have* 16 sts.

» **RNDS 11–14:** Sc in each sc around. At the end of Rnd 14, join with slip st in next st. Fasten off, leaving a length for sewing.

continued on next page

Crocheting the Back Ridges *(make 5)*

» (Ch 3, slip in 2nd ch from hook) 20 times, ch 1. Fasten off, leaving a long length for sewing.

Crocheting the Eyes *(make 2)*

» Begin with your choice of ring.

» **RND 1:** Work 6 sc in ring. *You now have* 6 sts.

» **RND 2:** 2 sc in each sc around. *You now have* 12 sts.

» **RND 3:** (Sc in next 2 sts, 2 sc in next sc) around. *You now have* 16 sts.

» **RNDS 4 AND 5:** Sc in each sc around. At the end of Rnd 5, join with slip st to next st. Fasten off, leaving a length for sewing.

Crocheting the Nostrils *(make 2)*

» Ch 4, sc in 2nd ch from hook, sc in next ch, (sc, slip st) in last ch. Fasten off, leaving a length for sewing.

Finishing

» Stuff and then sew the legs to the bottom of the crocodile. The curved tail will be facing upward. Sew the head to the end of the body. Insert the safety eyes between Rounds 2 and 3 of the eyes. Stuff and then sew the eyes to the top of the head over Rounds 21 through 26. Sew the nostrils to the end of the nose.

» Center a back ridge down the length of the back from the neck almost to the tip of the tail. Sew in place. Sew two more ridges on each side of the center ridge with about ¾"–1"/2–2.5 cm between ridges.

Lucky Dog
Designed by Deb Richey

Lucky is the child who receives this dog as a gift! Like the others in this series, the toy is irresistibly cute and completely child-safe.

FINISHED MEASUREMENTS
Approximately 7"/18 cm tall

YARN
Red Heart Stripes, 100% acrylic, 170 yds (155 m)/3.5 oz (100 g), Color 0936 Latte Stripe

CROCHET HOOK
US G/6 (4 mm) *or size you need to obtain correct gauge*

GAUGE
18 single crochet and 20 rounds = 4"/10 cm (*Note:* Exact gauge is not crucial for this project; however, the tighter you crochet, the less stuffing you'll see through the stitches.)

OTHER SUPPLIES
Stitch markers; fiberfill for stuffing; two 12 mm black safety eyes or buttons; yarn needle

❋ **SEE MAKING AMIGURUMI TOYS ON PAGE 211.**

Crocheting the Head

» Starting at front of head, begin with your choice of ring.

» **RND 1:** Work 6 sc in ring. *You now have* 6 sts. Place marker at the first st of the round and move it up as you work the rounds.

» **RND 2:** 2 sc in each sc around. *You now have* 12 sts.

» **RND 3:** (Sc in next sc, 2 sc in next sc) around. *You now have* 18 sts.

» **RND 4:** (2 sc in next sc, sc in next 2 sc) around. *You now have* 24 sts.

» **RNDS 5–8:** Sc in each sc around.

» **RND 9:** (Sc in next 4 sc, sc2tog) around. *You now have* 20 sts.

» **RND 10:** (Sc in next sc, 2 sc in next sc) around. *You now have* 30 sts.

» **RND 11:** (Sc in next 2 sts, 2 sc in next sc) five times, sc in next 15 sc. *You now have* 35 sts.

» **RNDS 12–21:** Sc in each st around. If using safety eyes, insert them in Rnd 11 in the 2nd and 4th 2-sc clusters.

» **RND 22:** (Sc2tog, sc in next 5 sc) around. *You now have* 30 sts. Begin and continue to stuff the head.

» **RND 23:** (Sc in next 3 sc, sc2tog) around. *You now have* 24 sts.

» **RND 24:** (Sc2tog, sc in next 2 sc) around. *You now have* 18 sts.

» **RND 25:** (Sc in next sc, sc2tog) around. *You now have* 12 sts.

» **RND 26:** Sc2tog around, join with slip st to next st. *You now have* 6 sts. Fasten off, leaving a long length for sewing. Sew hole closed.

223

Crocheting the Body

» Starting at the bottom, begin with your choice of ring.

» **RND 1:** Work 6 sc in ring. *You now have* 6 sts. Place marker at the first st of the round and move it up as you work the rounds.

» **RND 2:** 2 sc in each sc around. *You now have* 12 sts.

» **RND 3:** (Sc in next sc, 2 sc in next sc) around. *You now have* 18 sts.

» **RND 4:** (2 sc in next sc, sc in next 2 sc) around. *You now have* 24 sts.

» **RND 5:** (Sc in next 3 sc, 2 sc in next sc) around. *You now have* 30 sts.

» **RND 6:** Sc in next 2 sc, (2 sc in next sc, sc in next 4 sc) five times, 2 sc in next sc, sc in next 2 sts. *You now have* 36 sts.

» **RND 7:** (Sc in next 5 sc, 2 sc in next sc) around. *You now have* 42 sts.

» **RNDS 8–15:** Sc in each sc around.

» **RND 16:** (Sc2tog, sc in next 4 sc) three times, sc2tog, sc in next 22 sc. *You now have* 38 sts.

» **RND 17:** Sc in each sc around.

» **RND 18:** (Sc in next 2 sc, sc2tog) four times, sc in next 22 sts. *You now have* 34 sts.

» **RND 19:** Sc in each sc around.

» **RND 20:** Sc in next sc, (sc2tog, sc in next 2 sc) three times, sc2tog, sc in next 19 sc. *You now have* 30 sts.

» **RND 21:** Sc in each sc around.

» **RND 22:** (Sc in next st, sc2tog) four times, sc in next 18 sts. *You now have* 26 sts.

» **RND 23:** Sc in each sc around.

» **RND 24:** (Sc in next 11 sts, sc2tog) twice. *You now have* 24 sts.

» **RND 25:** Sc in each sc around.

» **RND 26:** (Sc in next 10 sts, sc2tog) twice. *You now have* 22 sts.

» **RND 27:** Sc in each sc around.

» **RND 28:** Sc in next 11 sts, join with slip st in next st. Fasten off, leaving remaining sts unworked and a long length of yarn for sewing.

Crocheting the Ears
(make 2)

» Begin with your choice of ring.

» **RND 1:** Work 6 sc in ring. *You now have* 6 sts. Place marker at the first st of the round and move it up as you work the rounds.

» **RND 2:** 2 sc in each sc around. *You now have* 12 sts.

» **RND 3:** (Sc in next sc, 2 sc in next sc) around. *You now have* 18 sts.

» **RND 4:** (2 sc in next sc, sc in next 2 sts) around. *You now have* 24 sts.

» **RNDS 5–8:** Sc in each sc around.

» **RND 9:** (Sc in next 10 sc, sc2tog) twice. *You now have* 22 sts.

» **RND 10:** Sc in each sc around.

» **RND 11:** (Sc in next 9 sc, sc2tog) twice. *You now have* 20 sts.

» **RND 12:** Sc in each sc around.

» **RND 13:** (Sc in next 8 sc, sc2tog) twice. *You now have* 18 sts.

» **RND 14:** Sc in each sc around.

» **RND 15:** (Sc in next 7 sc, sc2tog) twice. *You now have* 16 sts.

» **RND 16:** Sc in each sc around.

» **RND 17:** (Sc in next 6 sc, sc2tog) twice. *You now have* 14 sts.

» **RNDS 18–21:** Sc in each sc around.

» **RND 22:** Sc in next 6 sc, join with slip st to next st. Fasten off, leaving remaining sts unworked and a length of yarn for sewing.

Crocheting the Front Legs
(make 2)

» Begin with your choice of ring.

» **RND 1:** Work 6 sc in ring. *You now have* 6 sts. Place marker at the first st of the round and move it up as you work the rounds.

» **RND 2:** 2 sc in each sc around. *You now have* 12 sts.

» **RND 3:** (Sc in next sc, 2 sc in next sc) around. *You now have* 18 sts.

» **RNDS 4–6:** Sc in each sc around.

» **RND 7:** Sc in next 5 sc, (sc2tog) four times, sc in next 5 sc. *You now have* 14 sts.

» **RND 8:** Sc in each sc around.

» **RND 9:** Sc in next 3 sc, sc2tog, sc in next 4 sc, sc2tog, sc in next 3 sc. *You now have* 12 sts.

» **RNDS 10 AND 11:** Sc in each sc around. Begin and continue to stuff the front leg.

» **RND 12:** (Sc in next 4 sc, sc2tog) twice. *You now have* 10 sts.

» **RNDS 13–18:** Sc in each sc around.

» **RND 19:** Sc2tog around, join with slip st to next st. *You now have* 5 sts. Fasten off, leaving a long length of yarn for sewing. Sew hole closed.

Crocheting the Back Legs
(make 2)

» Begin with your choice of ring.

» **RND 1:** Work 6 sc in ring. *You now have* 6 sts. Place marker at the first st of the round and move it up as you work the rounds.

» **RND 2:** 2 sc in each sc around. *You now have* 12 sts.

» **RND 3:** (Sc in next sc, 2 sc in next sc) around. *You now have* 18 sts.

» **RNDS 4–6:** Sc in each sc around.

» **RND 7:** Sc in next 5 sc, (sc2tog) four times, sc in next 5 sc. *You now have* 14 sts.

» **RND 8:** Sc in next 3 sc, sc2tog, sc in next 4 sc, sc2tog, sc in next 3 sc. *You now have* 12 sts.

» **RND 9:** Sc in each sc around, join with slip st to next st. Fasten off, leaving a long length of yarn for sewing.

Crocheting the Tail

» Begin with your choice of ring.

» **RND 1:** Work 5 sc in ring. *You now have* 5 sts.

» **RND 2:** Sc in next 2 sc, 2 sc in next sc, sc in next 2 sts. *You now have* 6 sts.

» **RND 3:** (Sc in next 2 sc, 2 sc in next sc) twice. *You now have* 8 sts.

» **RND 4:** Sc in next 4 sc, hdc in next sc, 2 hdc in next 2 sc, hdc in next sc. *You now have* 10 sts.

» **RNDS 5 AND 6:** Sc in next 5 sts, hdc in next 5 sts. *You now have* 10 sts.

» **RND 7:** Sc in next 5 sts, hdc in next st, 2 hdc in next 2 sts, hdc in next st, sc in next st. *You now have* 12 sts.

continued on next page

» **RNDS 8 AND 9:** Sc in next 5 sts, hdc in next 6 sts, sc in next st.

» **RND 10:** Sc in next 6 sts, hdc in next st, 2 hdc in next 2 sts, hdc in next st, sc in next 2 sts. *You now have* 14 sts.

» **RNDS 11 AND 12:** Sc in next 6 sts, hdc in next 6 sts, sc in next 2 sts.

» **RND 13:** (Sc in next 2 sts, 2 sc in next st) twice, 2 sc in next 3 sts, sc in next 2 sts, 2 sc in next st, sc in next 2 sts. *You now have* 20 sts. Join with slip st to next st. Fasten off, leaving a long length of yarn for sewing.

Finishing

» Stuff the body. Sew the head to the body. The body will slope outward to the back. If you didn't use safety eyes, embroider or sew buttons on for eyes. Embroider a mouth and nose if desired. Flatten the ears and with the 6 sts from Rnd 22 across the top, sew the ears to the sides of the head.

» Sew the front legs to the front of the body, placing legs so that the bottoms of the feet are even with the bottom of the body. Stuff and then sew the back legs to the front sides of the body so that the bottoms of the legs are even with the bottom of the body. Sew the tail on the back of the body so that it points upward and the bottom of the tail is even with the bottom of the body.

Bernie the Bunny

Designed by Deb Richey

Bernie the Bunny is quick and easy to crochet, and his floppy ears will undoubtedly become handles by which to carry him everywhere your child goes.

FINISHED MEASUREMENTS
Approximately 11"/28 cm long

YARN
Universal Cotton Supreme Batik, 100% cotton, 180 yds (165 m)/3.5 oz (100 g), Color 26 Summer Camp

CROCHET HOOK
US G/6 (4 mm) *or size you need to obtain correct gauge*

GAUGE
18 stitches and 20 rounds = 4"/10 cm in single crochet (*Note:* Exact gauge is not crucial for this project; however, the tighter you crochet, the less stuffing you'll see through the stitches.)

OTHER SUPPLIES
Stitch markers, fiberfill for stuffing, two 12 mm black buttons or safety eyes (optional), yarn needle, row counter (optional)

❋ **SEE MAKING AMIGURUMI TOYS ON PAGE 211.**

Crocheting the Head

Note: The head looks best when started with a light-colored section of the yarn. If your yarn begins with a darker color, make the nose or another body part before beginning the head.

» Starting at front of head, begin with your choice of ring.

» **RND 1:** Work 6 sc in ring. *You now have* 6 sts. Place marker at the first st of the round and move it up as you work the rounds.

» **RND 2:** 2 sc in each sc around. *You now have* 12 sts.

» **RND 3:** (Sc in next sc, 2 sc in next sc) around. *You now have* 18 sts.

» **RND 4:** (2 sc in next sc, sc in next 2 sc) around. *You now have* 24 sts.

» **RND 5:** Sc in each sc around.

» **RND 6:** (Sc in next 3 sc, 2 sc in next sc) around. *You now have* 30 sts.

» **RND 7:** (Sc in next 3 sc, 2 sc in next sc) five times, sc in next 10 sc. *You now have* 35 sts.

» **RNDS 8–16:** Sc in each sc around. Begin and continue to stuff the head as you work. Insert the eyes between Rnds 8 and 9 with 6 sts between them. The top of the head is the area of Rnd 7 that has the increases. Be sure to insert the eyes

above either side of the center 2-sc increase of that round.

» **RND 17:** (Sc in next 5 sc, sc2tog) around. *You now have* 30 sts.

» **RND 18:** Sc in next 2 sc, (sc2tog, sc in next 4 sc) four times, sc2tog, sc in next 2 sc. *You now have* 25 sts.

» **RND 19:** (Sc in next 3 sc, sc2tog) around. *You now have 20 sts.*

» **RND 20:** (Sc2tog, sc in next 2 sc) around. *You now have 15 sts.*

» **RND 21:** (Sc in next sc, sc2tog) around. *You now have 10 sts.*

» **RND 22:** Sc2tog around. Fasten off, leaving a length of yarn for sewing. Sew the hole closed.

Crocheting the Nose

» Use a section of color that contrasts with Rnds 1–10 of the head. Before starting the different body parts, check the color. If it contrasts with the head, make the nose.

» Begin with your choice of ring.

» **RND 1:** Work 6 sc in ring. *You now have 6 sts.*

» **RND 2:** [(Sc, ch 1, sc) in next sc, sc in next sc] around. Join and fasten off, leaving a length of yarn for sewing.

Crocheting the Body

» Starting at bottom, begin with your choice of ring.

» **RND 1:** Work 6 sc in ring. *You now have 6 sts.*

» **RND 2:** 2 sc in each sc around. *You now have 12 sts.*

» **RND 3:** (Sc in next sc, 2 sc in next sc) around. *You now have 18 sts.*

» **RND 4:** (2 sc in next sc, sc in next 2 sc) around. *You now have 24 sts.*

» **RND 5:** (Sc in next 3 sc, 2 sc in next sc) around. *You now have 30 sts.*

» **RND 6:** (Sc in next 9 sc, 2 sc in next sc) around. *You now have 33 sts.*

» **RNDS 7–12:** Sc in each sc around.

» **RND 13:** (Sc in next 9 sc, sc2tog) around. *You now have 30 sts.*

» **RND 14:** Sc in each sc around.

» **RND 15:** (Sc in next 3 sc, sc2tog) around. *You now have 24 sts.*

» **RNDS 16 AND 17:** Sc in each sc around.

» **RND 18:** (Sc in next 6 sc, sc2tog) around. *You now have 21 sts.*

» **RNDS 19–22:** Sc in each sc around. At the end of Rnd 22, join with slip st in next st. Fasten off, leaving a long length of yarn for sewing.

Crocheting the Ears
(make 2)

» Begin with your choice of ring.

» **RND 1:** Work 6 sc in ring. *You now have 6 sts.*

» **RND 2:** (2 sc in next 2 sc, sc in next sc) twice. *You now have 10 sts.*

» **RND 3:** (Sc in next 4 sc, 2 sc in next sc) twice. *You now have 12 sts.*

» **RND 4:** (Sc in next 5 sc, 2 sc in next sc) twice. *You now have 14 sts.*

» **RND 5:** (Sc in next 6 sc, 2 sc in next sc) twice. *You now have 16 sts.*

» **RND 6:** (Sc in next 7 sc, 2 sc in next sc) twice. *You now have 18 sts.*

» **RND 7:** (Sc in next 8 sc, 2 sc in next sc) twice. *You now have 20 sts.*

» **RND 8:** (Sc in next 9 sc, 2 sc in next sc) twice. *You now have 22 sts.*

» **RND 9:** (Sc in next 10 sc, 2 sc in next sc) twice. *You now have 24 sts.*

- » **RNDS 10–19:** Sc in each sc around.
- » **RND 20:** (Sc in next 10 sc, sc2tog) twice. *You now have* 22 sts.
- » **RND 21:** (Sc in next 9 sc, sc2tog) twice. *You now have* 20 sts.
- » **RND 22:** Sc in each sc around.
- » **RND 23:** (Sc in next 8 sc, sc2tog) twice. *You now have* 18 sts.
- » **RND 24:** (Sc in next 7 sc, sc2tog) twice. *You now have* 16 sts.
- » **RND 25:** Sc in each sc around.
- » **RND 26:** (Sc in next 6 sc, sc2tog) twice. *You now have* 14 sts.
- » **RND 27:** (Sc in next 5 sc, sc2tog) twice. *You now have* 12 sts.
- » **RNDS 28–30:** Sc in each sc around. At the end of Rnd 30, join with slip st in next st. Fasten off, leaving a long length of yarn for sewing. Do not stuff the ears.

Crocheting the Arms
(make 2)

- » Begin with your choice of ring.
- » **RND 1:** Work 6 sc in ring. *You now have* 6 sts.
- » **RND 2:** (2 sc in next 2 sc, sc in next sc) twice. *You now have* 10 sts.
- » **RND 3:** (Sc in next 4 sc, 2 sc in next sc) twice. *You now have* 12 sts.
- » **RND 4:** (Sc in next 3 sc, 2 sc in next sc) around. *You now have* 15 sts.
- » **RNDS 5 AND 6:** Sc in each sc around.

- » **RND 7:** (Sc in next 3 sc, sc2tog) around. *You now have* 12 sts.
- » **RND 8:** (Sc in next 4 sc, sc2tog) twice. *You now have* 10 sts.
- » **RND 9:** (Sc in next 3 sc, sc2tog) twice. *You now have* 8 sts. Stuff Rnds 1–9 only.
- » **RNDS 10–21:** Sc in each sc around.

continued on next page

» **RND 22:** (Sc2tog, sc in next 2 sc) twice, join with slip st in next st. Fasten off, leaving a long length of yarn for sewing.

Crocheting the Legs *(make 2)*

» Begin with your choice of ring.

» **RND 1:** Work 6 sc in ring. *You now have 6 sts.*

» **RND 2:** 2 sc in each sc around. *You now have* 12 sts.

» **RND 3:** (Sc in next sc, 2 sc in next sc) around. *You now have* 18 sts.

» **RND 4:** Sc in next 6 sc, 2 sc in next sc, sc in next 4 sc, 2 sc in next sc, sc in next 6 sc. *You now have* 20 sts.

» **RNDS 5 AND 6:** Sc in each sc around.

» **RND 7:** Sc in next 6 sc, (sc2tog) four times, sc in next 6 sc. *You now have* 16 sts.

» **RND 8:** Sc in each sc around.

» **RND 9:** Sc in next 6 sc, (sc2tog) twice, sc in next 6 sc. *You now have* 14 sts.

» **RNDS 10–12:** Sc in each sc around. Begin and continue to stuff the legs.

» **RND 13:** (Sc in next 5 sc, sc2tog) twice. *You now have* 12 sts.

» **RNDS 14–17:** Sc in each sc around.

» **RND 18:** (Sc in next 4 sc, sc2tog) twice. *You now have* 10 sts.

» **RNDS 19–28:** Sc in each sc around. At the end of Rnd 28, join with slip st to next st. Fasten off, leaving a long length of yarn for sewing.

Making the Tail

» Wrap yarn around two fingers approximately 20 times. With a separate piece of yarn, tie the wrapped yarn tightly in the center (forming two sets of loops) to secure.

Finishing

» Stuff the body. With yarn needle, sew the nose to the front of the head with the bottom of the nose in the center of Rnd 1 and the top of the nose over Rnd 4. Do not fasten off. With remaining nose yarn, embroider a line from the bottom of the nose to 2 rounds below for a mouth.

» Sew the head to the top of the body. Sew the ears to the top of the head. Sew the arms to the sides of the body. Sew the legs to the bottom of the body. Sew the tail to the back of the body.

Robotic

Designed by Deb Richey

Who knew a robot could be cute and cuddly? Crocheted and stuffed with fiberfill, this creature is downright huggable — and easy to crochet, too.

FINISHED MEASUREMENTS

Approximately 8"/20.5 cm tall

YARN

Lion Brand Vanna's Choice, 100% acrylic, 170 yds (155 m)/3.5 oz (100 g), Color 108 Dusty Blue

CROCHET HOOK

US G/6 (4 mm) *or size you need to obtain correct gauge*

GAUGE

20 single crochet and 23 rounds = 4"/10 cm in pattern (*Note:* Exact gauge is not crucial for this project; however, the tighter you crochet, the less stuffing you'll see through the stitches.)

OTHER SUPPLIES

Stitch markers, fiberfill for stuffing, 3" × 3"/8 × 8 cm piece of plastic canvas or lightweight cardboard, yarn needle, two 1"/2.5 cm buttons or safety eyes

✳ **SEE MAKING AMIGURUMI TOYS ON PAGE 211.**

Crocheting the Head and Body

» Starting at top, chain 6.

» **RND 1:** 3 sc in 2nd ch from hook, sc in next 3 ch, 3 sc in last ch; working on opposite side of foundation ch, sc in next 3 ch. *You now have* 12 sc. Place marker at the first st of the round and move it up as you work the rounds.

» **RND 2:** (2 sc in next 3 sc, sc in next 3 sc) twice. *You now have* 18 sts.

» **RND 3:** [(Sc in next sc, 2 sc in next sc) three times, sc in next 3 sc] twice. *You now have* 24 sts.

» **RND 4:** [(2 sc in next sc, sc in next 2 sc) three times, sc in next 3 sc] twice. *You now have* 30 sts.

» **RND 5:** [(Sc in next 3 sc, 2 sc in next sc) three times, sc in next 3 sc] twice. *You now have* 36 sts.

» **RND 6:** Sc in each sc around.

» **RND 7:** [(Sc in next 4 sc, 2 sc in next sc) three times, sc in next 3 sc] twice. *You now have* 42 sts.

» **RND 8:** [(Sc in next 5 sc, 2 sc in next sc) three times, sc in next 3 sc] twice. *You now have* 48 sts.

» **RNDS 9–31:** Sc in each sc around. At the end of Rnd 31, join with slip st to next st. Fasten off, leaving a long length of yarn for sewing.

Crocheting the Body Base

» Chain 6.

» **RND 1:** 3 sc in 2nd ch from hook, sc in next 3 ch, 3 sc in last ch; working on opposite side of foundation ch, sc in next 3. *You now have* 12 sc. Place marker in first st of the round and move it up as you work the rounds.

» **RND 2:** (2 sc in next 3 sc, sc in next 3 sc) twice. *You now have* 18 sts.

» **RND 3:** [(Sc in next sc, 2 sc in next sc) three times, sc in next 3 sc] twice. *You now have* 24 sts.

» **RND 4:** [(2 sc in next sc, sc in next 2 sc) three times, sc in next 3 sc] twice. *You now have* 30 sts.

» **RND 5:** [(Sc in next 3 sc, 2 sc in next sc) three times, sc in next 3 sc] twice. *You now have* 36 sts.

» **RND 6:** Sc in next 2 sc, (2 sc in next sc, sc in next 4 sc) twice, 2 sc in next sc, sc in next 6 sc, (2 sc in next sc, sc in next 4 sc) twice, 2 sc in next st, sc in next 6 sc. *You now have* 42 sts.

» **RND 7:** [(Sc in next 5 sc, 2 sc in next sc) three times, sc in next 3 sc] twice. *You now have* 48 sts.

Crocheting the Legs *(make 2)*

» Begin with your choice of ring.

» **RND 1:** Work 6 sc in ring. *You now have* 6 sts.

» **RND 2:** 2 sc in each sc around. *You now have* 12 sts.

» **RND 3:** (Sc in next sc, 2 sc in next sc) around. *You now have* 18 sts.

» **RND 4:** (2 sc in next sc, sc in next 2 sc) around. *You now have* 24 sts.

» **RND 5:** Working in back loops only, sc in each sc around.

» **RNDS 6 AND 7:** Sc in each sc around.

» **RND 8:** (Sc2tog, sc in next sc) around. *You now have* 16 sts.

» **RND 9:** (Sc in next 2 sc, sc2tog) around. *You now have* 12 sts.

» **RNDS 10–18:** Sc in each sc around. Begin and continue to stuff the legs. At the end of Rnd 18, join with slip st to first sc. Fasten off, leaving a length of yarn for sewing.

Crocheting the Arms
(make 2)

» Begin with your choice of ring.

» **RND 1:** Work 6 sc in ring. *You now have* 6 sts.

» **RND 2:** 2 sc in each sc around. *You now have* 12 sts.

» **RND 3:** (Sc in next sc, 2 sc in next sc) around. *You now have* 18 sts.

» **RND 4:** (2 sc in next sc, sc in next 2 sc) around. *You now have* 24 sts.

» **RND 5:** Sc in each sc around.

» **RND 6:** (Sc2tog, sc in next 2 sc) around. *You now have* 18 sts.

» **RND 7:** Sc in next 2 sc, (sc2tog, sc in next 4 sc) twice, sc2tog, sc in next 2 sc. *You now have* 15 sts.

» **RND 8:** (Sc in next 3 sc, sc2tog) around. *You now have* 12 sts.

» **RNDS 9–16:** Sc in each sc around. Begin and continue to stuff the arms. At the end of Rnd 16, join with slip st to next st. Fasten off, leaving a length of yarn for sewing.

Crocheting the Shoulders *(make 2)*

» Begin with your choice of ring.

» **RND 1:** Work 6 sc in ring. *You now have* 6 sts.

» **RND 2:** 2 sc in each sc around. *You now have* 12 sts.

» **RND 3:** (Sc in next sc, 2 sc in next sc) around. *You now have* 18 sts.

» **RND 4:** (Sc in next 5 sc, 2 sc in next sc) around. *You now have* 21 sts.

» **RNDS 5–8:** Sc in each sc around. At the end of Rnd 8, join with slip st to next st. Fasten off, leaving a length of yarn for sewing.

Finishing

» Stuff the body. Cut a piece of plastic canvas or cardboard slightly smaller than the bottom of the body and set it on top of the body base so that when it is sewn together, the crocheted piece will be on the outside. Line up the body base with the body. Sew together, fully stuffing before finishing.

» Stuff, then sew shoulders, one on each side of the body over Rnds 13–20. Sew an arm to the bottom of each shoulder. Sew the legs to bottom of the body. Sew on buttons for eyes.

Louis the Lobster

Designed by Susan Timmons

Louis the Lobster is named for Fortress Louisbourg in Cape Breton, Canada. Lobster is very common and a large part of the culture on the east coast of Canada and in New England. The pattern for Louis is easy to read and understand, and it shows different techniques for creating amigurumi shapes.

FINISHED MEASUREMENTS
8"/20.5 cm long, including claws

YARN
Red Heart Super Saver, 100% acrylic, 364 yds
  (333 m)/7 oz (198 g), Color 0319 Cherry Red

CROCHET HOOK
US D/3 (3.25 mm) *or size you need to obtain correct gauge*

GAUGE
20 stitches and 25 rounds = 4"/10 cm in single crochet

OTHER SUPPLIES
Yarn needle, fiberfill for stuffing, two 6 mm black safety eyes

✳ **NOTES:**
• The body is worked in the round without joining at the end of each round.
• The claws are formed in two parts, and the two parts are crocheted together.
• The antennae and legs are formed as part of the body, not as separate pieces to be joined later.
• The tail ends are sewn, and there is detailing between the body and the tail created with back post single crochet (BPsc).
• Louis takes about ½ oz (14 g) of yarn, and the pieces (other than the tail pieces) should be stuffed as they are worked.

✳ **SEE MAKING AMIGURUMI TOYS ON PAGE 211.**

Crocheting the Large Claw

MAKING PART 1

» **RND 1:** Ch 2, 6 sc in 2nd ch from hook, do not join. *You now have 6 sts.*

» **RND 2:** Sc in each st around.

» **RND 3:** (Sc in next sc, 2 sc in next sc) three times. *You now have 9 sts.*

» **RND 4:** Sc in each sc around.

» **RND 5:** (Sc in next 2 sc, 2 sc in next sc) three times. *You now have 12 sts.*

» **RND 6:** (Sc in next 3 sc, 2 sc in next sc) three times. *You now have 15 sts.*

» **RND 7:** (Sc in next 4 sc, 2 sc in next sc) three times. *You now have 18 sts.*

» **RNDS 8–10:** Sc in each sc around. At end of Rnd 10, join with slip st to next st. Fasten off.

MAKING PART 2

» **RND 1:** Ch 2, 6 sc in 2nd ch from hook. *You now have* 6 sts.

» **RND 2:** Sc in each sc around.

» **RND 3:** (Sc in next sc, 2 sc in next sc) three times. *You now have* 9 sts.

» **RND 4:** (Sc in next 2 sc, 2 sc in next sc) three times. *You now have* 12 sts.

» **RNDS 5 AND 6:** Sc in each st around.

» **RND 7:** Hold Part 1 in front of Part 2 (RS together); working through both pieces (through the inside of Part 1 and outside of Part 2), slip st in 2 sts to join both parts — these sts will not be part of the round and should be ignored. Working in Part 2, sc in 4 next sc, sc2tog, sc in next 4 sc; working in Part 1, sc in next 7 sc, sc2tog, sc in next 7 sc, do not join. *You now have* 24 sts in a round.

» **RND 8:** (Sc2tog, sc in next 6 sc) three times. *You now have* 21 sts.

» **RND 9:** (Sc2tog, sc in next 5 sc) three times. *You now have* 18 sts.

» **RND 10:** (Sc2tog, sc in next sc) six times. *You now have* 12 sts.

» **RND 11:** (Sc2tog, sc in next sc) four times. *You now have* 8 sts.

» **RNDS 12-18:** Sc in each sc around. At end of Rnd 18, join with slip st to next st. Fasten off, leaving long tail of yarn to sew the claw to the body. Stuff firmly.

Crocheting the Small Claw

MAKING PART 1

» **RND 1:** Ch 2, 6 sc in 2nd ch from hook. *You now have* 6 sts.

» **RND 2:** Sc in each sc around.

» **RND 3:** (Sc in next sc, 2 sc in next sc) three times. *You now have* 9 sts.

» **RND 4:** Sc in each sc around.

» **RND 5:** (Sc in next 2 sc, 2 sc in next sc) three times. *You now have* 12 sts.

» **RND 6:** (Sc in next 3 sc, 2 sc in next sc) three times. *You now have* 15 sts.

» **RNDS 7 AND 8:** Sc in each sc around. At end of Rnd 8, join with slip st to next st. Fasten off.

MAKING PART 2

» **RND 1:** Ch 2, 6 sc in 2nd ch from hook. *You now have* 6 sts.

» **RND 2:** Sc in each sc.

» **RND 3:** (Sc in next sc, 2 sc in next sc) three times. *You now have* 9 sts.

» **RND 4:** (Sc in next 2 sc, 2 sc in next sc) three times. *You now have* 12 sts.

» **RND 5:** Sc in each sc around.

» **RND 6:** Holding Part 1 in front of Part 2, join both parts by sc in 2 sts working through both parts — these sts will not be part of the round and should be ignored. Working in Part 2, sc in next 4 sc, sc2tog, sc in next 4 sc; working in Part 1, sc in next 5 sc, sc2tog, sc in next 6 sc. *You now have* 21 sts in a round.

» **RND 7:** (Sc2tog, sc in next 5 sc) three times. *You now have* 18 sts.

» **RND 8:** (Sc2tog, sc in next sc) six times. *You now have* 12 sts.

» **RND 9:** (Sc2tog, sc in next sc) four times. *You now have* 8 sts.

» **RND 10:** (Sc in next 3 sc, 2 sc in next sc) two times. *You now have* 10 sts.

» **RNDS 11–16:** Sc in each sc around. At end of Rnd 16, join with slip st to next st. Fasten off, leaving long tail of yarn to sew the claw to the body. Stuff firmly.

Crocheting the Head and Body

» **FORM ANTENNAE:** (Ch 15, slip st in 2nd ch from hook and in next 14 ch) twice.

» **RND 1:** Ch 2, 6 sc in 2nd ch from hook. *You now have* 6 sts.

» **RND 2:** Skipping antennae, (sc in next sc, 2 sc in next sc) three times. *You now have* 9 sts.

» **RND 3:** (Sc in next 2 sc, 2 sc in next sc) three times. *You now have* 12 sts.

» **RND 4:** (Sc in next 3 sc, 2 sc in next sc) three times. *You now have* 15 sts.

» **RND 5:** (Sc in next 4 sc, 2 sc in next sc) three times. *You now have* 18 sts.

» **RND 6:** (Sc in next 5 sc, 2 sc in next sc) three times. *You now have* 21 sts.

» Attach eyes ½"/13 mm apart in Rnd 3 of head.

» **RND 7:** (Sc in next 6 sc, 2 sc in next sc) three times. *You now have* 24 sts. Mark Rnd 7 for attaching claws.

» **RND 8:** (Sc in next 3 sc, 2 sc in next sc) six times. *You now have* 30 sts.

» **RNDS 9–11:** Sc in each st around.

» **RND 12:** (Sc2tog, sc in next 3 sc) six times. *You now have* 24 sts.

» **RND 13:** Sc in next 16 sc, [ch 9, slip st in 2nd ch from hook and in next 7 ch sts — *leg made* (don't count leg as part of round and skip the leg in next round)], sc in next 7 sts, make second leg, sc in next st.

» **RNDS 14–16:** Repeat Rnd 13. Sew claws onto Rnd 7, using photo as a guide for placement.

» **RND 17:** Sc in each sc around.

» **RND 18:** BPsc in each sc around.

» **RND 19:** (Sc2tog, sc in next 2 sc) six times. *You now have* 18 sts.

» **RNDS 20–30:** Sc in each st around. Mark Rnd 29 for attaching tail pieces.

» **RND 31:** (Sc2tog, sc in next sc) six times. *You now have* 12 sts.

» **RND 32:** Sc2tog six times. *You now have* 6 sts. Fasten off, leaving a long tail of yarn for sewing the tail closed. Stuff the body firmly and sew closed.

Crocheting the Tail
(make 3)

» **RND 1:** Ch 2, 6 sc in 2nd ch from hook. *You now have* 6 sts.

» **RND 2:** 2 sc in each st around.

» **RND 3:** (Sc in next sc, 2 sc in next sc) six times. *You now have* 18 sts.

» **RNDS 4 AND 5:** Sc in each sc around.

» **RND 6:** (Sc2tog, sc in next sc) six times. *You now have* 12 sts.

» **RND 7:** Sc2tog six times. *You now have* 6 sts. Fold flat and fasten off, leaving a long tail of yarn to sew to body.

» Sew tail pieces to marked Rnd 29 of body.

Tunisian Pot Holders

Designed by Diana Foster

Almost too pretty to actually use in the kitchen, these pot holders are worked in Tunisian simple stitch, which produces a surface that looks woven. They look equally good when worked in a solid or a multicolored yarn, and they are double-layered for extra protection.

Crocheting the Pot Holder

» With afghan hook, ch 24.

» Work even in Tunisian simple stitch (TSS) (see page 274) for 20 rows, ending on a return row. Change to smaller crochet hook.

» Ch 1 (counts as first st), slip st in each vertical bar across, working down side edge, slip st in each row-end st across, working across bottom edge, slip st in each ch across, working down side edge, slip st in each row-end st across to beginning, slip st in first slip st. *You now have 88 slip sts.*

» Fasten off and weave in ends.

Joining the Two Sides

» Hold pieces with WS together. Leaving a 30"/76 cm tail for the hanging loop, join yarn with slip st in upper right corner; working through double thickness in back loops only of front piece and front loops only of back piece, ch 1, *3 sc in corner st, sc in each st to next corner; repeat from * around, join with slip st in first sc. Do not fasten off.

Making the Hanging Loop

» Holding working yarn and long tail together, ch 14; join with slip st to first sc to form a loop.

Entwine Trivets

Designed by René E. Wells

These trivets, worked with front and back post double crochet, will look handsome on your table while they wait for a hot dish. One skein of yarn will make two trivets.

Crocheting the Trivets
(make 2)

» Chain 32.

» **ROW 1:** Dc in 4th chain from hook and in each ch across. *You now have 30 dc.*

» **ROW 2:** Ch 3 (counts as dc), *FPdc around next dc, BPdc around next dc, repeat from * across to last st, FPdc around ch-3 space, turn.

» **ROW 3:** Ch 3 (counts as dc), *BPdc around next st, FPdc around next st; repeat from * across to last st, BPdc around ch-3 space, turn.

» **ROW 4:** Ch 3 (counts as dc), *FPdc around next st, BPdc around next st; repeat from * across to last st, FPdc around ch-3 space, turn.

» Repeat Rows 3 and 4 until piece measures 6½"/16.5 cm. Fasten off. Weave in ends.

FINISHED MEASUREMENTS
Approximately 6½"/16.5 cm square

YARN
Reynolds Saucy, 100% mercerized cotton, 185 yds (169 m)/3.5 oz (100 g), Color 820

CROCHET HOOK
US G/6 (4 mm) *or size you need to obtain correct gauge*

GAUGE
18 stitches and 12 rows = 4"/10 cm in pattern

OTHER SUPPLIES
Yarn needle

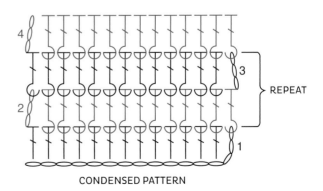

CONDENSED PATTERN

Lodge Pillow

Designed by Sandy Scoville

"Lodge Pillow" is a good name for this cushion — the neutral-colored tweedy yarn has a casual and cozy feel, and the knotted straps complete the weekend cabin style.

FINISHED MEASUREMENTS
Covers a 12"/30.5 cm square pillow

YARN
Red Heart Super Saver, 96% acrylic/4% other fibers, 260 yds (238 m)/5 oz (141 g), Color 4313 Aran Fleck

CROCHET HOOK
US I/9 (5.5 mm) *or size you need to obtain correct gauge*

GAUGE
12 stitches and 6 rows = 4"/10 cm in double crochet

OTHER SUPPLIES
Yarn needle, 12"/30.5 cm square pillow form

Crocheting the Front and Back *(make 2)*

» Chain 40.

» **ROW 1 (RS):** Sc in 2nd ch from hook and in each remaining ch, turn. *You now have 39 sc.*

» **ROW 2 (WS):** Ch 2 (counts as dc on this and following rows), *BLdc in next sc, FLdc in next sc; repeat from * across, turn.

» **ROW 3:** Ch 2, *BLdc in next dc, FLdc in next dc, repeat from * across, turn.

» **ROWS 4–20:** Repeat Row 3.

» **ROW 21:** Ch 1, FLsc in first dc, *BLsc in next dc, FLsc in next dc; repeat from * across. Do not turn.

» **FIRST SIDE EDGE (RS):** Ch 1, working along side edge, skip Row 21, work 2 sc in side of each dc to Row 1, sc in side of sc on Row 1. *You now have 41 sc.* Fasten off.

» **SECOND SIDE EDGE (RS):** Make slip knot and place loop on hook, join with sc in side of sc in Row 1, 2 sc in side of each dc to Row 21, join with slip st to first sc on Row 21. *You now have 41 sc.* Fasten off and weave in ends.

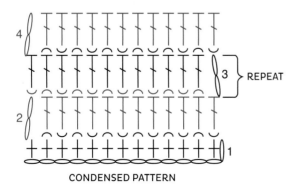

4
3 } REPEAT
2
1

CONDENSED PATTERN

Crocheting the Knotted Straps

(make 2)

» Chain 50.

» **ROW 1 (RS):** Sc in 2nd ch from hook and in each ch across, turn. *You now have* 49 sc.

» **ROW 2:** Ch 1, skip first sc, sc in next 47 sc, slip st in next sc, turn.

» **ROW 3:** Ch 1, skip slip st and next sc, sc in next 45 sc, slip st in next sc. *Do not turn.*

» **EDGE ROW (RS):** Ch 1, skip slip st at end of Row 3, slip st in edge of Rows 2 and 1, ch 1, slip st in each unused loop of beg ch, slip st in edge of Rows 1 and 2, join to beg ch-1 of Row 3. Fasten off, leaving an 8"/20.5 cm yarn tail for sewing.

Finishing

» Tie each strap with an overhand knot at center, and twist slightly so RS of each end of tie is facing you.

» Referring to photo above, lay pillow front piece with RS facing you. Pin one strap from center top to right-hand side edge, and one strap from center bottom to left-hand side edge, matching angle of strap to edge of pillow. Sew straps in place with yarn needle.

» With RS of front and back pieces held together and beginning at lower edge, sew together along side and top edges. Turn RS out and insert pillow form. Sew pillow top closed along lower edge. Weave in ends.

E-Reader Cover

Designed by Rebecca Averill

This cushy cover features an interesting texture that makes it fun to hold. It stretches to accommodate any small e-reader, and you can also add or subtract stitches or rows to fit your other devices as well.

PATTERN ESSENTIALS

Hdc ch st Work hdc in horizontal thread behind top of st. The top of the hdc will be pushed forward, creating a chain-type texture on the front of the fabric.

Sc ch st Work sc in horizontal thread behind top of st.

✳ NOTES:
• The cover begins with a foundation single crochet (fsc), then Round 1 is worked around both sides of the foundation in order to form a tube.
• Do not turn at the end of each round; work in rounds, moving a stitch marker up at the end of each round.

FINISHED MEASUREMENTS
4½"/11.5 cm wide and 8"/20.5 cm long, unstretched

YARN
TLC Cotton Plus, 51% cotton/49% acrylic, 178 yds (163 m)/3.5 oz (100 g), Color 3643 Kiwi

CROCHET HOOK
US H/8 (5 mm) *or size you need to obtain correct gauge*

GAUGE
15 stitches and 13 rows = 4"/10 cm in Half Double Crochet Chain Stitch; exact gauge is not critical for this project, as cover is very stretchy

OTHER SUPPLIES
Yarn needle

Crocheting the Cover

» Fsc 16 or to desired width (see page 273).

» **RND 1:** Ch 2 (does not count as hdc), working along top of fsc, hdc in each st across, 2 hdc in side of last st; working along opposite side of fsc, hdc in each st across, 2 hdc in side of last st. Do not join. *You now have* 36 hdc.

» **RNDS 2–23:** Working in a spiral, work hdc ch st in each st around.

» **RND 24 (OR TO ABOUT 1"/2.5 CM FROM DESIRED LENGTH):** Continuing in the spiral, sc ch st in each st around.

» **RNDS 25 AND 26:** Sc in each st around.

» **RND 27:** Slip st around in back loop only of each st.

» Fasten off. Weave in ends.

Bulky Weight

Möbius Cowl ∗ Button-Flap Cape ∗ Ribbed Wristlets ∗
November Mittens ∗ Quinby ∗ Men's Snow Sports Headband ∗
Felted Clutch ∗ Handpainted Shoulder Bag ∗ Fuzzy Tea Cozy ∗
Spike & Loopy, Felted Twins

Möbius Cowl

Designed by Andrea Lyn Van Benschoten

A cowl is a great way to enjoy the warmth of a scarf without the extra length. The texture of back-loop stitches adds additional twist to the Möbius design.

FINISHED MEASUREMENTS

Approximately 24"/61 cm in circumference and 8"/20.5 cm wide

YARN

Lion Brand Wool-Ease Thick & Quick Prints, 80% acrylic/20% wool, 87 yds (80 m)/5 oz (141 g), Color 501 Sequoia

CROCHET HOOK

US N/13 (9 mm) *or size you need to obtain correct gauge*

GAUGE

8 stitches and 4 rows = 4"/10 cm in double crochet

OTHER SUPPLIES

Yarn needle

Crocheting the Cowl

» Chain 17.

» **ROW 1:** Dc in 2nd ch from hook and in each ch across, turn. *You now have* 15 dc.

» **ROWS 2–41:** Ch 3 (counts as dc), BLdc in each st across, turn.

Finishing

» With WS facing, fold top right corner to bottom left corner, working through double thickness of last row and foundation ch, slip st in each st across short side. Weave in ends. Turn RS out.

Button-Flap Cape

Designed by Patricia Colloton-Walsh

Made with a bulky-weight yarn, this cape is a one-size-fits-most! Worked in the round from the top down, it features a button-down flap, which adds interest to the design. Appropriate for beginning to intermediate crocheters, this project is perfect for a quick gift.

Crocheting the Cape

» Chain 30. Place marker in first chain. Being careful not to twist chain, join with a slip st in first chain to form a circle.

» **RND 1:** Ch 1, sc in each ch around, join with slip st to top of ch-2. *You now have* 30 sts.

FINISHED MEASUREMENTS

Approximately 20"/51 cm around at neck edge, 58"/147 cm around at bottom edge, and 11"/28 cm long

YARN

Brown Sheep Burly Spun, 100% wool, 132 yds (121 m)/8 oz (226 g), Color 181 Prairie Fire

CROCHET HOOK

US S (19 mm) *or size you need to obtain correct gauge*

GAUGE

5 stitches and 3 rows = 4"/10 cm in double crochet, blocked

OTHER SUPPLIES

Split stitch marker, yarn needle, two 1½"/3.8 cm buttons

» **RND 2:** Ch 3 (counts as dc here and throughout), dc in same st, *dc in next st, 2 dc in next st; repeat from * to last st, 2 dc in last st, join with slip st to top of ch-3. *You now have 46 sts.*

» **RND 3:** Ch 3, dc in each st around, join with slip st to top of ch-3.

» Work now progresses in rows.

» **ROW 4:** Ch 3, dc in next 2 dc, 2 dc in next dc, *dc in next 3 dc, 2 dc in next dc; repeat from * to last 2 sts, dc in next 2 sts, turn. *You now have 57 sts.*

Crocheting the Flap

» **ROW 1:** Ch 5 loosely, dc in 3rd ch from hook, dc in next 2 ch, dc in each st across Row 4, turn.

» **ROW 2:** Ch 3 (counts as dc), dc in each dc across. Fasten off.

Finishing

» **EDGING:** With RS facing, join yarn to the bottom corner of cape, *ch 3, slip st in next st, repeat from * around lower edge of cape, around corner of flap, up the side and across the top of flap. Fasten off. Weave in ends. Block and pull out or pin the ch-3 edging loops at the bottom of the cape as it dries. Sew top edge of flap to cape at base of ch-3 loops. Sew two buttons to cape underneath flap, using ch-3 loops as buttonholes.

Ribbed Wristlets

Designed by Janet M. Spirik

This pattern uses double crochet, single crochet, and front post double crochet. It's a great stash buster as it only uses about three ounces (85 g) of bulky-weight yarn. The pattern is fairly simple and works up very quickly.

FINISHED MEASUREMENTS
6"–7" (7"–8")/15–18 (18–20) cm wrist circumference

❋ **NOTE:** The gloves will stretch over the wide part of the hand, so base size on wrist measurement.

YARN
Lion Brand Tweed Stripes, 100% acrylic, 144 yds (132 m)/3 oz (85 g), Color 206 Woodlands

CROCHET HOOK
US G/6 (4 mm) *or size you need to obtain correct gauge*

GAUGE
13 stitches and 14 rows = 4"/10 cm in ribbed pattern

OTHER SUPPLIES
Yarn needle, two 1"/2.5 cm buttons, sewing needle, coordinating thread

Crocheting the Wristlet *(make 2)*

» Chain 24 (26). Being careful not to twist chain, join with slip st to first ch to form a circle.

» **RND 1:** Ch 3 (counts as dc), dc in each ch around, join with slip st to top of ch-3. *You now have 24 (26) dc.*

» **RND 2:** Ch 1, sc in same st, FPdc in next dc, *sc in next dc, FPdc in next dc; repeat from * around, join with slip st to first sc. *You now have* 12 (13) FPdc and 12 (13) sc.

» **RND 3:** Ch 1, sc in same st, FPdc in next st, *sc in next st, FPdc in next st; repeat from * around, join with slip st to first sc.

» Repeat Rnd 3 until piece measures 5"/12.5 cm or desired length from cuff to thumb.

WORKING THE THUMB OPENING

» **RND 1 (THUMB OPENING):** Ch 1, sc in same st, FPdc in next st, ch 5, skip 6 sts, *sc in next sc, FPdc in next st; repeat from * around, join with slip st to first sc.

» **NEXT RND:** Ch 1, sc in same st, FPdc in next st, (sc, dc) three times in next ch-5 space, *sc in next sc, FPdc in next st; repeat from * around, join with slip st to first sc.

CONTINUING THE HAND

» **NEXT RND:** Ch 1, sc in same st, FPdc in next st, *sc in next sc, FPdc in next st; repeat from * around, join with slip st to first sc. *You now have* 12 (13) FPdc and 12 (13) sc.

» Repeat the previous round until glove measures 2"/5 cm from thumb opening to the top of wristlet. Fasten off. Weave in ends.

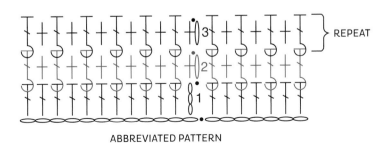

REPEAT

ABBREVIATED PATTERN

continued on next page

Making the Decorative Band *(make 2)*

» Ch 4, leaving a long tail for sewing.

» **ROW 1:** Sc in 2nd ch from hook and in next 2 ch, turn. *You now have 3 sc.*

» **ROW 2:** Ch 1, sc in each sc across, turn.

» Repeat Row 2 until band measures 5"/12.5 cm from beginning. Fasten off.

Assembling the Wristlet

» With yarn needle, sew end of each band about ½"/13 mm up from the wrist edge and centered under the thumb opening. With sewing needle and thread, sew buttons on the opposite edge of the band and to the wristlet. Be sure to lay your gloves side by side with the thumbholes facing, then fold the band to the outside edge, so you have a right and left glove.

November Mittens

Brenda K. B. Anderson

These chunky mittens feature a ribbed cuff, and the hand can be lengthened or shortened for a custom fit. The addition of a strap attached with steampunk-style buttons makes this classic mitten very up-to-date.

FINISHED MEASUREMENTS
8"/20.5 cm in circumference and 10¾"/27.5 cm in length, or as desired

YARN
Knit Picks Swish Bulky, 100% superwash merino wool, 137 yds (126 m)/3.5 oz (100 g), Brindle Heather

CROCHET HOOK
US K/10½ (6.5 mm) *or size you need to obtain correct gauge*

GAUGE
12 stitches and 12 rows = 4"/10 cm in pattern

OTHER SUPPLIES
Two stitch markers, yarn needle, four ⅞"/22 mm buttons, sewing needle and coordinating thread

✽ **NOTES:**

· The ribbed cuff is worked back and forth in rows and then slipstitched to form a tube. The body of the mitten is then worked in a spiral from the ribbing up to the top.

· Right and left mittens are the same, except that the button straps are stitched onto opposite sides.

· You will need to unravel your gauge swatch in order to have enough yarn to complete these mittens.

Crocheting the Cuff

(make 2)

» Chain 7.

» **ROW 1:** Working into the back bump of the chains, slip st in 2nd ch from hook, slip st in next 2 ch, sc in next 3 ch, turn. *You now have 6 sts.*

» **ROW 2:** Ch 1, BLsc in next 3 sts, BLslip st in next 3 sts, turn.

» **ROW 3:** Ch 1, BLslip st in next 3 sts, BLsc in next 3 sts, turn.

» Repeat Rows 2 and 3 thirteen more times.

» Hold ribbing with crochet hook on the RS of your work as though you are about to work another row; fold first row of ribbing up in front so that short edges of ribbing are aligned; insert hook into back loop of foundation ch and through back loop of the next stitch on the previous row, yo and pull loop through both stitches and through loop on hook to slipstitch layers together; continue to slip st layers together across row. Do not fasten off. Turn ribbing inside out so that the slip-st row is on the inside. RS is now facing.

Crocheting the Mitten Body

» **RND 1:** Ch 1, work 20 sc evenly spaced around top edge of ribbing tube; do not join. Place marker at the first st of the round and move up as you work the rounds. *You now have 20 sts.*

» **RNDS 2 AND 3:** BLsc into each st around.

» **RND 4:** (BLsc in next 3 sts, 2 BLsc in next st) five times. *You now have 25 sts.*

» **RND 5:** (BLsc in next 1 st, 2 BLsc in next st, BLsc into next 3 sts) five times. *You now have 30 sts.*

» **RND 6:** (BLsc in next 9 sts, 2 BLsc in next st) three times. *You now have 33 sts.*

continued on next page

» **RNDS 7–11:** BLsc into each st around.

» **RND 12:** BLsc in next 12 sts, skip next 9 sts (for thumb opening), BLsc in next 12 sts. *You now have* 24 sts, not including thumb.

» **RNDS 13–22:** BLsc in each st around.

» **RND 23:** (BLsc in next 2 sts, BLsc2tog) six times. *You now have* 18 sts.

» **RND 24:** BLsc into each st around.

» **RND 25:** (BLsc2tog, BLsc in next st) six times. *You now have* 12 sts.

» **RND 26:** (BLsc2tog) six times. *You now have* 6 sts.

» Fasten off, leaving an 8"/20.5 cm tail. Using yarn needle, thread yarn tail through the front loop of the remaining 6 sts and gather tightly to close top of mitten. Weave in ends.

Crocheting the Thumb

» **RND 1:** Pull up a loop of yarn in any st at thumbhole, BLsc in each of the 9 skipped sts, adding 1 st at thumb crotch. (Let the beginning yarn tail dangle on the outside of your work. Later you can use it to stitch closed any small holes that occur.) *You now have* 10 sts.

» **RNDS 2–6:** BLsc into each st around.

» **RND 7:** (BLsc2tog) five times. *You now have* 5 sts.

» Fasten off, leaving an 8"/20.5 cm tail. Using yarn needle, thread yarn tail through the front loop of the remaining 5 sts and gather tightly to close top of thumb. Weave in ends.

Crocheting the Button Strap *(make 2)*

» Ch 8, making sure that the 8th ch st is loose enough to get your hook into it later.

» **RND 1:** Sc in 2nd ch from hook and in next 5 ch, 3 sc in last ch; working on opposite side of foundation ch, sc in next 6 ch, 3 sc in last chain of foundation chain. Do not join.

» **RND 2:** Sc in next 7 sc, 3 sc in next sc, sc in next 8 sc, 3 sc in next sc, slip st to next sc. Fasten off.

Finishing

» Weave in ends. Use yarn tail to stitch closed the small hole between the thumb and the hand. Secure button straps in place (at wrists of mittens) by stitching a button to each end through both thicknesses.

Quinby

Designed by Sara Kay Hartmann

Quinby is a classic watchcap constructed with a twist. You'll crochet a circle and make a long chain, then work back-loop ribbing sideways around the circle, joining as you go. This results in a totally seamless project. A change of yarn changes the look, making Quinby a great pattern for men and women.

SIZES AND FINISHED MEASUREMENTS

To fit adult head size 22"–23"/56–58 cm, approximately 20"/51 cm in circumference

YARN

Yarn Bee Andes Alpaca, 85% acrylic/15% alpaca, 102 yds (93 m)/3 oz (85 g), Color 730 Damson

CROCHET HOOK

US J/10 (6 mm) *or size you need to obtain correct gauge*

GAUGE

12 stitches and 7 rows = 4"/10 cm in ribbed pattern

OTHER SUPPLIES

Locking stitch marker, yarn needle

Crocheting the Crown

- » Chain 4, slip st in first ch to form a ring.

- » **RND 1:** Ch 3 (counts as dc here and through-out), 11 dc in ring, join with slip st to top of ch-3. *You now have* 12 dc.

- » **RND 2:** Ch 3, dc in same st, 2 dc in each st around, join with slip st to top of ch-3. *You now have* 24 dc.

- » **RND 3:** Ch 3, 2 dc in next dc, *dc in next dc, 2 dc in next dc; repeat from * around, join with slip st to top of ch-3. *You now have* 36 dc. Do not fasten off.

Crocheting the Body

- » **SETUP ROW:** Ch 24. Beginning in 3rd ch from hook, work 1 BLhdc in each ch across, pm in final hdc. *You now have* 22 hdc.

- » Working counterclockwise around the crown, skip first dc of the crown, slip st to 2nd dc, turn.

- » **ROW 1:** Work 1 BLhdc into marked hdc (move marker to BLhdc just made) and in each hdc across, turn.

- » **ROW 2:** Ch 2, work 1 BLhdc in each BLhdc across, skip 1 crown dc, slip st into next dc, turn.

- » Repeat Rows 1 and 2 seventeen times more.

- » **FINAL ROW:** Working through double thick-ness in back loops of last row and in front loops of foundation ch, slip st in each pair of sts across.

Finishing

- » Fasten off. Weave in ends.

Men's Snow Sports Headband

Designed by Nancy Brown

An alpaca-blend headband will keep your favorite man's ears warm while he's skiing, sledding, skating — or during any other wintertime outdoor activity. This one is crocheted from the center back and seamed, then edged on both sides.

FINISHED MEASUREMENTS
Approximately 20"/51 cm in circumference, unstretched, and 5"/12.5 cm wide at widest point

YARN
Bernat Alpaca Natural Blends, 70% acrylic/30% alpaca, 120 yds (110 m)/3.5 oz (100 g), Color 93040 Ebony

CROCHET HOOK
US J/10 (6 mm) *or size you need to obtain correct gauge*

GAUGE
12 stitches and 8 rows = 4"/10 cm in half double crochet

OTHER SUPPLIES
Yarn needle

PATTERN ESSENTIALS

BLhdc2tog Yo, draw up a loop in back loop of next st, yo and draw up a loop in back loop of next st, yo and draw through all 5 loops.

Join yarn with sc Make a slip knot on hook, insert hook in st, yo, pull up a loop, yo, draw through both loops.

Crocheting the Headband

» Beginning at center back, ch 9.

» **ROW 1:** BLhdc in 2nd ch from hook and in each ch across, turn. *You now have* 8 sts.

» **ROWS 2 AND 3:** Ch 1 (does not count as a st on next rows), BLhdc in each st across, turn.

» **ROW 4:** Ch 1, BLhdc in first st, 2 BLhdc in next st — *increase made*, BLhdc in each st across, turn. *You now have* 9 sts.

» **ROW 5:** Ch 1, BLhdc in each st to last 2 sts, 2 BLhdc in next st, BLhdc in last st, turn. *You now have* 10 sts.

» **ROWS 6 AND 8:** Repeat Row 4.

» **ROWS 7 AND 9:** Repeat Row 5. *You now have* 14 sts at the end of Row 9.

» **ROWS 10, 12, AND 14:** Ch 1, BLhdc in first st, BLhdc2tog, BLhdc in each st across, turn.

» **ROWS 11, 13, AND 15:** Ch 1, BLhdc in each st to last 3 sts, BLhdc2tog, BLhdc in last st, turn. *You now have* 8 sts at the end of Row 15.

» **ROWS 16–26:** Work even.

» **ROW 27:** Repeat Row 5. *You now have* 9 sts.

» **ROW 28:** Repeat Row 4. *You now have* 10 sts.

» **ROWS 29 AND 31:** Repeat Row 5.

» **ROWS 30 AND 32:** Repeat Row 4. *You now have* 14 sts at the end of Row 32.

» **ROWS 33, 35, AND 37:** Repeat Row 11.

» **ROWS 34, 36, AND 38:** Repeat Row 10. *You now have* 8 sts at the end of Row 38.

» **ROWS 39 AND 40:** Work even, ending with Row 40 at top edge of headband. With RS of headband facing and working through double thickness of last row and foundation ch, slip st in each st across for back seam, ending at bottom edge of headband. Do not fasten off.

Working the Bottom Edging

» With RS facing, ch 1, sc in each row-end st around; join with slip st in first sc. Fasten off.

Working the Top Edging

» With RS facing, join yarn with sc (see Pattern Essentials) in end of row to the left of back seam, sc in each row-end st around; join with slip st in first sc. Fasten off. Weave in ends.

Felted Clutch

Designed by Patricia Colloton-Walsh

This felted clutch is versatile and can be embellished before or after felting. Because this is felted, the crocheting can be done looser than usual. This is a perfect pattern for a novice crocheter and pattern reader.

FINISHED MEASUREMENTS

Approximately 10"/25.5 cm wide and 8"/20.5 cm tall

YARN

Brown Sheep Lamb's Pride Bulky, 85% wool, 15% mohair, 125 yds (114 m)/4 oz (113 g), Color 191 Kiwi

CROCHET HOOKS

US N/13 (10 mm) *or size you need to obtain correct gauge* and US J/10 (6 mm) for flower (optional)

GAUGE

Approximately 10 stitches and 6 rows = 4"/10 cm in pattern before felting

OTHER SUPPLIES

Locking stitch marker, yarn needle, one 1"/2.5 cm button (optional)

Crocheting the Clutch

» Chain 60. Being careful not to twist the chain, join with a slip st in first ch to form a circle. Place marker at the first st of the round and move it up as you work the rounds.

» **RND 1:** Ch 1, sc in each ch around, join with slip st to first sc. *You now have 60 sts.*

» **RND 2:** Ch 1, BLsc in each sc around, join with slip st to first sc.

» **RNDS 3–8:** Repeat Rnd 2.

» **RND 9:** Ch 1, *BLsc in next 8 sc, BLsc2tog; repeat from * around, join with slip st to first sc. *You now have 54 sts.*

- » **RNDS 10–12:** Repeat Rnd 2.

- » **RND 13:** Ch 1, *BLsc in next 7 sc, BLsc2tog; repeat from * around, join with slip st to first sc. *You now have 48 sts.*

- » **RND 14:** Repeat Rnd 2.

- » **RND 15:** Ch 1, *BLsc in next 8 sc, ch 8, skip 8 sc, BLsc in next 8 sc; repeat from * once more, join with slip st to first sc.

- » **RND 16:** Ch 1, BLsc in every sc and 8 sc in each ch-space around, join with slip st to first sc.

- » **RND 17:** Ch 1, slip st in each st around. Fasten off.

Finishing

- » Weave in ends. Sew or crochet the bottom seam closed. Turn the bag inside out. From the inside of the bag, flatten the bottom seam and form triangles at the base's edges. Sew a small seam with the yarn at the base of the triangles (about 1"/2.5 cm in length) to square off the bottom of the bag. Felt (see page 275) the bag to desired size.

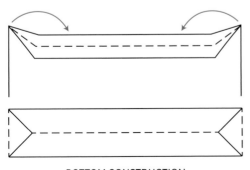

BOTTOM CONSTRUCTION

Crocheting the Flower *(optional)*

- » Leaving a 6"/15 cm sewing length, ch 2.

- » **RND 1:** 6 sc in 2nd ch from hook, join with slip st to first sc, pm. *You now have* 6 sts.

- » **RND 2:** Ch 2 (counts as hdc), hdc in same st, 2 hdc in next 5 sts, join with slip st to top of ch-2. *You now have* 12 sts.

- » **RND 3:** *Ch 3, slip st in next st; repeat from * around, ending with ch 1, join with hdc to first ch.

- » **RND 4:** *Ch 5, slip st in next space; repeat from * around, join with slip st to top of first ch. Fasten off.

- » Sew flower to clutch with decorative button in the center, if desired.

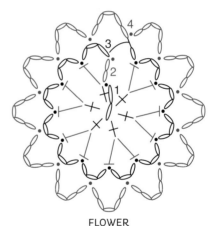

FLOWER

255

Handpainted Shoulder Bag

Designed by Reneé Rodgers

This clever pattern makes effective use of the color changes in handpainted yarn by utilizing a spike stitch, which allows the color to be more fully revealed in the fabric. The bulky-weight yarn creates a sturdy purse that will carry whatever you need in style.

FINISHED MEASUREMENTS
Approximately 11"/28 cm wide and
  9"/23 cm tall excluding strap

YARN
Brown Sheep Lanaloft Bulky Handpaint,
  100% wool, 160 yds (146 m)/7 oz (198 g),
  Color LL222 Precious Stones

CROCHET HOOK
US K/10½ (6.5 mm) *or size you need
  to obtain correct gauge*

GAUGE
10 stitches and 12 rows = 4"/10 cm in pattern

OTHER SUPPLIES
Yarn needle, one 1½"/3.8 cm button

PATTERN ESSENTIALS

Spike st Insert hook in next sc 4 rows below, yo
  and pull up a loop, yo and pull through both
  loops on hook to complete sc, skip st behind
  spike st in previous row.

Crocheting the Bag

See chart on page 258.

» Chain 26.

» **ROW 1 (WS):** Sc in 2nd ch from hook and in each ch across, turn. *You now have 25 sc.*

» **ROWS 2–5:** Ch 1, sc in each st across, turn.

» **ROW 6 (RS):** Ch 1, sc in next 2 sc, spike st 4 rows below, *sc in next 3 sc, spike st 4 rows below; repeat from * four times, sc in last 2 sc, turn.

» **ROWS 7–10:** Ch 1, sc in each sc across, turn.

» **ROW 11:** Repeat Row 6.

» **ROWS 12–51:** Repeat Rows 7–11 eight times.

» **ROW 52:** Ch 1, sc in each sc across, turn.

» **ROWS 53–55:** Ch 1, sc2tog, sc in each sc across to last 2 sc, sc2tog, turn. *You now have 19 sc at the end of Row 55.*

» **ROW 56:** Ch 1, sc2tog, sc in next sc, spike st 4 rows below, *sc in next 3 sc, spike st 4 rows below; repeat from * two more times, sc in next sc, sc2tog, turn. *You now have 17 sc.*

» **ROWS 57–60:** Ch 1, sc2tog, sc in each sc across to last 2 sc, sc2tog, turn. *You now have* 9 sc at the end of Row 60.

» **ROW 61:** Ch 1, sc2tog, spike st 4 rows below, sc in next 3 sc, spike st 4 rows below, sc2tog, turn. *You now have* 7 sc.

» **ROWS 62 AND 63:** Repeat Row 57. *You now have* 3 sc.

» **ROW 64:** Ch 1, sc3tog, ch 15, slip st to base of chain. Fasten off.

Crocheting the Strap

» Chain 91.

» **ROW 1:** Sc in 2nd ch from hook and in each ch across, turn. *You now have* 90 sc.

» **ROWS 2 AND 3:** Ch 1, sc in each sc across, ch 1, turn. Fasten off at end of Row 3.

Assembling the Bag

» With RS facing, fold up 8"/20.5 cm from the beginning edge. Sew the sides together using yarn and a yarn needle. Turn RS out. Sew the button in place opposite button loop. Sew the strap onto the sides of the bag on the WS. Weave in ends.

continued on next page

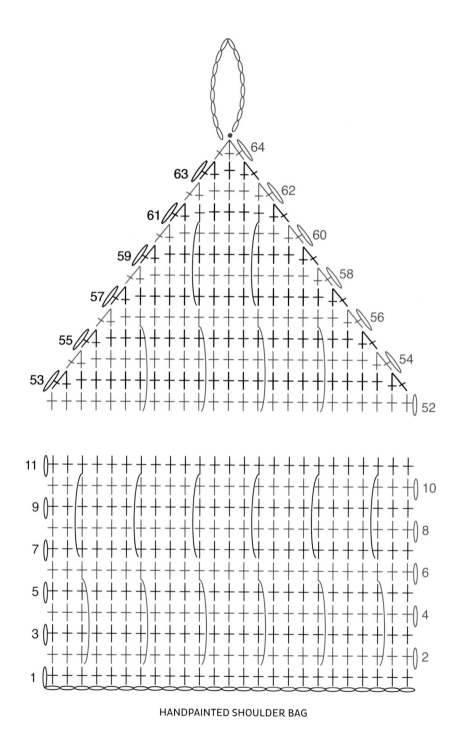

HANDPAINTED SHOULDER BAG

Fuzzy Tea Cozy

Designed by Melinda A. Sheehan

This fuzzy and thick cozy will keep your tea warm through several book chapters or a long conversation with a friend. The circles are dyed with food colors and attached to the cozy with coordinating buttons.

FINISHED MEASUREMENTS
11"/28 cm wide and 10"/25.5 cm tall after felting

YARN
Bartlettyarn Maine Wool, 100% wool, 200 yd
  (183 m)/4 oz (113 g), Color 209 Oatmeal

CROCHET HOOK
US K/10½ (6.5 mm) *or size you need to obtain correct gauge*

GAUGE
18 stitches and 8 rows = 5"/12.5 cm in
  double crochet before felting

OTHER SUPPLIES
Yarn needle, assorted food colors, seven ⅝"/16 mm
  buttons, sewing needle, coordinating sewing thread

Crocheting the Cozy *(make 2)*

» Chain 43.

» **ROW 1:** Dc in 4th ch from hook and in each ch to end, turn. *You now have* 41 dc.

» **ROW 2:** Ch 3 (counts as dc), BLdc in each st across, turn.

» **ROWS 3–9:** Repeat Row 2.

» **ROW 10:** Ch 3 (counts as dc), dc2tog, BLdc in each st to last 2 sts, dc2tog, turn. *You now have* 39 dc.

» **ROWS 11–17:** Repeat Row 10. *You now have* 25 dc.

» **ROW 18:** Ch 1, sc2tog, sc in each st to last 2 sts, sc2tog. *You now have* 23 dc. Fasten off.

Finishing

» Felt the cozy to desired size (see page 275). While still wet, gently stretch to block it, then dry flat. Once dry, single crochet the edges of the two pieces together. Cut one length of yarn 36"/91 cm long and set aside for sewing the cuff in place. Use the remaining yarn to crochet decorative circles.

Crocheting the Large Circle

» Begin with adjustable ring (see page 271). Ch 3 (counts as dc), 17 dc in ring, join with slip st to top of ch-3. Fasten off.

Crocheting the Medium Circle

» Begin with adjustable ring. Ch 2 (counts as hdc), 17 hdc in ring, join with slip st to top of ch-2. Fasten off.

Crocheting the Small Circle

» Begin with adjustable ring. Ch 1, 15 sc in ring, join with slip st to top of first sc. Fasten off.

Dyeing the Sewing Yarn and Circles

» Cover working area with paper towels or a plastic tablecloth. Soak the 36"/91 cm piece of yarn and circles in a solution of one part white vinegar to three parts water for 30 minutes. While pieces are soaking, in separate microwavable containers mix 1 teaspoon (5 mL) vinegar and desired number of drops of food colors with ½ cup (118 mL) boiling water. After 30 minutes, gently squeeze out excess vinegar solution from each piece and submerge them in the various dye baths. Place each dye bath in the microwave and cook on high for 1 minute. Use tongs to lift the pieces out of the dye to check for color saturation. Continue to microwave pieces in 30-second intervals until desired color is reached. Rinse pieces in tepid water until water runs clear; dry flat.

Finishing

» Fold up the cuff to desired height and use the dyed length of the yarn to loosely stitch it in place. Arrange circles on front of cozy, with a single button in the center of each circle. With sewing needle and coordinating thread, sew buttons and circles onto cozy in desired pattern.

Spike & Loopy, Felted Twins

Designed by Janet Brani

Spike and Loopy are twins! They share the same "mama skein" but have very different hairstyles. These felted vessels are fun to make and take just a couple of hours to crochet. The only thing better than a one-skein project is getting two projects from one skein.

FINISHED MEASUREMENTS
Spike: 3½"/9 cm in diameter and 5"/12.5 cm high
Loopy: 4"/10 cm in diameter and 3½"/9 cm high

YARN
Brown Sheep Lamb's Pride Bulky, 85% wool/15% mohair, 125 yds (114 m)/4 oz (113 g), Color M-10 Cream

CROCHET HOOK
US L/11 (8 mm) *or size you need to obtain correct gauge*

GAUGE
8 stitches and 8 rounds = 4"/10 cm in single crochet before felting

OTHER SUPPLIES
Yarn needle

Crocheting Spike

» Begin with an adjustable ring (see page 271).

» **RND 1:** Ch 1, 6 sc in ring, join with slip st to first sc, turn. *You now have 6 sc.*

» **RND 2:** Ch 1, 2 sc in each sc around, join with slip st to first sc, turn. *You now have 12 sc.*

» **RND 3:** Ch 1, (2 sc in next 3 sc, sc in next sc) three times, join with slip st to first sc, turn. *You now have 21 sc.*

» **RND 4:** Ch 1, (2 sc in next sc, sc in next 2 sc) seven times, join with slip st to first sc, turn. *You now have 28 sc.*

» **RND 5:** Ch 1, BLsc in each st around — this creates a ridge at the base of the bowl, join with slip st to first sc, turn.

continued on next page

» **RNDS 6–17:** Ch 1, sc in each st around, join with slip st to first sc, turn. Do not turn at end of Rnd 17.

MAKING THE SPIKES

» **RND 18:** *Ch 6, slip st in 2nd ch from hook and in next 4 ch, slip st in next 2 sc in Rnd 17, ch 7, slip st in 2nd ch from hook and in next 5 ch, slip st in next 2 sc in Rnd 17, ch 8, slip st in 2nd ch from hook and in the next 6 ch, slip st in next 2 sc in Rnd 17; repeat from * four times; ch 7, slip st in 2nd ch from hook and in next 5 ch, slip st in next 2 sc in Rnd 17, ch 8, slip st in 2nd ch from hook and in the next 6 ch, slip st in next 2 sc in Rnd 17 — *14 spikes made.* Fasten off. Weave in ends.

Finishing

» Felt (see page 275) tightly, shape, and dry.

Crocheting Loopy

» Begin with an adjustable ring (see page 271).

» **RND 1:** Ch 1, 6 sc in ring, join with slip st to first sc, turn. *You now have* 6 sc.

» **RND 2:** Ch 1, 2 sc in each sc around, join with slip st to first sc, turn. *You now have* 12 sc.

» **RND 3:** Ch 1, (2 sc in next 3 sc, sc in next sc) three times, join with slip st to first sc, turn. *You now have* 21 sc.

» **RND 4:** Ch 1, (2 sc in next sc, sc in next 2 sc) seven times, join with slip st to first sc, turn. *You now have* 28 sc.

» **RND 5:** Ch 1, (2 sc in next sc, sc in next 3 sc) seven times, join with slip st to first sc, *do not turn.* (Note that the Spike bowl did turn at this point in the pattern.) *You now have* 35 sc.

» **RND 6:** Ch 1, BLsc in each st around — this creates a ridge at the base of the bowl, join with slip st to first sc, turn.

» **RNDS 7–12:** Ch 1, sc in each st around, join with slip st to first sc, turn.

» **RND 13:** Ch 1, (sc in next 5 sc, sc2tog) five times, join with slip st to first sc, *do not turn. You now have* 30 sc.

MAKING THE LOOPS

» **RND 14:** (Ch 8, slip st in the next sc, ch 10, slip st in the next sc, ch 12, slip st in the next sc) 10 times, for a total of 30 loops. End with a slip st at the base of the first loop. Fasten off and weave in tails.

Finishing

» Felt (see page 275) tightly, shape, and dry.

Appendix

About the Designers

Jenny Allbritain

Jenny has been crocheting since the age of ten. In 2009 Jenny began designing and opened her pattern shop, Injenuity, on Etsy. Among her most popular designs are the vintage-inspired "Li'l Jackie Hat" and the "Seamus Scally Cap," an innovative take on the classic flat cap. When she isn't crocheting, Jenny enjoys reading and writing fiction. You can find her designs on the web: *www.injenuity.etsy.com* or *www.ravelry.com/designers/jenny-allbritain*. Or, search "Injenuity" on Facebook.

Brenda K. B. Anderson

Brenda's work has been published in *Interweave Crochet*, *Crochet Today*, *Knitscene*, and *Your Knitting Life*. She lives in a little house (with a lot of yarn) that she shares with her handsome husband and one naughty kitty. You can find her on Ravelry as Yarnville.

Rebecca Averill

Rebecca's been wielding the hook off and on since she was in junior high school. In recent years she's joined the ranks of the crochet obsessed. Rebecca relishes designing hats, bags, cozies, shrugs . . . anything that's fun, fast, and useful!

Annelies Baes

Annelies is the mother of two great sons, Viç and Arno, who are her inspiration. Her designer name is vicarno's mama and you can find her at *www.vicarnosmama.blogspot.com*.

Sharon Ballsmith

Sharon is an avid crocheter and freelance designer. Her designs have appeared in magazines such as *Interweave Crochet*, *Crochet!*, and *Tangled*. She also has designs in *Oh Baby! Crochet* (DRG, 2010) as well as designs in upcoming books by Cooperative Press and Storey Publishing. You can find her on Ravelry as stitchesandstones.

Donna Barranti

Donna was born in Seattle, Washington, grew up in California, and now lives in North Florida with her husband, Michael, and their dog, Shelby. At the age of eleven, her grandmother taught her to crochet pineapple sachets, but she soon found great pleasure in creating afghans. Her afghan designs are inspired by quilt patterns and a technique that produces a seamless, reversible blanket. She has published patterns in *Crochet World*, *Crochet with Heart*, and *Warm & Cuddly: Afghans for All Seasons*, Book 3. Donna's most recent design patterns include afghans, shoulder bags, and table runners and can be found online at Knit Picks and Ravelry.

Laura Biondi

Laura discovered the joy of crocheting when she first picked up a hook in 2005. She likes the challenge of creating a new pattern and enjoys sharing her passion for the craft with her students. She teaches crochet classes for all skill levels at the Red Thread in Warrenton, Virginia. You can also find her online at *www.ravelry.com/people/blacksheepcrochet*.

Julie Blagojevich

Julie's been crocheting since she was eight years old. She currently works with a community of knitters at Haus of Yarn in Nashville, Tennessee, and is continually inspired by the talent and creativity of the group. Accessories are her favorite projects, especially shawlettes, necklaces, and purses.

Janet Brani
OneLoopShy Designs
www.oneloopshy.com

Janet adores luxury yarns and loves the challenge of creating accessories using just a skein or two. "Looping" off and on since the age of eight, she is happily caught up in this new wave of crochet enthusiasm and enjoying the ride. Her design work can be seen in *Interweave Crochet*, *Interweave Crochet Accessories*, *Crochet!*, *Crochet World*, and now in this wonderful book. Her pattern line is available to the wholesale industry through Deep South Fibers.

Jane M. Brown
Craftique/Never Enough Knitting

In business at the same location in Wheaton, Illinois, for eighteen years, Craftique/Never Enough Knitting specializes in knitting, quilting, and crocheting, originating many patterns in all these crafts. Jane is a retired teacher who takes advantage of her master's degree in fine arts to develop new ideas and methods to assist customers in developing new skills.

Nancy Brown

Nancy is a widely published knit and crochet designer. Having taught herself to crochet as a teenager, Nancy admits she's been "crocheting for decades." She is a member and past president of the Crochet Guild of America (CGOA). She lives on the Kitsap Peninsula of Washington State.

Bendy Carter

Bendy began designing full-time in 1999. She enjoys crocheting, designing, and crocheting her own designs. Her crochet books include *Baby Shower Cakes*, *When Granny Meets Filet*, *Charted Picture Afghans*, and a light murder mystery called *Dying to Crochet*. She hopes everyone enjoys her Lacy Pineapple Belt.

Yvonne Cherry
Brooklyn Crochet

Yvonne designs and crochets all kinds of things: hats, scarves, clothes, curtains, rugs, dog sweaters, etc. Her grandma, Mema, was always doing all kinds of crafts, sewing, needlepoint, quilting, and crochet. She taught Yvonne to crochet when she was eight years old. Now she's crocheting with her grand-daughters, to whom she taught Tunisian crochet. Yvonne is a member of the Crochet Guild of America, NYC Crochet Guild, and the Harlem Knitting Circle. As a member of the NYC Crochet Guild, she worked on the Hyperbolic Crochet Coral Reef Project. She loves to teach and recently started Brooklyn Crochet Connection, a fun, free intergenerational program geared toward passing on the skills, gifts, and talents of our elders to our youth through crochet. They meet at the Walt Whitman Library in Fort Greene, Brooklyn. You can contact Yvonne at *www.brooklyncrochet.com*.

Patricia Colloton-Walsh

A former instructor at Loop Yarn Shop in Milwaukee, Patricia is an avid knitter and crocheter. Inspired by natural fibers and yarns of all types, she turns to crochet to design quick gifts for family and friends. Projects include baby hats and sweaters, amigurumi, borders on dish towels, cowls, and scarves. Her crochet hooks are always as close as her knitting needles.

Sylvie Damey

Sylvie is an avid crafter who started publishing her own knitting and crochet patterns back in 2005 under the name "Chez Plum." Follow her yarny adventures in the French Alps via her blog *http://chezplum.com/blog*.

Tamara Del Sonno

Tamara has worked for several yarn shops and currently has patterns on Ravelry and Craftsy. She loves the shape, size, color, and texture of knit and crochet, but loves her children and wonderful grandchildren more.

Judith Durant

Judith has been up to yarny things for almost fifty years. Editor of the One-Skein Wonders series and author of several other books about knitting and beadwork, she can be found on the Web at *www.judithdurant.com*.

Robin Dykema

Robin Dykema began tweaking designs, which soon led to creating original designs, and she has more than thirty to date. She is thrilled to be included in this book. "I learn something new with every new design — whether it starts as a vague idea or a more complete image."

Edie Eckman

Edie likes to crochet, knit, sew, teach, design, write, and edit, not necessarily in that order. She is the author of four best-selling crochet books, *Connect the Shapes Crochet Motifs*, *Beyond the Square Crochet Motifs*, *Around the Corner Crochet Borders*, and *The Crochet Answer Book*. She is on a mission to make crochet patterns as understandable as possible to as many crocheters as possible. Edie is co-editor of *Crochet One-Skein Wonders*.

Diana Foster

Diana, owner and designer for Lowellmountain Wools, LLC, a farm shop with sheep in the Northeast Kingdom of Vermont that offers classes in knitting. She is a member of the Knitting Guild Association and is a knitting instructor at The Old Stone House Museum.

Melody Fulone

Melody is a self-taught designer, specializing in crochet and jewelry designs, and sometimes combining the two. A native of New England, she spends her days at a bookstore and her nights creating new, original ideas.

Ellen Gormley

Ellen stitched more than eighty afghans before beginning her design career in 2004. She has now sold more than two hundred designs and been published numerous times in many crochet magazines including *Interweave Crochet*, *Crochet Today*, *Crochet!*, *Crochet World* and *Inside Crochet*. Her designs have been shown on the PBS show *Knit and Crochet Now!* Her two books are *Go Crochet! Afghan Design Workbook* and *Learn Bruges Lace*. You can follow Ellen on her blog at *www.gocrochet.com* and as GoCrochet on Twitter and Ravelry.

Beth Graham

Affiliated with Shall We Knit? in Waterloo, Ontario, Beth is an elementary school supply teacher in southwestern Ontario. She is also a lifelong learner who enjoys sharing her discoveries with others. In her spare time she teaches crochet at her local yarn shop and designs many of her patterns as teaching tools to introduce the crafter to new techniques in a clear and (she hopes!) relatively painless way. Her work can also be found in the Fresh Designs crochet series (Cooperative Press), *Crochet!* magazine, and online via Ravelry.

Sarah Grieve

Sarah has been stitching since she was a wee girl, and she loves to design. She is continually inspired by nature and always trying something new. She can be found at *www.asarahgrieveproduction.com*.

Pam Grushkin

Pam shares her passion for knitting and crochet through teaching and designing. Her designs have been published in *Vogue Knitting*, *Knitting Socks with Hand-painted Yarn*, *One + One Hats*, and independently as Knits with a Twist. She lives in Connecticut where she is rarely seen without a hook or needles in her hands. For more information visit *www.pamgrushkin.com*.

Sara Kay Hartmann

Sara Kay designs crochet and knitting patterns for the modern crafter. See her designs at *www.sara-kayknitandcrochet.com*. She lives with her wonderful husband in central Illinois.

Ryan Hollist

Ryan's designing crochet patterns started as an act of financial desperation. However, making the step into professional crafting has brought a greater love for the work. Visit him at Blazing Needles, *www.blazing-needles.com*.

Laura Hontz

Laura is a lifelong crocheter and knitter who enjoys working with color, pattern, and texture. She hopes to outlive her yarn stash but says, "I may have to live forever!"

Akua Lezli Hope

Akua Lezli began crocheting at age twelve and creates wild hats for herself and her friends in New York City. Her participation lapsed until she reconnected with dimensional crochet in the late 1990s and soon after found freeform. Her crochet designs have been included in the *Crochet* 2010 and 2011 calendars, *Interweave Crochet*, *Knit Picks IDP*, *Sanguine Gryphon*, and *Tangled* magazine. Her crochet patterns are available on Ravelry, Etsy, Craftsy, and DaWanda. An Associate Professional member of the Crochet Guild of America, her crochet blog is *www.zencrochet.blogspot.com*. Her fiber love extends to hand papermaking. She also creates using glass, wire, words, and sound. A NEA award-winning poet, her work is included in several groundbreaking collections.

Adrienne Hopkins

Adrienne is a self-taught crochet artist who designs, creates, and felts handmade slippers. As a mother of four, she has a lot of toes to practice on. Adrienne's other slipper styles can be found at *www.handmadebyade.etsy.com*.

Mike Horwath

Mike eats, sleeps, and breathes fiber arts. While he has crocheted since he was young, machine knitting is his growing passion, and he just can't get enough. He has made it his mission to enlighten others on what machine knitting is all about. He works an office job by day, and is often seen wearing a suit on the commuter train and pulling out his crochet. It never fails to get a comment. Mike is glad to help educate anyone who wants to know, and is just as eager to learn from others. Watch for more from this budding designer.

Erica Jackofsky

More of Erica's designs can be found on her website at *www.fiddleknits.com*.

Justyna Kacprzak

Justyna is a designer, mother, and wife from the oldest town in Poland. She tries to keep her designs cute and useful at the same time. Visit her at *www.cuteandkaboodle.com*.

Nirmal Kaur Khalsa

Since she could never manage to follow crochet directions without changing something (for the better, of course), Nirmal decided it was time to create her own patterns. You can find more of her work on Ravelry under the name nirmal.

Barbara Khouri

Barbara started the conversion from hobby to profession many years ago when she knitted model sweaters for Deb Newton. She then worked as technical director at JCA Knitting Yarn division for about nine years and is currently doing freelance technical work while also working a "real" job as a lab tech at a local hospital.

Susan Levin

Susan is the owner of K1C2, LLC. Her knitting and crocheting patterns have been published in major magazines, and she is the author of four craft-related books, including *Crochet Your Way* with Gloria Tracy. Susan has invented numerous craft products and is a consultant to several major craft companies.

Susan McCabe

Stay-at-home mom of two, Susan started crocheting to make a monkey hat for Halloween and has been addicted ever since.

Caissa McClinton

Caissa has been crafting her entire life, blogging at *www.artlikebread.com* since 2007, and crocheting since 2008. An educator by day, she's also a proud member of the Crochet Guild of America (CGOA). She sends love to her fellow Mount Holyoke alumnae.

Melinda Miller

Melinda is a self-taught crocheter who was inspired to learn from her great-grandmother. Her very first project was a christening set for her son's baptism. After a house fire years ago, she still has the smoke-stained jacket as a keepsake. The Miller family is the Brady Bunch of their family tree, raising six children between them both. In the evening, Melinda loves to crochet while her husband, Craig, knits.

Dorian Owen

As a teenager, Dorian learned to crochet from her grandma. Originally from Alaska, she now makes her home in Colorado, where she enjoys crocheting and craft beer.

Anastasia Popova

Anastasia is a contributor to the soon-to-be-published Fresh Design Crochet book series by Cooperative Press. Her crochet career began when she designed and produced a line of kids' clothes and accessories for local boutiques. Catch up with Anastasia at *www.anastasiapopova.com*.

Deb Richey

Deb loves to design crocheted patterns. She especially likes to create fun, quirky, and original dolls that are not always cute and cuddly. Her patterns have appeared in crochet magazines and craft companies such as Caron International, Mary Maxim, Herrshner's, Joann's, and Annie's Attic. More of her designs can be found at *www.craftydeb.com* and you can follow her blog at *http://yarn-or-fabric.weebly.com/crafty-blog.html*.

Reneé Rodgers

Reneé has been designing professionally for more than five years. She crochets, spins, knits, and dyes in the heart of the Ozarks. Keep up with what she's up to at *www.crochetrenee.com*.

Annalee Rose

Annalee has been a crocheter for more than forty years, and she especially enjoys creating new designs. Being newly retired, she is looking forward to having more time to read and sew as well. Surrounded by many fiber-creative women, Annalee hopes to now learn rug hooking.

Sandy Scoville

Sandy is the multipublished author of dozens of crochet and knit designs and patterns. Her collections are favorites among handknitters and crocheters all over the world.

Melinda A. Sheehan

Melinda started at Storey Publishing in 2005 as an intern from the Massachusetts College of Liberal Arts and is currently the associate production editor. In the eight years since she started at Storey, she has worked on every book in the One-Skein Wonders series and is ecstatic to have her very first design, the Fuzzy Tea Cozy, featured in this newest edition to the series.

Marcia Sommerkamp

Marcia is living proof to every crafter that you *can* do it! She has owned a yarn shop; sold the first design she ever submitted (to Plymouth Yarns); and has just started a new company called Sommerkamp Designs. Now if she could find someone to drive her car on her three-hour commute to her "real" job . . . just imagine what she could accomplish for her charity knitting group.

Janet Spirik

Janet is known by her friends and family for being crafty and creative. She has always loved crocheting and knitting, and loves doing so in her favorite spot in front of the fireplace. Recently she began to design her own patterns in the hopes of sharing her passions with others. Janet lives near Pittsburg with her husband and three daughters, where despite the cold winters, she dreams of sunny beaches and warm weather. See more of her creations at *www.jspirik.etsy.com*, or on Ravelry under designer jspirik.

Gwen Steege

A confirmed fiber fanatic since childhood, Gwen has edited more than two dozen books on crochet, knitting, spinning, weaving, and dyeing, and has contributed designs to several of them. She shares her passion for fiber in her book, *The Knitter's Life List* (Storey, 2011). She lives in Williamstown, Massachusetts, and blogs at *http://theknitterslifelist. wordpress.com*.

Lindsey Stephens

Lindsey is the crochet and knit designer behind *www.poetryinyarn.com*. From her home in Connecticut, Lindsey creates designs for Poetry in Yarn, magazines, and yarn companies. She loves yarn and has the growing stash to prove it. When she's not stitching, Lindsey also teaches and does web design.

Kristen Stoltzfus

Kristen lives on an organic farm in Pennsylvania's Cumberland Valley and has been designing since she was nineteen years old. Her designs have been featured by multiple magazines and yarn companies. She can't function without crochet.

Deb Swinski

A third-generation crocheter, Deb began to design patterns as soon as she picked up a hook. When not answering phones at WEBS, Deb also enjoys jewelry making and karaoke.

Gail Tanquary

Gail learned to crochet as a child, and was fortunate to be able to open a yarn shop in 1972 where she could pursue her passion for all things yarn and share that love of the art with others. After trying to retire in 2001, Gail reopened a shop in her new town where she continues to design and work with yarns and people every day.

Pam Thompson

Pam, a project editor at Storey Publishing, is happy to have a professional reason to carry around needles, hooks, and yarn at all times.

Susan Timmons

Susan's babysitter taught her the basics of crocheting twenty-three years ago when she was seven years old, and she started crocheting professionally four years ago with The Silver Hook. Mermaids were her first amigurumi designs, and she is always working on new ideas and techniques for her patterns.

Birgit Tüchsen

Birgit is a crochet designer from Copenhagen. You can find crochet tutorials and free patterns on her blog *http://bynumber19.com*.

Kennita Tully

Kennita is a freelance designer living in Manhattan, Kansas. She publishes her own pattern line, Wildflower knitwear, and owns a yarn shop, Wildflower yarns and knitwear. Check it out at *www.wildflowerknits.com.*

Andrea Lyn Van Benschoten

Andrea Lyn is a professional member of the CGOA and has designed patterns for publishers and yarn companies alike in both the United States and England. Her fiber arts work has been on display at Lafayette College, the Catskill Fly Fishing Center & Museum, and Peters Valley Craft Center in Layton, New Jersey. She lives in New Jersey with her husband, Glenn, and her cockatiel, Mendelssohn. Her website is at *www.alvbfiberart.com* and her blog is at *www.thefiberforum.com.*

René E. Wells

The joy of fiber began for René when she was seven years old. After teaching her the chain stitch, Grandma offered to teach her more if she would chain the whole skein. She did and went on to crochet, knit, sew on a treadle machine, and embroider. In recent years René has enjoyed learning to quilt, tat, and spin. She is a member of TNNA, TKGA, and is published in *Luxury Yarn One-Skein Wonders* (Storey, 2008) and *Sock Yarn One-Skein Wonders* (Storey, 2010), and has patterns available through Sporfarm Just for EWE, Wolle's Yarn Creations, and on Ravelry under grannanmedesigns. René holds small group classes through Tea Time Knitters with Chocolate or one-on-one.

Jana Whittle

Jana has been crocheting for several years. When she couldn't find a pattern she liked for a cute pair of gloves, her first design was born.

Myra Wood

Myra is an internationally known fiber and bead artist, teacher, and author. She teaches a wide range of classes in crochet, knitting, beading, and embroidery, specializing in creative expression. She has appeared on a number of episodes of *Knit and Crochet Today*, *Knitty Gritty*, and *Uncommon Threads* for PBS, DIY, and HGTV networks and has published numerous crochet, knit, jewelry, and wearable art patterns in a wide range of books and magazines. Her books, *Creative Crochet Lace* and *Crazy Lace* are available on Amazon and through local yarn and book stores. Myra has been crocheting, sewing, and crafting since she was young and enjoys any opportunity to inspire others creatively. Visit her at *www.myrawood.com.*

Glossary

2-dc cluster Yo, insert hook into stitch indicated and pull up a loop, yo and pull through 2 loops on hook, yo, insert hook into same stitch and pull up a loop, yo and pull through 2 loops, yo and pull through all 3 loops on hook.

3-dc cluster Yo, insert hook into stitch indicated and pull up a loop, yo and pull through 2 loops on hook, (yo, insert hook into same stitch and pull up a loop, yo and pull through 2 loops) two times, yo and pull through all 4 loops on hook.

adjustable ring Leaving a 6"/15 cm tail, form a loop in the yarn and hold it in your left hand with the working yarn over your index finger (figure 1). Draw the working yarn through the loop so you have 1 loop on the hook (figure 2). Work the appropriate number of build-up chains for the first stitch (figure 2), then work stitches into the ring as instructed (i.e. single, double, or treble crochet), working each stitch over the loop yarn and the tail yarn (figures 3 and 4). When you've crocheted the last stitch, separate the tail from the loop and pull it up to close the loop. You may leave an open hole in the center or pull it up tightly to close the ring.

back loop vs. front loop The back loop is the one farther away as you look at the work. The front loop is the one closer to you.

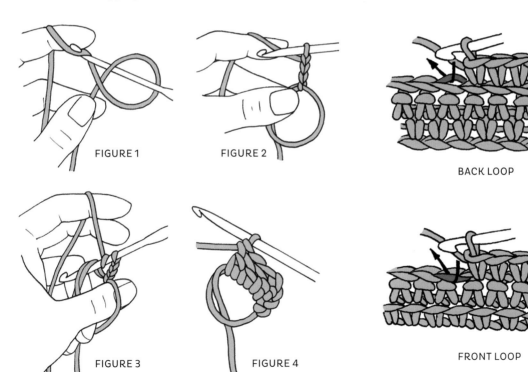

FIGURE 1

FIGURE 2

FIGURE 3

FIGURE 4

BACK LOOP

FRONT LOOP

BLdc (back loop double crochet) Work 1 double crochet into the back loop only.

BLhdc (back loop half double crochet) Work 1 half double crochet into the back loop only.

BLhdc2tog (back loop half double crochet 2 stitches together) Yarn over, insert hook into back loop of next stitch and pull up a loop, yarn over, insert hook into back loop of next stitch and pull up a loop, yarn over and pull through all 5 loops on hook.

BLsc (back loop single crochet) Work 1 single crochet into the back loop only.

BLsc2tog (back loop single crochet 2 stitches together) (Insert hook into back loop of next st and pull up a loop) two times, yarn over and pull through all 3 loops on hook.

BL slip st (back loop slip st) Work 1 slip stitch into the back loop only.

back post vs. front post
To work a back post stitch, insert the hook from back to front to back around post of stitch indicated.

To work a front post stitch, insert the hook from front to back to front around post of stitch indicated.

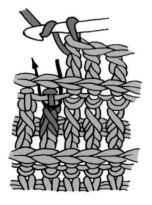

BACK POST

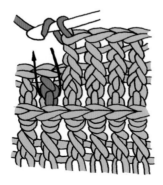

FRONT POST

BPdc (back post double crochet) Yarn over, insert hook from back to front to back around post of stitch indicated and pull up a loop, (yarn over and pull through 2 loops on hook) two times.

BPsc (back post single crochet) Insert hook from back to front to back around post of stitch indicated and pull up a loop, yarn over and pull through 2 loops on hook.

BPtr (back post treble crochet) (Yarn over) two times, insert hook from back to front to back around post of stitch indicated and pull up a loop (yarn over and pull through 2 loops on hook) three times.

dc (double crochet) Yarn over, insert hook into stitch or space indicated, pull up a loop — 3 loops on hook, (yarn over, pull yarn through 2 loops on hook) two times.

dc2tog (double crochet 2 together) (Yarn over, insert hook into next stitch or space and pull up a loop, yarn over, pull through 2 loops) two times, yarn over and pull through all 3 loops on hook.

dc3tog (double crochet 3 together) (Yarn over, insert hook into next stitch or space and pull up a loop, yarn over, pull through 2 loops) three times, yarn over and pull through all 4 loops on hook.

dtr (double treble) (Yarn over) three times, insert hook into stitch or space indicated and pull up a loop, (yarn over and pull through 2 loops on hook) four times.

fdc (foundation double crochet) Begin with slip knot on hook, chain 3, yarn over, insert hook in 3rd chain from hook, yarn over and pull up loop, yarn over and draw through 1 loop — *chain made*, (yarn over and draw through 2 loops) two times — *double crochet made*. For each subsequent fdc, yarn over, insert hook under 2 loops of chain at the bottom of stitch just made, yarn over and pull up loop, yarn over and draw through 1 loop — *chain made*, (yarn over and draw through 2 loops) two times — *double crochet made*.

FLdc (front loop double crochet) Work 1 double crochet into the front loop only.

FLhdc (front loop half double crochet) Work 1 half double crochet into the front loop only.

FLsc (front loop single crochet) Work 1 single crochet into the front loop only.

FPdc (front post double crochet) Yarn over, insert hook from front to back to front around post of stitch indicated and pull up a loop, (yarn over and pull through 2 loops on hook) two times.

FPtr (front post treble crochet) (Yarn over) two times, insert hook from front to back to front around post of stitch indicated and pull up a loop (yarn over and pull through 2 loops on hook) three times.

FPtr2tog (front post treble crochet 2 together) (Yarn over) two times, insert hook from front to back to front around post of stitch indicated and pull up a loop (yarn over and pull through 2 loops on hook) two times; (yarn over) two times, insert hook from front to back to front around post of next stitch and pull up a loop (yarn over and pull through 2 loops on hook) two times, yarn over and pull through all 3 loops on hook.

fsc (foundation single crochet) Begin with slip knot on hook, chain 2, insert hook into 2nd chain from hook, *yarn over and pull up a loop, yarn over and pull through 1 loop — *1 chain made*, yarn over and pull through 2 loops — *1 fsc made**. For each subsequent fsc, insert hook into chain at base of previous fsc, repeat from * to ** for desired length.

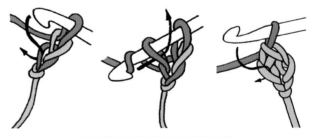

FOUNDATION SINGLE CROCHET

front loop: See back loop vs. front loop.

front post: See back post vs. front post.

hdc (half double crochet) Yarn over, insert hook into stitch or space indicated and pull up a loop — *3 loops on hook,* yarn over and pull through all 3 loops on hook.

hdc2tog (half double crochet 2 together): (Yarn over, insert hook into next stitch and pull up a loop) two times, yarn over and pull through all 5 loops on hook.

273

picot-2 Chain 2, slip stitch in 2nd chain from hook.

picot-3 Chain 3, slip stitch in 3rd chain from hook.

picot-4 Chain 4, slip stitch in 4th chain from hook.

sc (single crochet) Insert hook into stitch or space indicated, yarn over, pull up a loop — *2 loops on hook,* yarn over and pull through both loops on hook.

sc2tog (single crochet 2 stitches together) (Insert hook into next stitch and pull up a loop) two times, yarn over and pull through all 3 loops on hook.

sc3tog (single crochet 3 stitches together) (Insert hook into next stitch and pull up a loop) three times, yarn over and pull through all 4 loops on hook.

slip st (slip stitch) Insert hook into stitch or space indicated, yarn over and pull through all loops on hook.

tight picot-3: Ch 3, slip stitch in stitch at base of chain.

tr (treble crochet) (Yarn over) two times, insert hook into stitch or space indicated, pull up a loop — *(4 loops on hook),* (yarn over and pull through 2 loops on hook) three times.

TSS (Tunisian simple stitch) Chain desired number.
  ROW 1: Insert hook in 2nd chain from hook, yarn over and pull up a loop, (insert hook into next chain, yarn over, pull up a loop) across — *forward row complete;* yarn over, pull through 1 loop on hook, (yarn over, pull through 2 loops on hook) until 1 loop remains — *return row complete.*
  ROW 2: Skip first vertical bar, insert hook under next vertical bar, yarn over, pull up loop (insert hook under next vertical bar, yarn over, pull up loop) across; work loops off using return row. Repeat Row 2 for pattern.

TSS ROW 1 FORWARD

TSS ROW 1 RETURN

TSS ROW 2 FORWARD

TSS bind off (worked on forward row) Insert hook under second vertical bar from hook, yarn over, pull through both loops. You now have 1 loop on hook. *Insert hook under next vertical bar, yarn over, pull through both loops; repeat from * until all stitches are bound off.

Other Techniques

Felting Place item in a pillowcase and close it with a rubber band. Place the pillowcase in washing machine with pair of jeans to add to the agitation. Set the washing machine to the hottest temperature and lowest water level. Add a small amount of soap and begin the wash cycle. Before the cycle ends, stop the machine and check the felting progress. If more is needed, reset the wash cycle and continue. It's important to check the felting progress often, about every 5 to 10 minutes, to ensure you get the desired size. Measure the dimensions at each check.

Using Markers in Rounds Place marker at the first stitch of the round and move it up as you work the rounds.

Whipstitch Also known as overcast stitch. Holding the two pieces to be joined together, insert needle from back to front through one stitch on each piece; repeat until the pieces are joined.

Working into Back of Chain With the wrong side of the chain facing, insert hook into the bumps on the back of the chain. (The right side of the chain is a series of Vs.)

Guide to Yarn Weights

This system of categorizing yarn, gauge ranges, and recommended needle and hook sizes was developed by the Craft Yarn Council and was used to classify the projects in this book.

	TYPES OF YARN	STITCHES IN 4" (10 CM)	RECOMMENDED HOOK SIZE
0 LACE	(10-count crochet thread, lace*, fingering)	32–42 dc	steel 6, 7, 8 (1.6–1.4 mm), regular B–1 (2.25 mm)
1 SUPER FINE	(sock, fingering, baby)	21–32 sc	B–1 to E–4 (2.25–3.5 mm)
2 FINE	(sport, baby)	16–20 sc	E–4 to 7 (3.5–4.5 mm)
3 LIGHT	(DK, light worsted)	12–17 sc	7 to I–9 (4.5–5.5 mm)
4 MEDIUM	(worsted)	11–14 sc	I–9 to K–10½ (5.5–6.5 mm)
5 BULKY	(chunky, craft)	8–11 sc	K–10½ to M–13 (6.5–9 mm)

✳ *Lace weight yarns are usually crocheted on larger hooks to create lacy openwork patterns. Accordingly, a gauge range is difficult to determine. Always follow the gauge stated in your pattern.*

Abbreviations

beg	begin(ning)
BLdc	back loop double crochet
BLhdc	back loop half double crochet
BLhdc2tog	back loop half double crochet 2 together
BLsc	back loop single crochet
BLsc2tog	back loop single crochet 2 together
BLslip st	back loop slip stitch
BPdc	back post double crochet
BPsc	back post single crochet
BPtr	back post treble crochet
ch	chain
dc	double crochet
dc2tog	double crochet 2 together
dc3tog	double crochet 3 together
dtr	double treble crochet
fdc	foundation double crochet
FLdc	front loop double crochet
FLhdc	front loop half double crochet

FLsc	front loop single crochet
FPdc	front post double crochet
FPtr	front post treble crochet
FPtr2tog	front post treble crochet 2 together
fsc	foundation single crochet
hdc	half double crochet
hdc2tog	half double crochet 2 together
pm	place marker
RS	right side of work
sc	single crochet
sc2tog	single crochet 2 together
sc3tog	single crochet 3 together
slip st	slip stitch
st(s)	stitch(es)
tr	treble crochet
TSS	Tunisian simple stitch
WS	wrong side of work
yo	yarn over hook

Symbol Key

◠ = chain (ch)

◗ = work into ch not space

• = slip stitch (sl st)

+ = single crochet (sc)

⊤ = half double crochet (hdc)

= double crochet (dc)

= treble crochet (tr)

= double treble crochet (dtr)

= foundation single crochet (fsc)

= foundation double crochet (fdc)

= spike st

= back post double crochet (BPdc)

= front post double crochet (FPdc)

= back post treble crochet (BPtr)

= front post treble crochet (FPtr)

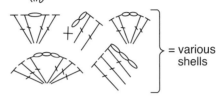

= beginning V-stitch (beg V-st)

or = V-stitch (V-st)

= beginning shell (beg shell)

} = various shells

= large shell

or = picot shell

= crossed dc

= sc2tog

= sc/dc cluster

= dc2tog

= dc3tog

= FPtr2tog

= 2-dc cluster

= 3-dc cluster

= double treble cluster (dtr-cl)

or = puff stitch

= beginning popcorn

= popcorn

= Dot stitch (Dot st)

• = bead

= Beaded ch (Bch)

= Beaded single crochet (Bsc)

= Beaded treble crochet (Btr)

= picot-3

= tight picot-3

or = picot-4

= bead picot

⌒ = worked in back loop

⌣ = worked in front loop

◎ = adjustable ring

= blanket stitch (embroidery)

✳ = marker

⇄ = directional arrows

277

Index

Page numbers in *italics* indicate illustrations, page numbers in **bold** indicate charts.

Are you a knitter, too?
Then welcome to the world of One-Skein Wonders!

Judith Durant's best-selling One-Skein Wonders books each come with 101 unique projects for using those spare skeins or giving you a reason to buy more! From scarves to baby clothes and dog sweaters to lampshades, there are so many fabulous projects in each book, you'll want to buy them all!

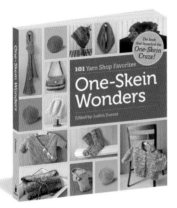

One-Skein Wonders
240 pages. Paper. ISBN 978-1-58017-645-3.

Luxury Yarn One-Skein Wonders
272 pages. Paper. ISBN 978-1-60342-079-2.

Sock Yarn One-Skein Wonders
288 pages. Paper. ISBN 978-1-60342-579-7.

101 Designer One-Skein Wonders
256 pages. Paper. ISBN 978-1-58017-688-0.

Ready to go beyond one skein?

Then Edie Eckman has the motifs and techniques to guide you on your next project. Edie Eckman's best-selling crochet books offer hundreds of beautiful motifs and the techniques you need to make your projects unique. Look to *The Crochet Answer Book* when you have questions about all things crochet — from counting stitches to blocking and joining. Learn how to put the finishing touch on the edges of any fiber project with *Around the Corner Borders*. With *Beyond the Square Crochet Motifs*, experiment with color combinations and different sizes of the 144 motif designs. With *Connect the Shapes Crochet Motifs*, you will find 101 new motifs and learn ways to join them to create completely new patterns.

The Crochet Answer Book
320 pages. Flexibind.
ISBN 978-1-58017-598-2.

Around the Corner Crochet Borders
320 pages. Paper. ISBN 978-1-60342-538-4.

Beyond the Square Crochet Motifs
208 pages. Hardcover with concealed wire-o.
ISBN 978-1-60342-039-6.

Connect the Shapes Crochet Motifs
272 pages. Hardcover with concealed wire-o.
ISBN 978-1-60342-973-3.

These and other books from Storey Publishing are available wherever quality books are sold or by calling 1-800-441-5700. Visit us at *www.storey.com* or sign up for our newsletter at *www.storey.com/signup*.